HOW TO PAY ZERO ESTATE TAXES

Jeff A. Schnepper

Also by Jeff A. Schnepper:

How to Pay Zero Taxes
(now in its seventeenth annual edition)

HOW TO PAY ZERO ESTATE TAXES

Jeff A. Schnepper

McGraw-Hill

New York   San Francisco   Washington, D.C.   Auckland   Bogotá
Caracas   Lisbon   London   Madrid   Mexico City   Milan
Montreal   New Delhi   San Juan   Singapore
Sydney   Tokyo   Toronto

McGraw-Hill

*A Division of The **McGraw·Hill** Companies*

1 2 3 4 5 6 7 8 9 0 DOC/DOC 0 9 8 7 6 5 4 3 2 1 0

ISBN 0-07-134513-2

This book was set in Baskerville by North Market Street Graphics.

Printed and bound by R. R. Donnelley & Sons Company.

McGraw-Hill books are available at special quantity discounts to use as premiums and sales promotions, or for use in corporate training programs. For more information, please write to the Director of Special Sales, Professional Publishing, McGraw-Hill, Two Penn Plaza, New York, NY 10121-2298. Or contact your local bookstore.

This book is printed on recycled, acid-free paper containing a minimum of 50% recycled, de-inked fiber.

Dedicated to my two daughters, Brandy and Allison; my two sons, Josh and Mario; and the reason for my being—my Barbara Alice—and her kitten, Fred, just beclaws.

Contents

Acknowledgments

I wish to thank Philip Ruppel, who insisted I write this book; Noel Day, who transformed my mumblings into words; Stephanie S. Landis, who translated those words into understandable sentences; and Paul Malagoli; Sayes B. Block; Frank Kesselman; Sri Haran, CPA; and John Oxley for their professional guidance and encouragement.

I also want to thank President Clinton, without whose veto this book would not have been needed.

Jeff Schnepper

Introduction

You work all your life to accumulate a degree of wealth. You, not the bank, now own your house. You even have some investments—bought with money on which you have already paid your income taxes.

Nobody gave you these assets. You worked hard for them and paid your dues every April 15. Now, if you want some of these assets to go to your kids, the IRS is going to tax you *again!*

You see, we have a dual system of taxation in this country. We have an income tax, which is imposed on the income you earn, and a *second* tax on the "transfer of wealth." If you transfer money or property during your lifetime, it's called the *gift tax*. If the transfer is at death, it's called the *estate tax*.

Don't say you already paid taxes on this property—they were income taxes. Don't ask how the government can tax you for giving your *own money* or property to your kids—or to anyone else, for that matter. That's exactly what the law does.

Moreover, the tax rates are outrageous. You begin paying taxes at a rate of 37 percent, and the rate goes up as high as 55 percent. That means that you may end up paying taxes of $37,000 on your first $100,000 in taxable transfers and as much as $55,000 on your last $100,000 in taxable transfers.

But all is not lost. You have bought this book (which is income tax deductible) to help you find the cracks in the Code. *How to Pay Zero Estate Taxes* recognizes something that our government doesn't want you to know—that the gift and estate taxes are really *voluntary* taxes. I don't mean you aren't required to pay the taxes. What I do mean is that the taxes are mostly paid by the uninformed or the uneducated.

How to Pay Zero Estate Taxes will educate you as to the various strategies and techniques that can be used to reduce these taxes to zero. Some of these techniques have been congressionally legislated, while others are the result of judicial validation of sophisticated financial planning strategies. They are all legal—backed up by reference to a specific Code section or court case. Some of the techniques found in this book are the result of mixing complicated and convoluted Tax Code sections, but all of them are completely valid. Some are legal not because Congress intended them to be there, but because both Congress and the Internal Revenue Service were lax in their homework and the Tax Code language allowing them is there. Until the Code is changed, it is fully within the legal rights of the American taxpayer to use such Code combinations to reduce, minimize, or even completely eliminate taxes. Each individual must pay taxes, but not one penny more than the law requires. If you want to make voluntary transfer tax contributions to our federal treasury, you have bought the wrong book.

How to Pay Zero Estate Taxes is structured to save you tax dollars. We will do this in two ways. Our first approach will be to use various techniques to cut up and remove different properties from your taxable estate. For example, life insurance may not be taxable for income tax purposes, but it is taxable as part of your gross estate. If you own a $500,000 life insurance policy, your kids may only get $250,000. But if that life insurance is set up in an Irrevocable Life Insurance Trust (ILIT), it escapes taxation. *How to Pay Zero Estate Taxes* not only will show you how to set up that trust, but will give you a sample form.

Next, *How to Pay Zero Estate Taxes* will show you how to discount the taxable value of what you want transferred. The lower the value, the lower the tax. If we can lower the value enough through various discounts, the tax may be zero. We will use various techniques to lower the value of what is being transferred. For example, the appropriate use of a Family Limited Partnership (FLIP) will discount the value of the property transferred by a historical average of 40 percent. That means that if you know the rules and play the game right, you can immediately cut your potential tax by as much as 40 percent.

A Family Limited Partnership is a complicated document. Not only will we explain it in simple English, but *How to Pay Zero Estate Taxes* will provide a sample form for your use.

We'll start with an examination of the basic structure of our gift and estate tax system. We will focus on the process itself and on the interrelationship between the gift and estate taxes. Only by understanding the mechanics of the system can we truly begin to plan to avoid its traps.

We will examine what's included in your estate and discuss what can be excluded and how. Then we will talk about the credits against your gift and estate taxes. A credit is a dollar-for-dollar reduction in your tax. A $100 deduction reduces your tax by $50 in the 50 percent tax bracket, but a $100 credit reduces your tax by a full $100 no matter what bracket you're in.

Then we will turn to your Testamentary Will as your primary weapon against the estate tax. Appropriately structured, your Will can exclude as much as $1.35 million in 2000 and $2 million if you die in 2006 or later. *How to Pay Zero Estate Taxes* will examine those things that should be in your Testamentary Will and reveal those things that should not be there.

We will then turn to alternatives to Testamentary Wills. In some states, revocable trusts can save significant probate costs and provide the same benefits as

Testamentary Wills. *How to Pay Zero Estate Taxes* will not only explain the benefits and limitations of these documents, but will provide samples for your use as well.

Not all of your estate property transfers are governed by your Testamentary Will. Such things as life insurance and retirement plans go outside your Will. *How to Pay Zero Estate Taxes* will show you ways to eliminate all taxes on your life insurance and a special sophisticated technique that can enable you to avoid both income and estate taxes on your retirement plans (see page 112).

We will then come to the real value of this book. *How to Pay Zero Estate Taxes* will explain, demonstrate, and document those superstrategies for which financial and estate planners are currently charging multiple thousands of dollars. We will look at charitable techniques, private annuities, installment sales, Personal Residence Trusts, Grantor Retained Annuity Trusts (GRATs), Grantor Retained Unitrusts (GRUTs), and all that stuff.

While the arcane and apparently endless gobbledygook and the unintelligible acronyms have little meaning to you now, *How to Pay Zero Estate Taxes* will translate them into simple English and show you how to use these instruments to eliminate your estate tax. These strategies and techniques have all been court tested and validated.

We will conclude with a chapter on audit avoidance and what to do if and when you get audited.

Taxpayers who can afford expensive, professional tax planning don't pay high transfer taxes. The goal of *How to Pay Zero Estate Taxes* is to provide that planning and those techniques to middle-income taxpayers who are unknowingly overpaying. Former Supreme Court Justice George Sutherland once remarked: "The legal right of a taxpayer to decrease his taxes or to altogether avoid them by means which the law permits cannot be doubted."[1] *How to Pay Zero Estate Taxes* is dedicated to that ideal.

---

[1] Gregory v. Helvering, 35-1, USTC Par. 9043, 293 U.S. 463, 469 (1935).

Samples of the documents discussed in this book are available for download at

http://www.books.mcgraw-hill.com/business/download/

CHAPTER 1

How Estate Taxes Work

Our goal is to eliminate the burden of the estate tax from your beneficiaries' bank accounts. To accomplish this goal, we need a blueprint to construct your estate plan. We need to draft a design to determine the best strategies to reach this goal—at the least cost to you. This design must be flexible to react to changing legal and economic conditions and must be modifiable to conform with changing laws.

Remember our two basic approaches to estate tax minimization—first, cut up your estate to remove assets with special shelters that may be legally structured to escape taxation, and second, discount the value of whatever is left and subject to tax.

But, in order to successfully attack the system, we must first understand how the system works. That's the function of this chapter—to educate you as to the skeletal structure of the gift and estate tax system. Once you know how the system works, then you can plan to beat it.

The History and Mechanics of the Federal Estate Tax

The estate tax, also known as a death tax, is simply a tax imposed upon wealth transfers made at death. Death taxes have taken on several different forms in the United States at both the state and federal levels. Three times in this nation's history, a federal death tax has been imposed only to be repealed shortly thereafter. In each instance, the estate tax was implemented to provide revenue on a short-term basis to finance military action.

The first death tax in this country was a death "stamp" tax established in 1797 to pay for a naval buildup in response to heightened tensions with France. This tax was abolished just five years later, in 1802. The federal death tax was absent for the next 60 years until Congress reenacted it in 1862 to raise revenue for the Civil War. After the war ended, Congress repealed the tax in 1870. The third federal death tax was enacted in 1898 to finance the Spanish-American War. As before, the estate tax was abolished after the war in 1902. While prior death taxes were primarily imposed to finance warfare, President Theodore Roosevelt proposed in 1906 a progressive tax on all lifetime gifts and deathtime bequests to limit the amount that one individual could transfer to another, although no legislation immediately resulted from such proposal.

The commencement of World War I caused revenues from tariffs to fall. In response to this, the federal government, in 1916, adopted a progressive estate tax on all property owned by a decedent at his or her death, certain lifetime transfers that were for inadequate consideration, transfers not intended to take effect until death, and transfers made in contemplation of death.

Under the Revenue Act of 1918, estate tax rates upon transfers under $1 million were reduced, but the tax was extended to life insurance proceeds in excess of $40,000 that were receivable by the estate or its executor and properties subject to a general Power of Appointment.

In 1924, the estate tax was changed by:

1. Increasing the maximum rate to 40 percent;

2. Broadening properties subject to the tax to include jointly owned property and property subject to a power (such as a Power of Appointment) retained by the decedent to alter, amend, or revoke the beneficial enjoyment of the property; *and*

3. Allowing a credit for state death taxes for up to 25 percent of the federal tax. In addition, the first gift tax was imposed.

In 1926 the gift tax was repealed and estate taxes were reduced to a maximum of 20 percent on transfers over $10 million. The exemption was increased from $50,000 to $100,000 and the credit for state death taxes was increased to 80 percent of the federal tax.

In 1932, with the advent of the Depression, which reduced revenues from other sources and increased the need for revenues for new government projects, the state tax rates were increased, with a top rate of 45 percent on transfers over $10 million. The tax was made applicable to lifetime transfers in which the transferrer retained the life estate with the power to control who would benefit from the property or income therefrom. The exemption was reduced to $50,000 and the federal gift tax was reimposed (at 75 percent of the estate tax rates) for cumulative lifetime gifts in excess of $5,000 per year.

The state and gift tax rates were increased in 1934 to top rates of 60 percent and 45 percent, respectively, on transfers in excess of $10 million and again in 1935 to top rates of 70 percent and 52.5 percent, respectively, on transfers in excess of $50 million. The exemptions for both estate and gift taxes were reduced in 1935 to $40,000 each.

In 1940, a 10 percent surcharge was imposed on both income and estate and gift taxes in light of the need for additional revenue caused by the military buildup just prior to World War II. Estate and gift tax rates were increased in 1941, with a top estate tax rate of 77 percent on transfers in excess of $50 million.

In 1942, Congress again altered estate and gift taxes by:

1. Setting the exemption from the estate tax at $60,000, setting the lifetime exemption from the gift tax at $30,000, and providing an annual gift tax exclusion of $3,000; *and*

2. Attempting to equate property owned in community property states with property owned in non-community property states by providing that in both community property states and non-community property states each spouse would be taxed on the portion he or she contributed toward the acquisition cost of jointly owned or community property.

The 1942 solution to the community property problem was viewed as complex. Congress provided a different solution in 1948 for equating community property states and non-community property states by providing the decedent or donor spouse a marital deduction for 50 percent of the property transferred to the other spouse and thus effectively allowing both spouses to be taxed on one-half of the property's value.

In 1954, the estate tax treatment of life insurance was changed to subject life insurance proceeds to the estate tax if the proceeds were paid to the decedent's estate or executor or if the decedent retained "incidents of ownership" in the life insurance policy.

The Small Business Revision Act of 1958 provided for payment of federal estate tax on certain closely held businesses in installments over a 10-year period.

In the Tax Reform Act of 1976, Congress substantially revised gift and estate taxes by:

1. Providing for a single unified rate structure for cumulative lifetime and deathtime transfers;

2. Providing an exemption in the form of a credit (called the *unified credit*) that exempted $175,625 of transfers from tax when fully phased in;

3. Revising and lowering the unified rate structure such that the maximum tax rate was 70 percent;

4. Changing the income tax rules applicable to the disposition of inherited assets from a rule that stipulated only tax post death appreciation (i.e., the basis in the hands of the heir was stepped up to its value on the date of the

decedent's death) to one that provided that the heir's basis generally would be the same as the basis to the decedent (i.e., the decedent's basis in the property would carry over to be the basis to the heir);

5. Providing a 100 percent marital deduction for the first $250,000 of property transferred to a surviving spouse;

6. Changing the treatment of gifts made in contemplation of death from a rebuttable presumption that gifts made within three years of death would be subject to estate tax to a rule that subjects all gifts made within three years of death to the estate tax;

7. Providing that each spouse was rebuttably presumed to have contributed equally to the acquisition cost of jointly held property;

8. Providing that a farm or other real property used in a closely held business could be valued at its "current use value" instead of its "highest and best used value" so long as the heirs continued to so use the property for 15 years after the decedent's death;

9. Providing a limited deduction for bequests to children with no living parents (the so-called orphan's deduction);

10. Providing a new transfer tax on generation-skipping transfers basically equal to the additional estate or gift tax that the decedent's children would have paid if the property had passed directly to the children instead of in a form where the children received only an income interest or power to control the enjoyment of the property; *and*

11. Providing statutory rules governing the disclaimer of gifts and bequests under which an unqualified, irrevocable refusal to accept any benefits from the gift or bequest generally within nine months of the creation of the transferee's interest is not treated as a gift by the disclaiming individual, and liberalizing the provision that permits installment payment of estate tax on closely held businesses by providing that only interest need be paid for the first 4 years after death and lengthening the period of installment an additional 4 years to 14 years.

In 1980, the carry-over basis rule was retroactively repealed and replaced by the stepped-up basis rules that applied before the 1976 legislation.

The Economic Recovery Act of 1981 made the following changes to the estate and gift taxes:

1. Increased the unified credit such that when fully phased in in 1987 it effectively exempted the first $600,000 of transfers from the unified estate and gift tax;

2. Reduced the top unified estate and gift tax rate from 70 percent to 50 percent over a four-year period (1982–1985);

3. Provided for an unlimited deduction for transfers to spouses and permitted such a deduction (the so-called QTIP deduction) even where the donee spouse could not control disposition of the property after that spouse's death, so long as that spouse had an income interest in that property and that property was subject to that spouse's estate and gift tax;

4. Increased the annual gift tax exemption from $3,000 per year per donee to $10,000 per year per donee;

5. Changed the presumption that each spouse equally provided for the acquisition cost of jointly held property to an irrebuttable presumption;

6. Modified the "current use" valuation rules by shortening to 10 years the period for which heirs who inherit farms or other real property used in a closely held business are required to so use the property and by increasing the maximum reduction in the value of such property from $500,000 to $750,000;

7. Repealed the so-called orphan's deduction;

8. Delayed the effective date of the generation-skipping transfer tax; *and*

9. Further liberalized and simplified the rules that permit the installment payment of estate tax on closely held businesses.

The Deficit Reduction Act of 1984:

1. Delayed for three years the scheduled reduction of the maximum gift and estate tax rates (such that the maximum rate remained at 55 percent until 1988);

2. Eliminated the exclusion for interest in qualified pension plans;

3. Provided rules for the gift tax treatment of below-market-rate loans; *and*

4. Extended the rules that permit the installment payment of estate taxes on closely held businesses to certain holding companies.

The Tax Reform Act of 1986 substantially revised the tax on generation-skipping transfers by applying a single rate equal to the highest estate tax rate (i.e., 55 percent) to all generation-skipping transfers in excess of $1 million and by broadening the definition of a generation-skipping transfer to include direct transfers from a grandparent to a grandchild (i.e., direct skips).

The Omnibus Budget Reconciliation Act of 1987 made the following modifications:

1. Provided special rules for the so-called estate freeze transactions under which the person who engaged in such a transaction would be subject to estate tax on the value of such property;

2. Provided a higher estate or gift tax rate on transfers in excess of $10 million to phase out the unified credit and rate brackets lower than 55 percent; *and*

3. Again delayed for five years the scheduled reduction in estate and gift tax rates from 55 percent to 50 percent.

The Omnibus Budget Reconciliation Act of 1990 replaced the special rules for estate freeze transactions with a new set of rules that effectively subject to the gift tax the full value of interest in property, unless retained interest in that property takes certain specified forms.

The maximum estate, gift, and generation-skipping transfer tax rate dropped to 50 percent after December 31, 1992, but the Omnibus Budget Reconciliation Act of 1993 restored the 55 percent top rate retroactively to January 1, 1993 and made that top rate permanent. The Taxpayer Relief Act of 1997 provided for gradual increases in the unified credit, new exclusions for family-owned businesses and for certain land subject to permanent conservation easements, and a number of other changes.

So Where Do We Stand Now?

Today the gift tax and the estate tax are the same tax. It is a cumulative tax. What that means is that estate transfers are added on top of gift transfers to determine the tax due, subject to progressive, increasing rates (see Table 1.1). The advantage of the estate tax is that wealth subject to it receives a step up in basis at your death. That means if you buy stock at $10 a share and die when it is $15 a share, your beneficiaries take the $15 per share fair market value at your death (or the value six months later if the alternative valuation date is elected) as their basis.

Table 1.1   Unified Transfer Tax Rate Schedule

Taxable Estate		Tentative Tax		
Over	But Not Over	Tax	Plus	Of Excess Over
$ 0	$ 10,000	$ 0	18%	$ 0
10,000	20,000	1,800	20%	10,000
20,000	40,000	3,800	22%	20,000
40,000	60,000	8,200	24%	40,000
60,000	80,000	13,000	26%	60,000
80,000	100,000	18,200	28%	80,000
100,000	150,000	23,800	30%	100,000
150,000	250,000	38,800	32%	150,000
250,000	500,000	70,800	34%	250,000
500,000	750,000	155,800	37%	500,000
750,000	1,000,000	248,300	39%	750,000
1,000,000	1,250,000	345,800	41%	1,000,000
1,250,000	1,500,000	448,300	43%	1,250,000
1,500,000	2,000,000	555,800	45%	1,500,000
2,000,000	2,500,000	780,800	49%	2,000,000
2,500,000	3,000,000	1,025,800	53%	2,500,000
3,000,000	10,000,000	1,290,800	55%	3,000,000
10,000,000	17,184,000	5,140,800	60%*	10,000,000
17,184,000		9,451,200	55%	17,184,000

*The benefits from the graduated rates are phased out for taxable estates between $10,000,000 and $17,184,000.

Unified Credit

Each person has a unified credit that will reduce the amount of estate or gift tax that must be paid. For 2000, this credit is $220,550, equivalent to having $675,000 of assets not subject to federal estate tax. Since 1998, the unified credit has increased as the equivalent amount of estate assets not subject to the estate tax (the applicable exclusion amount) has changed. The following table shows these and future changes.

Year	Unified Credit	Applicable Exclusion Amount
1998	$202,050	$625,000
1999	$211,300	$650,000
2000 and 2001	$220,550	$675,000
2002 and 2003	$229,800	$700,000
2004	$287,300	$850,000
2005	$326,300	$950,000
2006 and later	$345,800	$1 million

No income tax is ever imposed on the $5 of appreciation during your lifetime—but you have to die to get it! With any transfers during your lifetime, your donees take your basis ($10 a share) as their basis. It's called *substituted basis*.

The advantage of making lifetime gifts subject to the gift tax is that the payment of the gift tax itself during your lifetime reduces your estate for the estate tax by the amount of the gift tax paid. There is no deduction for any estate taxes paid.

Let's take a closer look at the gift and estate tax. If you give someone money or property during your life, you may be subject to a federal gift tax. The money and property you own when you die (your estate) may be subject to a federal estate tax.

Most gifts are not subject to the gift tax and most estates are not subject to the estate tax. For example, there is usually no tax if you make a gift to your spouse or if your estate goes to your spouse at your death. If you make a gift to someone else, the gift tax does not apply to the first $10,000 you give that person each year.

Even if tax applies to your gifts or your estate, it may be eliminated by the unified credit. For 2000, the unified credit eliminates any tax on the first $675,000 of your lifetime taxable gifts or your taxable estate. This credit is scheduled to increase to $1 million by 2006.

The person who receives your gift or estate will *not* have to pay any gift or estate tax because of it. Also, that person will *not* have to pay any income tax on the value of the gift or inheritance received.

Making a gift or leaving your estate to your heirs does not ordinarily affect your federal income tax. You cannot deduct the value of gifts you made (other than gifts that are deductible charitable contributions).

The Federal Gift Tax

The gift tax applies to the transfer by gift of any property. You make a gift if you give property (including money) or the use of or income from property without expecting to receive something of at least equal value in return. If you sell something at less than its full value or if you make an interest-free or reduced-interest loan, you may be making a gift.

The general rule is that any gift is a taxable gift; however, there are many exceptions to this rule.

Generally, the following gifts are not taxable gifts:

1. The first $10,000 you give someone during a calendar year (the annual exclusion);

2. Tuition or medical expenses you pay for someone (the tuition and educational exclusions);

3. Gifts to your spouse;

4. Gifts to a political organization for its use; *and*

5. Gifts to charity.

A separate $10,000 annual exclusion applies to each person to whom you make a gift. Therefore, you can generally give up to $10,000 each to any number of people each year without having to pay tax on any of the gifts. If you are married, both you and your spouse can separately give up to $10,000 to the same person each year without making a taxable gift. If one of you gives more than $10,000 to the same person during the year, you may be able to avoid tax by splitting the gift (see the following text).

Example 1: You give your nephew a cash gift of $9,000. It is your only gift to him this year. The gift is not a taxable gift because it is not more than the $10,000 annual exclusion.

Example 2: You pay the $12,000 college tuition of your friend. Because the payment qualifies for the tuition exclusion, the gift is not a taxable gift.

Example 3: You give $25,000 to your 25-year-old daughter. The first $10,000 of your gift is not subject to the gift tax because of the $10,000 annual exclusion. The remaining $15,000 is a taxable gift. You may not have to pay the tax on the remaining $15,000 if you have any unused unified credit available. You can use the credit to pay the gift tax; however, you do have to file a gift tax return.

Alternatively, if you or your spouse make a gift to a third party, the gift can be considered as made one-half by you and one-half by your spouse. This is known as *gift splitting*. Both of you must consent (agree) to split the gift. If you do, you each can take the annual $10,000 exclusion for your part of the gift. Gift splitting allows married couples to give up to $20,000 to the same person annually without making a taxable gift.

If you split a gift you made, you must file a gift tax return to show that you both consent to use gift splitting. You must file a return even if half the split gift is less than $10,000.

Example 4: Jeff and his wife, Barbara, agree to use gift splitting so each of them can make a gift of more than $10,000 during the year without making a taxable gift. Jeff gives his nephew, Ben, $17,000 and Barbara gives her niece, Elizabeth, $12,000. Although each gift is more than $10,000, by gift splitting they can make these gifts without making a taxable gift. Jeff's gift to Ben is treated as one-half ($8,500) from Jeff and one-half ($8,500) from Barbara. Barbara's gift to Elizabeth is also treated as one-half ($6,000) from Barbara and one-half ($6,000) from Jeff. In each case, because one-half of the split gift is not more than the $10,000 annual exclusion, it is not a taxable gift.

As explained earlier, the unified credit eliminates the gift tax on the first $675,000 (in 2000; going to $1 million in 2006) of taxable gifts you make during your lifetime.

After you determine which of your gifts are taxable, you figure the amount of gift tax on the total taxable gifts and then apply your unified credit.

Example 5: You give your niece, Emily, a cash gift of $8,000. It is your only gift to her this year. You pay the $11,000 college tuition of your friend, David. You give your 25-year-old daughter, Brandy, $25,000. You also give your 27-year-old son, Joshua, $25,000. Before this year, you had never given a taxable gift. You apply the exceptions to the gift tax and the unified credit as follows:

1. Apply the educational exclusion. Payment of tuition is not subject to the gift tax; therefore the gift to David is not a taxable gift.

2. Apply the $10,000 annual exclusion. The first $10,000 you give someone during the year is not a taxable gift. Therefore, your $8,000 gift to Emily, the first $10,000 of your gift to Brandy, and the first $10,000 of your gift to Joshua are not taxable gifts.

3. Apply the unified credit. The gift tax on $30,000 ($15,000 remaining from your gift to Brandy plus $15,000 remaining from your gift to Joshua) is $6,000. You subtract the $6,000 from your unified credit and that leaves you with the amount of unified credit that you have left for future use.

Generally, you must file a gift tax return on Form 709 if:

1. You give more than $10,000 during the year to someone (other than your spouse);

2. You and your spouse are splitting a gift;

3. You give someone (other than your spouse) a gift that he or she cannot actually possess, enjoy, or receive income from until some time in the future; *or*

4. You give your spouse an interest in property that will be ended by some future event.

You do not have to file a gift tax return to report gifts to (or for the use of) political organizations, gifts to charitable organizations, or gifts made by paying someone's tuition or medical expenses.

You may use Form 709-A if you and your spouse are splitting a gift and that is the only reason you must file a gift tax return. This form is shorter and simpler than Form 709.

The Federal Estate Tax

An estate tax will apply to your taxable estate at your death. Your taxable estate is your gross estate less allowable deductions.

If you have not used any of your unified credit to eliminate gift taxes, no estate tax will have to be paid unless your taxable estate is more than $675,000 in 2000 (going to $1 million by 2006).

Your gross estate includes the value of all property in which you had an interest at the time of death. Your gross estate also includes:

1. The value of property you sold (or otherwise transferred) for less than its full value when you were alive, if you kept any interest in the property;

2. The value of property you own jointly with another person;

3. Life insurance proceeds payable to your estate, or if you owned the policy or had any incidents of ownership to your heirs;

4. The value of certain annuities payable to your estate or your heirs;

5. The value of community property to the extent of your interest under local law;

6. The value of any other property that you have the power to give yourself or someone else;

7. Gift taxes paid by you or your estate on gifts made by you or your spouse within three years before your death; *and*

8. The value of certain other property you transferred within three years before your death.

Your taxable estate is your gross estate reduced by:

1. Funeral expenses paid out of your estate;

2. Expenses for administrating your estate;

3. Debts you owe at the time of death;

4. Casualty and theft losses that occur during settlement of your estate;

5. Charitable contributions made by your estate; *and*

6. The marital deduction (generally the value of the property that passes from your estate to your surviving spouse).

As explained in the preceding text, any of your unified credit not used to eliminate gift tax can be used to eliminate or reduce estate tax.

Example 6: Mike gives his son, Ben, $100,000, which is Mike's first taxable gift. Mike files a gift tax return. He subtracts the $10,000 annual exclusion from the $100,000 gift to figure the amount of his taxable gift—$90,000. The gift tax on $90,000 is $21,000. Mike uses $21,000 of unified credit to eliminate the tax on the gift. Mike's wife has already given Ben $10,000, so splitting the gift will not help.

If Mike makes no other taxable gifts and his estate is not more than $585,000 in 2000 ($675,000 − $90,000), his remaining unified credit will eliminate any estate tax.

Example 7: Cory gives each of his five children $10,000 per year for 10 years. Since none of the gifts are more than the $10,000 exclusion, none of the gifts are taxable. Cory is able to give $500,000 tax free without using any of his unified credit.

If Cory makes no other gifts that are taxable and he leaves a taxable estate of $675,000 or less (in 2000), the unified credit will eliminate any tax on the estate. If Cory leaves a taxable estate of more than $675,000 (in 2000), the estate will have to pay estate tax only on the value of the estate that is more than $675,000.

An estate tax return Form 706 must be filed if the gross estate plus any additional taxable gifts and specific gift tax exemption is more than the credit equivalent ($675,000 for 2000, increasing to $1 million in 2006). Adjusted taxable gifts is the total of the taxable gifts you made after 1976 that are not included in your gross estate. The specific gift tax exemption applies only to gifts made after September 8, 1976 and before 1977.

Example 8: Ann's gross estate is worth $1,350,000. She dies in 2000 and leaves a total of $675,000 to her children and the remaining $675,000 to her husband, Mike. The amount that passes to Mike qualifies for the marital deduction and therefore is not included in the taxable estate. The taxable estate is therefore $675,000. Neither Ann nor Mike has ever made a taxable gift. An estate tax return has to be filed because the *gross estate* is more than $675,000. However, because Ann's *taxable estate* is not more than $675,000, Ann's unified credit eliminates all of the estate tax.

CHAPTER 2

This Book Will Save You Money

IF YOU ARE MARRIED AND PROPERLY EXECUTE AND FOLLOW THE DOCUMENTS IN THIS BOOK, YOU SHOULD PAY ZERO FEDERAL ESTATE TAXES ON ESTATES OF LESS THAN $3 MILLION!

I have thought long and hard about where I want to go with this book. Most tax guides are written to show how smart the author is. They are loaded with citations and written in unintelligible gobbledygook. Their assumption is that if you don't understand the text, it proves the author is smarter than you are.

Most estate tax guides are written by professionals for professionals. This book is different. This is an estate planning guide for all those with estates of $3 million or less. For you, if you follow the dictates of this book, your federal estate tax will disappear. That is what this book will do for you. For those with estates in excess of $3 million—get a lawyer! You can afford one, and a good one will save you hundreds of thousands of dollars in taxes. The strategies in *How to Pay Zero Estate Taxes* will eliminate the tax for the rest of us.

My colleagues have called this professional suicide, but growing up in the projects of East New York taught me that not everyone who needs a good estate planning attorney can afford $500 an hour. Here's how it's going to work.

The following chapters contain all of the documents necessary for a complete, professional estate plan. Each document will be introduced and explained. You will know *why* you need the document. You will next be given an analysis and translation into English of each document, paragraph by paragraph. You will then be presented with the full document.

All documents will also be available for download at

www.books.mcgraw-hill.com/business/download

WARNING: This book is structured to eliminate the federal estate tax. It is recommended that each reader have the forms reviewed by a competent attorney to make sure they conform to individual state requirements. However, a legal review and potential modification is substantially less expensive than the actual creation of the documents themselves.

CHAPTER 3

Living Wills

A Living Will is a document that, in effect, says that if you become a vegetable someone should pull the plug.

Living Wills authorize, but do not compel, the individual or individuals of your choice to direct a physician to terminate extraordinary measures to keep you alive.

There are many reasons for a Living Will. The one most often given is to preserve your estate for your beneficiaries rather than dissipating that estate through medical bills in a futile attempt to extend your life. Remember, a Living Will is a document that only applies when you have an extreme physical or mental disability with no reasonable expectation of recovery.

However, the real reason for a Living Will is to minimize the anguish of those you love. If you have an extreme physical disability from which there is no expectation of recovery, your family members have two choices—they can either come each day to the hospital and cry while watching you vegetate, or they can stay home and cry out of guilt for not coming to the hospital and watching you vegetate.

A Living Will is an act of love and mercy toward those who most care for you. It is sometimes referred to as an Advanced Health Directive.

It is important to remember that a Living Will only authorizes the individual or individuals to make the decision to pull the plug. It does not compel them to do so. However, without a properly drafted and executed Living Will, if your family members wanted to pull the plug, they would have to go to court and prove to the satisfaction of a judge that it was your intent and your desire, under these circumstances, to terminate such medical treatment. The creation and execution of the Living Will that follows will eliminate that burden from your family.

LIVING WILL

To My Family, My Physician, My Lawyer, and All Others Whom It May Concern

Death is as much a reality as birth, growth, maturity, and old age—it is the one certainty of life. If the time comes when I can no longer take part in decisions for my own future, let this statement stand as an expression of my wishes and directions while I am still of sound mind.

The first paragraph establishes your intent and the fact that you are competent at the time of expressing your intent.

If at such a time the situation should arise in which there is no reasonable expectation of my recovery from extreme physical or mental disability, I direct that I be allowed to die and not be kept alive by medications, artificial means, or "heroic measures." I do, however, ask that medication be mercifully administered to me to alleviate suffering even though this may shorten my remaining life.

This paragraph provides the specific instructions for those who are going to follow your Living Will. It provides for continuing medication to be mercifully administered to you to alleviate suffering, even though it may shorten your remaining life.

This statement is made after careful consideration and is in accordance with my strong convictions and beliefs. I want the wishes and directions here expressed to be carried out to the extent permitted by law. Insofar as they are not legally enforceable, I hope that those to whom this Will is addressed will regard themselves as morally bound by these provisions.

Living Wills are acceptable in all 50 states. I put this provision in in case you become ill or injured outside of the United States.

1. *I appoint my spouse, and if my spouse is not living or able, my children, age 18 or older, jointly, or, until there be any, (NAME), to make binding decisions concerning my medical treatment.*

Here you have appointed the specific individuals who make the decisions under this Living Will.

2. *Measures of artificial life support in the face of impending death that are especially abhorrent to me are:*

    a. *Electrical or mechanical resuscitation of my heart when it has stopped beating*

    b. *Nasogastric tube feedings when I am paralyzed and no longer able to swallow*

    c. *Mechanical respiration by machine when my brain can no longer sustain my breathing*

This paragraph specifically details those measures of artificial life support that you have clearly decided not to accept.

3. *If it does not jeopardize the chances of my recovery to a meaningful and sentient life or impose an undue burden on my family, I would like to live out my last days at home rather than in a hospital.*

The preceding paragraph allows you to spend your final days at home rather than in a hospital.

4. *If any of my tissues are sound and would be of value as transplants to help other people, I freely give my permission for such donation.*

This paragraph provides for organ and tissue donation, if so desired. If you choose not to donate your organs and tissues upon your death, this paragraph can be eliminated.

5. *No physician, hospital, or other health care provider who withholds or withdraws life-sustaining treatment in reliance on this Living Will shall have any liability or responsibility to me, my estate, or any other person for having complied with this document.*

This paragraph eliminates any doubts or questions with respect to the physician you are instructing.

(YOUR NAME)

Date:

Witness:

Witness:

Copies of this request have been given to:

_____

_____

_____

_____

STATE OF (YOUR STATE) _____

_____ *} ss.: Be it Remembered,*

COUNTY OF (YOUR COUNTY) _____

that on _____, *2000, before me, the subscriber, (YOUR NAME), personally appeared who, I am satisfied, is the person named in and who executed the within instrument, and thereupon said person acknowledged that said person signed, sealed, and delivered the same as the act and deed of said person, for the uses and purposes therein expressed.*

_____

Prepared by: _____

To complete the Living Will, it must be signed by you, dated, witnessed by at least two witnesses, and notarized. A notary is an individual authorized by your state who affirms that the person signing the document is truly that person whose signature appears on the document. In some states (for example, New Jersey), all attorneys are automatically notaries. If they sign as an attorney, they do not need the notary seal.

EXAMPLE

LIVING WILL

To My Family, My Physician, My Lawyer, and All Others Whom It May Concern

Death is as much a reality as birth, growth, maturity, and old age—it is the one certainty of life. If the time comes when I can no longer take part in decisions for my own future, let this statement stand as an expression of my wishes and directions while I am still of sound mind.

If at such a time the situation should arise in which there is no reasonable expectation of my recovery from extreme physical or mental disability, I direct that I be allowed to die and not be kept alive by medications, artificial means, or "heroic measures." I do, however, ask that medication be mercifully administered to me to alleviate suffering even though this may shorten my remaining life.

This statement is made after careful consideration and is in accordance with my strong convictions and beliefs. I want the wishes and directions here expressed to be carried out to the extent permitted by law. Insofar as they are not legally enforceable, I hope that those to whom this Will is addressed will regard themselves as morally bound by these provisions.

1. I appoint my spouse, and if my spouse is not living or able, my children, age 18 or older, jointly, or, until there be any, (NAME), to make binding decisions concerning my medical treatment.

2. Measures of artificial life support in the face of impending death that are especially abhorrent to me are:
   a. Electrical or mechanical resuscitation of my heart when it has stopped beating
   b. Nasogastric tube feedings when I am paralyzed and no longer able to swallow
   c. Mechanical respiration by machine when my brain can no longer sustain my breathing

3. If it does not jeopardize the chances of my recovery to a meaningful and sentient life or impose an undue burden on my family, I would like to live out my last days at home rather than in a hospital.

4. If any of my tissues are sound and would be of value as transplants to help other people, I freely give my permission for such donation.

5. No physician, hospital, or other health care provider who withholds or withdraws life-sustaining treatment in reliance on this Living Will shall have

any liability or responsibility to me, my estate, or any other person for having complied with this document.

_____
(YOUR NAME)

Date:

Witness:

Witness:

Copies of this request have been given to:

_____

_____

_____

_____

STATE OF (YOUR STATE)

_____ } ss.: Be it Remembered,

COUNTY OF (YOUR COUNTY)

that on   , 2000, before me, the subscriber, (YOUR NAME), personally appeared who, I am satisfied, is the person named in and who executed the within instrument, and thereupon said person acknowledged that said person signed, sealed, and delivered the same as the act and deed of said person, for the uses and purposes therein expressed.

_____

Prepared by: _____

CHAPTER 4

Durable Power of Attorney

The second document that you should have in an effective estate plan is a durable Power of Attorney. A Power of Attorney is a document that authorizes someone else to act for you. Normally that person would be your spouse if you are married. If you are not married, it would be someone in whom you have complete and absolute trust.

Why would you want a Power of Attorney? The answer most often given is to allow someone else to sign your name. For example, if you were out of town and had to have a joint tax return signed, this would allow your spouse to sign your name. Alternatively, if you were out of town and any other legal document required your signature, this would allow your spouse to do so.

However, the reality of the situation is that in most cases your spouse would just sign your name and, unless problems would subsequently arise, no one would ask or even question the signature. The true need would arise if you were to get into an accident and become disabled. In that case, your spouse would have to go into court and petition to be appointed guardian of your body and conservator of your estate. This could entail a legal bill of as much as $3,000 to $5,000. The existence of a properly executed Power of Attorney would eliminate that problem.

WARNING: Almost all states will automatically void any Power of Attorney you execute upon your disability. Their perspective is that if you are disabled, you no longer have the ability to withdraw your Power of Attorney, so the state will do it for you automatically.

To get around this, I suggest the execution of a *durable Power of Attorney*. This is a Power of Attorney that specifically declares that it will not be revoked upon your disability or incompetency.

Let's look at the following example.

Prepared by: _____
(Name of preparer)

POWER OF ATTORNEY

KNOW ALL MEN BY THESE PRESENTS, that I, (YOUR NAME), hereby revoke any general Power of Attorney that I have heretofore given to any person, and by these Presents do constitute, make, and appoint (SPOUSE/FRIEND'S NAME) my true and lawful attorney:

> The first paragraph defines whom you have appointed to be your attorney.

1. *To ask, demand, sue for, recover, and receive all sums of money, debts, goods, merchandise, chattels, effects, and things of whatsoever nature or description which are now or hereafter shall be or become owing, due, payable, or belonging to me in or by any right whatsoever, and upon receipt thereof, to make, sign, execute, and deliver such receipts, releases, or other discharges for the same, respectively, as the said attorney shall think fit.*

2. *To deposit any moneys which may come into said attorney's hands as such attorney with any bank or banker, either in my or said attorney's own name, and any of such money or any other money to which I am entitled which now is or shall be so deposited to withdraw as said attorney shall think fit; to sign mutual savings bank and federal savings and loan association withdraw orders; to sign and endorse checks payable to my order and to draw, accept, make, endorse, discount, or otherwise deal with any bills of exchange, checks, promissory notes, or other commercial or mercantile instruments; to borrow any sum or sums of money on such terms and with such security as said attorney may think fit and for that purpose to execute all notes or other instruments which may be necessary or proper; and to have access to any and all safe deposit boxes registered in my name. In the state of New Jersey, this is to be done with reference to N.J.S.A.46:2B-11.*

3. *To sell, assign, transfer, and dispose of any and all stocks, bonds (including U.S. Savings Bonds), loans, mortgages, or other securities registered in my name; and to collect and receipt for all interest and dividends due and payable to me.*

4. *To invest in my name in any stock, shares, bonds (including U.S. Treasury Bonds referred to as "flower bonds"), securities, or other property, real or personal, and to vary such investments as said attorney, in said attorney's sole discretion, may deem best; and to vote at meetings of shareholders or other meetings of any corporation or company and to execute any proxies or other instruments in connection therewith.*

5. *To enter into and upon my real estate, and to let, manage, and improve the same or any part thereof, and to repair or otherwise improve or alter and to insure any buildings thereon; to sell, either at public or private sale or exchange, any part or parts of my real estate or personal property for such consideration and upon such terms as said attorney shall think fit, and to execute and deliver good and sufficient deeds or other instruments for the convenience or transfer of the same, which such convenience of warranty or otherwise as said attorney shall see fit, and to give good and effectual receipt for all or any part of the purchase price or other consideration; and to mortgage my real estate and in connection therewith to execute bonds and warrants and all other necessary instruments and documents.*

6. *To contract with any person for leasing for such periods, at such rents and subject to such conditions as said attorney shall see fit, all or any of my said real estate; to give notice to quit to any tenant or occupier thereof; and to receive and recover from all tenants and occupiers thereof or of any part thereof all rents, arrears of rent, and sums of money which now are or shall hereafter become due and payable in respect thereof; and also on nonpayment thereof or of any part thereof to take all necessary or proper means and proceedings for determining the tenancy or occupation of such tenants or occupiers, and for ejecting the tenants or occupiers and recovering the possession thereof.*

7. *To commence, prosecute, discontinue, or defend all actions or other legal proceedings pertaining to me or my estate or any part thereof; to settle, compromise, or submit to arbitration any debt, demand, or other right or matter due me or concerning my estate as said attorney, in said attorney's sole discretion, shall deem best and for such purpose to execute and deliver such releases, discharges, or other instruments as said attorney may deem necessary and advisable; and to satisfy mortgages, including the execution of a good and sufficient release, or other discharge of such mortgage.*

8. *To execute, acknowledge, and file all federal, state, and local tax returns of every kind and nature, including without limitation income, gift, and property tax returns.*

9. *To engage, employ, and dismiss any agents, clerks, servants, or other persons as said attorney, in said attorney's sole discretion, shall deem necessary and advisable.*

10. *To make gifts to such individuals, including to said attorney, and in such amounts as said attorney in said attorney's sole discretion deems proper.*

11. *To make additions to any existing trust for my benefit and to withdraw and receive the income or corpus of a trust.*

12. *To disclaim any interest in property and to renounce fiduciary positions.*

13. *To authorize my admission to a medical, nursing, residential, or similar facility and to enter into agreements for my care, and to authorize medical and surgical procedures.*

14. *In general, to do all other acts, deeds, and matters whatsoever in or about my estate, all bank accounts, deposits, certificates of deposit, and property and affairs as fully and effectually to all intents and purposes as I could do myself as if personally present, giving to my said attorney power to make and substitute under said attorney an attorney or attorneys for all the purposes herein described, and I hereby ratify and confirm all that the said attorney or substitute or substitutes shall do therein by virtue of these Presents.*

All of what has been provided in the preceding text is not legally necessary. Your Power of Attorney will be completely legal/valid without paragraphs 1 through 14. However, in many cases you will be presenting this Power of Attorney to either a bureaucrat or a clerk in a financial institution. In both cases, you don't want to get into a position where you are debating the law with a low-level employee. Rather than having you argue as to whether or not this Power of Attorney specifically allows you to, for example, invest in U.S. Treasury Bonds or open a bank account, I have drafted the Power of Attorney to include every possible thing that I can imagine one might want to do. By loading the Power with specificity, I have eliminated the fatuous argument that the Power does not cover the specific thing that you wanted to do.

Also note that in paragraph 2, I have referenced the specific state statute. This is not necessary except in those states and in those instances where you wish to record your Power of Attorney. As long as your representative has an original copy, the Power does not have to be recorded in order to be effective.

15. *In addition to the powers and discretion herein specifically given and conferred upon my attorney, and notwithstanding any usage or custom to the contrary, my attorney shall have the full power, right, and authority to do, perform, and cause to be done and performed all such acts, deeds, and matters in connection with my property and estate as said attorney, in said attorney's sole discretion, shall deem reasonable, necessary, desirable, and proper, as fully, effectually, and absolutely as if said attorney were the absolute owner and possessor thereof.*

The preceding paragraph is all you need in order to have a valid Power of Attorney. However, I have included paragraphs 1 through 14 in order to avoid the specificity argument.

16. In the event of my disability or incompetency, from whatever cause, this Power of Attorney shall not thereby be revoked.

This is the durability clause. This is the clause that prevents your Power of Attorney from being automatically revoked upon your disability or incompetency.

There are two types of Powers of Attorney—an immediate Power of Attorney and a springing Power of Attorney. If you want your spouse to have immediate and full access to all of your assets, an immediate Power of Attorney would be appropriate. In some states, where there is no state inheritance or estate tax with respect to assets left to spouses, an immediate Power of Attorney allows you to take advantage of a major income tax loophole in the law.

Let me explain. Your estate includes not only all those assets that you own, but also all of those assets over which you have sufficient control to direct their disposition. This is known as a Power of Appointment. So, for example, if my spouse were to give me a Power of Attorney that contained a provision allowing me to gift her property to others—including to myself—that would constitute a Power of Appointment over her assets sufficient to include her assets in my estate upon my death.

Paragraph 10 in the Power of Attorney constitutes this Power of Appointment. If I have a Power of Attorney from my spouse with paragraph 10 in it, my spouse is giving me sufficient control over the disposition of her assets so that, if I died, those assets would be included in my estate.

But why would I want all of my spouse's assets to be included in my estate? Remember, we are dealing only with states where there is no state inheritance or estate tax between spouses. That means that this Power of Appointment will have no negative impact on my state inheritance tax. It will also not increase my federal estate tax if my Wills are appropriately drafted. The Wills that I will give you in the next chapter will provide for zero estate tax at the first death, no matter how big the estate is at that time.

But where's the advantage? Section 1014 of the Internal Revenue Code provides for a step up in basis for all assets included in your estate. The step up in basis mandates that fair market value be used rather than original cost basis for your beneficiaries. So, for example, if I bought an asset for $5 and that asset appreciated to $10 by the time of my death, the basis of that asset for my beneficiary would be $10. The $5 of appreciation is never taxed.

For estate tax purposes, your executor can use either fair market value at date of death or fair market value six months later. However, if you provide a Power of Appointment within your Power of Attorney, not only are all of *your* assets stepped up in basis to fair market value, but so too are all of *your spouse's* assets stepped up to fair market value. Clearly, the spouse expected to die first should have this Power of Appointment included in the Power of Attorney he or she receives from his/her spouse.

However, there may be situations where you might not be as comfortable as you would like in allowing your spouse full access and control over all of your assets immediately. In that case, rather than an immediate Power of Attorney, you would want a springing Power of Attorney. All that would be necessary would be the inclusion of paragraph 17, which follows. In this case I require a notarized statement by two medical doctors confirming your disability or incompetency prior to the Power of Attorney taking effect.

17. *This is a springing Power of Attorney. It shall only take effect upon my disability or incompetency. Said disability or incompetency shall be determined exclusively by the conclusive judgment of two medical doctors in a notarized statement to my above said attorney.*

IN WITNESS THEREOF, I have hereunto set my hand and seal this day of   , 2000.

_____(SEAL)

YOUR NAME

STATE OF (YOUR STATE) :

:SS

COUNTY OF (YOUR COUNTY) :

Before me, the undersigned, a Notary Public within and for the County of (Your County), State of (Your State), personally appeared (YOUR NAME), known to me to be the person whose name is subscribed to the within instrument, and acknowledged that said person executed the same for the purpose therein contained.

IN WITNESS THEREOF, I have hereunto set my hand and seal this day of , 2000.

—————————————————

This document also should be notarized.

EXAMPLE

Prepared by: _____
(Name of preparer)

POWER OF ATTORNEY

KNOW ALL MEN BY THESE PRESENTS, that I, (YOUR NAME), hereby revoke any general Power of Attorney that I have heretofore given to any person, and by these Presents do constitute, make, and appoint (SPOUSE/FRIEND'S NAME) my true and lawful attorney:

1. To ask, demand, sue for, recover, and receive all sums of money, debts, goods, merchandise, chattels, effects, and things of whatsoever nature or description which are now or hereafter shall be or become owing, due, payable, or belonging to me in or by any right whatsoever, and upon receipt thereof, to make, sign, execute, and deliver such receipts, releases, or other discharges for the same, respectively, as the said attorney shall think fit.

2. To deposit any moneys which may come into said attorney's hands as such attorney with any bank or banker, either in my or said attorney's own name, and any of such money or any other money to which I am entitled which now is or shall be so deposited to withdraw as said attorney shall think fit; to sign mutual savings bank and federal savings and loan association withdraw orders; to sign and endorse checks payable to my order and to draw, accept, make, endorse, discount, or otherwise deal with any bills of exchange, checks, promissory notes, or other commercial or mercantile instruments; to borrow any sum or sums of money on such terms and with such security as said attorney may think fit and for that purpose to execute all notes or other instruments which may be necessary or proper; and to have access to any and all safe deposit boxes registered in my name. In the state of New Jersey, this is to be done with reference to N.J.S.A.46:2B-11.

3. To sell, assign, transfer, and dispose of any and all stocks, bonds (including U.S. Savings Bonds), loans, mortgages, or other securities registered in my

name; and to collect and receipt for all interest and dividends due and payable to me.

4. To invest in my name in any stock, shares, bonds (including U.S. Treasury Bonds referred to as "flower bonds"), securities, or other property, real or personal, and to vary such investments as said attorney, and in said attorney's sole discretion, may deem best; and to vote at meetings of shareholders or other meetings of any corporation or company to execute any proxies or other instruments in connection therewith.

5. To enter into and upon my real estate, and to let, manage, and improve the same or any part thereof, and to repair or otherwise improve or alter and to insure any buildings thereon; to sell, either at public or private sale or exchange, any part or parts of my real estate or personal property for such consideration and upon such terms as said attorney shall think fit, and to execute and deliver good and sufficient deeds or other instruments for the convenience or transfer of the same, which such convenience of warranty or otherwise as said attorney shall see fit, and to give good and effectual receipt for all or any part of the purchase price or other consideration; and to mortgage my real estate and in connection therewith to execute bonds and warrants and all other necessary instruments and documents.

6. To contract with any person for leasing for such periods, at such rents and subject to such conditions as said attorney shall see fit, all or any of my said real estate; to give notice to quit to any tenant or occupier thereof; and to receive and recover from all tenants and occupiers thereof or of any part thereof all rents, arrears of rent, and sums of money which now are or shall hereafter become due and payable in respect thereof; and also on nonpayment thereof or of any part thereof to take all necessary or proper means and proceedings for determining the tenancy or occupation of such tenants or occupiers, and for ejecting the tenants or occupiers and recovering the possession thereof.

7. To commence, prosecute, discontinue, or defend all actions or other legal proceedings pertaining to me or my estate or any part thereof; to settle, compromise, or submit to arbitration any debt, demand, or other right or matter due me or concerning my estate as said attorney, in said attorney's sole discretion, shall deem best and for such purpose to execute and deliver such releases, discharges, or other instruments as said attorney may deem necessary and advisable; and to satisfy mortgages, including the execution of a good and sufficient release, or other discharge of such mortgage.

8. To execute, acknowledge, and file all federal, state, and local tax returns of every kind and nature, including without limitation income, gift, and property tax returns.

9. To engage, employ, and dismiss any agents, clerks, servants, or other persons as said attorney, in said attorney's sole discretion, shall deem necessary and advisable.

10. To make gifts to such individuals, including to said attorney, and in such amounts as said attorney in said attorney's sole discretion deems proper.

11. To make additions to any existing trust for my benefit and to withdraw and receive the income or corpus of a trust.

12. To disclaim any interest in property and to renounce fiduciary positions.

13. To authorize my admission to a medical, nursing, residential, or similar facility and to enter into agreements for my care, and to authorize medical and surgical procedures.

14. In general, to do all other acts, deeds, and matters whatsoever in or about my estate, all bank accounts, deposits, certificates of deposit, and property and affairs as fully and effectually to all intents and purposes as I could do myself as if personally present, giving to my said attorney power to make and substitute under said attorney an attorney or attorneys for all the purposes herein described, and I hereby ratify and confirm all that the said attorney or substitute or substitutes shall do therein by virtue of these Presents.

15. In addition to the powers and discretion herein specifically given and conferred upon my attorney, and notwithstanding any usage or custom to the contrary, my attorney shall have the full power, right, and authority to do, perform, and cause to be done and performed all such acts, deeds, and matters in connection with my property and estate as said attorney, in said attorney's sole discretion, shall deem reasonable, necessary, desirable, and proper, as fully, effectually, and absolutely as if said attorney were the absolute owner and possessor thereof.

16. In the event of my disability or incompetency, from whatever cause, this Power of Attorney shall not thereby be revoked.

17. This is a springing Power of Attorney. It shall only take effect upon my disability or incompetency. Said disability or incompetency shall be determined exclusively by the conclusive judgment of two medical doctors in a notarized statement to my above said attorney.

IN WITNESS THEREOF, I have hereunto set my hand and seal this day of   , 2000.

_____ (SEAL)

YOUR NAME

STATE OF (YOUR STATE)   :

                                           :SS

COUNTY OF (YOUR COUNTY)   :

Before me, the undersigned, a Notary Public within and for the County of (Your County), State of (Your State), personally appeared (YOUR NAME), known to me to be the person whose name is subscribed to the within instrument, and acknowledged that said person executed the same for the purpose therein contained.

IN WITNESS THEREOF, I have hereunto set my hand and official seal this day of   , 2000.

_____

CHAPTER 5

Testamentary Wills

This document is your Last Will and Testament. It is the document that directs the disposition of all of your assets upon your death. I will assume that you are married with children and that your primary objectives are as follows: (1) get as much to your spouse at your death as possible with minimal tax paid, and (2) transfer the remainder to your children.

What most people have is what I call an I Love You Will. In the examples that follow I will have the husband dying first. This is because traditionally husbands are older than and die before their wives, because men have shorter life expectancies than women, and because my wife has *guaranteed* that I will go first.

With an I Love You Will, the husband dies and leaves 100 percent of the estate to his spouse/wife.

$$H \rightarrow W$$

100% of assets <$675,000>

Because of the unlimited marital deduction, there is no tax at the first death.

When the wife dies, however, there will only be an exclusion of $675,000 worth of assets (in 2000; increasing to $1 million by 2006). Under this structure, the maximum that can be sheltered from tax is only $675,000.

What I would suggest instead is the following structure.

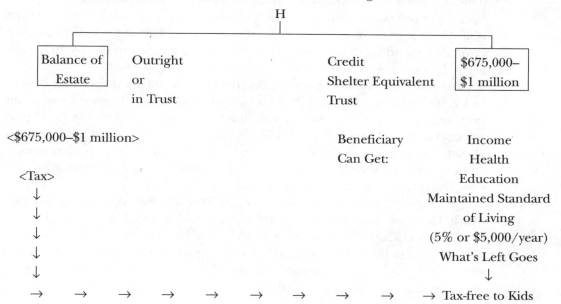

At the death of the first spouse, the executor divides the estate into two parts. The first part will be equal to whatever the exclusion amount is at the date of death. (For the year 2000, that amount is $675,000; it will go up to $1 million by 2006.) That amount is placed into what I refer to as a *credit shelter equivalent trust.* The remainder or the balance of the estate either goes outright or in a special trust to the surviving spouse.

Anything that is appropriately left to a surviving spouse is sheltered by the marital deduction and therefore will incur no tax. Therefore, at the first death there is no tax on what is left to the spouse. With respect to the $675,000–$1 million left in the credit shelter equivalent trust, the credit will pay the tax.

When I talk about credit, many people get confused. Rather than saying that the first $675,000 of your estate is not taxable in the year 2000, what Congress has done instead is to provide you with a credit of $220,550, which pays the tax on the first $675,000. By the year 2006, this credit increases to $345,800, which pays the tax on $1 million. So, for example, if you die in the year 2000 and put $675,000 into this credit shelter equivalent trust, the Internal Revenue Code provides you with a credit of $220,550 that pays the tax on that $675,000 in the trust. In other words, you pay no cash out of your pocket. As a result of this, at the first death, again zero estate taxes have been paid.

Out of this credit shelter equivalent trust, your spouse is entitled to all of the income, and anything he or she would need for health, education, or to maintain his or her standard of living. In addition, he or she has the right to invade the principal to the extent of $5,000 or 5 percent of that principal each year. These are what are known as ascertainable standards. If these ascertainable standards are adhered to, at the second death, whatever is in the credit shelter equivalent trust goes to your children tax free.

Your children receive the assets tax free because the assets come out of your estate (not your spouse's) and are taxed upon your death. However, the credit provided to you by Congress and contained in the Internal Revenue Code pays the tax on those assets at your death. Therefore, since the tax on these assets is already paid, and since these assets come to your children as secondary beneficiaries of your trust rather than through your spouse's estate, they come to your children with zero estate taxes to be paid.

With both this structure and the I Love You Will, no tax is paid at the first death. However, the result is vastly different at the second death.

At your spouse's death, he or she also has an exclusion amount of $675,000–$1 million. That means that if you structure your Will with the credit shelter trust, at a *minimum* you exclude from both estates $675,000 × 2 or

$1,350,000 (going to $2 million in 2006), as opposed to a maximum of $675,000 (going to a maximum of $1 million in 2006).

By structuring your Will this way, you double the amount that can be excluded. Moreover, remember that whatever is in the credit shelter equivalent trust at the second death goes to your children tax free. That means that if that trust grows to $10 million before the second death, all $10 million will go to your children or other beneficiaries without the imposition of an estate tax.

In order to get the benefits of this structure, you must have assets that passed through your estate by Will. Many married couples own all of their assets jointly. Unfortunately, if your estate exceeds the exclusion amount for that year ($675,000 in 2000, going to $1 million in 2006), jointly held assets are a recipe for disaster.

By operation of law, jointly held assets go to the survivor regardless of any directions to the contrary in your Will. That means that if all of your assets are held jointly, in effect you have created an I Love You Will. Everything must go to the surviving spouse. By doing this, you lose the benefit of the second exclusion amount.

In order to avoid this, if your joint estate, between husband and wife, is expected to exceed the exclusion amount prior to the death of the second spouse, then you should not own assets jointly. (In many states the joint owner-ship of assets between spouses is technically referred to as Tenancy by the Entireties.) Rather than owning assets jointly, you should own assets as Tenants in Common. Any accounts that you have and any property that you own should be changed to Tenants in Common so that those assets can pass through your Will and be available for the credit shelter equivalent trust.

Remember, the estate tax goes up as high as 55 percent. If you are only in the 50 percent bracket, the loss of a $1 million exclusion in the year 2006 will cost your children $500,000 in taxes that they should not have had to pay! In my opinion, an I Love You Will for an estate that is expected to exceed $675,000 is malpractice.

Let's look at an example of a Testamentary Will:

LAST WILL AND TESTAMENT
OF
(YOUR NAME)

I, (YOUR NAME), domiciled and residing at (Your Address), being of sound and disposing mind, memory, and understanding, do hereby make, publish, and declare this to be my Last Will and Testament, thereby revoking all Wills and codicils heretofore made by me.

> This paragraph establishes your residency and your competence and revokes all prior Wills and codicils. Any old Wills will automatically be revoked by this paragraph.

FIRST: I direct the payment of all my just debts and funeral and testamentary expenses as soon as convenient after my decease.

> This paragraph is important. In many cases, I see Wills that direct the payment of all just debts upon decease. This is another trap for the unwary. Inappropriately drafted, this paragraph would compel the payment in full of any outstanding debts, including mortgages and loans that you might not want to pay until maturity.

SECOND: If my spouse, (SPOUSE'S NAME), shall survive me by 30 days (720 hours), then I direct my Executor to divide the remainder of my estate, both real and personal, of or to which I am now or may hereafter become seized, possessed, or entitled, into two parts, so that the first part, hereinafter designated as SHARE A, shall constitute an amount of my adjusted gross estate as defined by the Internal Revenue Code and finally determined for federal estate tax purposes, to be computed by my Executor to total the then CURRENT maximum credit equivalent amount allowed by law. This amount shall be reduced by any credit equivalent amount used during my lifetime for inter vivos gifts.

> This paragraph divides the estate into two parts—one being the then current credit equivalent amount and the other being the balance of the estate. If the credit equivalent amount increases, this paragraph automatically will take into consideration the higher number.

Note that the amount going into the credit shelter equivalent trust is reduced by any inter vivos or lifetime gifts that were taxable and therefore used part of the credit in prior years.

The second part, hereinafter designated as SHARE B, shall constitute the entire balance of my said residuary estate. In allocating property to SHARE B, my Executor shall not use any property in respect of which no marital deduction is allowed. To the extent that other property qualifying for the marital deduction is available, my Executor shall not allocate to SHARE B: (a) assets with respect to which a credit for foreign taxes paid is allowable under the Internal Revenue Code: (b) assets which may be subject to both income and estate taxes and which may be eligible for a credit or deduction. SHARE A and SHARE B shall be disposed of as provided in Paragraphs THIRD and FOURTH of this Will.

This paragraph completes the division of assets between the credit shelter equivalent trust and those assets that are going outright to the spouse subject to the marital deduction.

It is my primary intent that the marital deduction bequest in SHARE B and the property comprising that share shall qualify for the federal estate tax marital deduction, notwithstanding any provision in my Will that might be construed as compromising this objective. All questions regarding the marital deduction bequest and this share shall be resolved accordingly. The powers and discretions of the Executor and Trustee with respect to administration of my estate and of said share shall not be exercised or exercisable except in a manner consistent with my intent as expressed in this paragraph. To the extent that any other provision of my Will conflicts with my primary intent as expressed in this paragraph, giving rise to an ambiguity, the ambiguity shall be resolved as directed in this paragraph. Should there be an ambiguity as to whether any provision necessary for qualification for the marital deduction is included in my Will, the ambiguity shall be resolved as directed in this paragraph. As regards the marital deduction, all other provisions of my Will are subordinate to this provision.

I call this my insurance paragraph. Basically it says that the most important thing in this Will is the marital deduction and if I have made any mistakes that might compromise the marital deduction bequest, those mistakes are to be ignored and any ambiguity is to be resolved in favor of the marital deduction. I have been practicing estate planning law for almost 30 years now and have yet to have any of my Wills challenged, but one never knows what he or she doesn't know. Therefore, I include this paragraph in all of my Wills simply because it adds an additional degree of confidence and security to the document.

THIRD: I give, devise, and bequeath SHARE B, my residuary estate, to my said spouse in fee simple without any restrictions whatsoever. It shall consist of, to the extent possible, my cash and liquid assets.

This is the outright bequest to the surviving spouse. All assets given to the surviving spouse are subject to the marital deduction and are therefore not taxable.

If my said spouse shall fail to survive me, then the bequest for the benefit of said spouse shall lapse and shall pass as part of SHARE A hereinafter disposed of.

If you have no surviving spouse, all of your assets are then put into trust for the benefit of your children.

FOURTH: I give, devise, and bequeath SHARE A to my hereinafter named TRUSTEE, IN TRUST, NEVERTHELESS, for the following uses and purposes:

(a) To invest in high-yield issues to the extent possible and reinvest the income and profits therefrom;

(b) Commencing with the date of my death, to pay to or apply for the benefit of my said spouse, at the request of said spouse, during the lifetime of said spouse, all the net income in convenient installments, at least as frequently as quarter-annually;

(c) In addition to the payment of such income, to pay to or apply for benefit of my said spouse during the whole lifetime, all or none of the principal of the Trust fund as my Trustee, in the Trustee's uncontrolled judgment and discretion, shall consider necessary or advisable for my said spouse's medical and educational needs and in order to maintain said spouse's current standard of living as of the date of my death. In addition, my spouse, (SPOUSE'S NAME), during the lifetime of said spouse, shall have the noncumulative right to withdraw each year from the principal of the Trust estate the sum of five thousand dollars ($5,000) or five percent (5%) of the then principal of the Trust estate, whichever amount shall be greater;

The preceding paragraphs detail the treatment of the credit shelter equivalent trust for the benefit of the surviving spouse. Note that the income will be paid to the surviving spouse, but only upon request. Here what you are doing is allowing your spouse to accumulate assets in the credit shelter equivalent trust while spending down the dollars and assets bequeathed directly to that spouse. Remember, those assets bequeathed directly are subject to estate tax to the extent that they exceed the exclusion amount. So, if your spouse dies in 2006, with $1.2 million in his or her estate, $1 million of that will be sheltered by the exclusion amount and $200,000 will be taxable. It would be to everyone's benefit if the surviving spouse would spend down the taxable $200,000 rather than spending down the assets or the income in the credit shelter equivalent trust, which goes to the children without the imposition of any tax.

(d) *Upon the death of my said spouse, to divide the then remaining principal of the Trust as follows:*

The remaining principal of the Trust shall be divided into so many equal shares that there shall be one of said equal shares for each child of mine then living and one for the then surviving issue, per stirpes, collectively of each child of mine who shall not be then living, and to set aside one of said shares for each child of mine then living and one of said shares for the then surviving issue, per stirpes, collectively of each child of mine who shall not be then living, and to hold, administer, and distribute each of said shares as provided in the following sections (e) and (f);·

The preceding paragraph then divides the remaining estate among your children. This division can be equal or unequal, and you can specifically exclude specific children, if that is your desire. In this case, I have made a division based upon a per stirpes allocation. That means that the dividing line is drawn at the level of your children.

Let me see if I can translate this paragraph into English. Assume you have four children. If at your death all four children are living, each one will get 25 percent of your estate. If one child should predecease you without issue, then the surviving three children each get one-third. If the child who predeceased you had issue (your grandchildren), then your three surviving children each get 25 percent and the issue of your deceased child share that child's 25 percent.

> As opposed to per stirpes, you can divide your estate on a per capita basis. In that case, if you have three surviving children with no issue and one deceased child with two children, you divide by the number of living persons in totality. In this case, your estate is divided into five parts, with each beneficiary getting 20 percent. Most people choose per stirpes as opposed to per capita.

(e)   As to the one share so set aside for the benefit of each child above living, each share is hereby given to my hereinafter TRUSTEE, IN TRUST, NEVERTHELESS, to hold and administer the same and to pay to or apply for the benefit of said children, equally, per stirpes, all the net income in convenient installments, at least as frequently as quarter-annually. In addition to the payment of such income, to pay to or apply for the benefit of said children, so much, all or none, of the principal of said equal share as my Trustee, in his or her uncontrolled judgment and discretion, shall consider necessary or advisable for the support, maintenance, and education of such children, and in order to maintain his or her current standard of living, said payments to be made subject to the schedule below, at which time the remainder of his or her respective share of my estate, with the accumulations, if any, shall be paid and distributed to him or her, or if he or she shall die before that time, shall be paid and distributed upon his or her death to his or her Executors or administrators, to be administered and distributed as part of his or her estate.

Age	Per Stirpes Share of Principal
18	5%
21	10%
25	25%
30	25%
35	35% (REMAINDER)

> The preceding paragraph provides for the payment of income and principal to your children by the trustee and the distribution of the assets to your children.
>
> In this Will, we have provided for an aging schedule for final asset distribution. In most states, if you say nothing, a beneficiary will receive full control of the assets upon his or her eighteenth birthday. I know that if I

had gotten my hands on $500,000 at age 18, I would have had a *great* year. However, I wouldn't have had $500,000 at age 19. In order to avoid this problem, and in order to avoid artificially enhancing the attractiveness of a beneficiary to a potential spouse for pecuniary rather than personality reasons, I suggest the spreading out of principal distributions over a period of years.

There is no one right answer. However, I suggest the following as a guideline for your own determination.

Remember, your children will get nothing until both you and your spouse are gone. In addition, all of their needs are taken care of. What we are talking about here are *only* discretionary distributions in excess of "needs." At age 18, I would give them 5 percent. They're going to college—let them buy a car. At age 21, give them another 10 percent. They've graduated college—let them take a trip overseas. At age 25, they're getting into business; give them 25 percent. At age 30, they're getting married, they're buying a house; give them 25 percent. At age 35—if they don't have it together by age 35, they probably never will—you might as well give them the remainder.

(f) As to the one share so set aside for the benefit of the then surviving issue, per stirpes, collectively of each child of mine who shall not be then living, to pay and distribute the same to the said then surviving issue of said children, per stirpes, for whom said share was so set aside, subject to the provisions of Paragraph FIFTH hereof, if any of such issue be then not yet 35 years of age;

FIFTH: If any part of my estate shall become payable or distributable at any time to the issue of my children who shall not yet be 35 years of age, then I give, devise, and bequeath his or her respective share of my estate to my hereinafter named TRUSTEE, IN TRUST, NEVERTHELESS, to hold and administer the same and to pay to or for the benefit of each such issue, so much, all or none, of said share, both income and principal, as my Trustee, in said Trustee's uncontrolled judgment and discretion, shall consider necessary or advisable for the support, maintenance, and education of such issue as per the schedule below, at which time the remainder of his or her respective share of my estate, with the accumulations, if any, shall be paid and distributed to him or her, or if he or she dies before that time, shall be paid and distributed upon his or her death to his or her Executors and administrators, to be administered and distributed as part of his or her estate.

Age	Per Stirpes Share of Principal
18	5%
21	10%
25	25%
30	25%
35	35% (REMAINDER)

The preceding paragraphs deal first with what happens if one or more of your children should predecease you (the assets go to their children) and then provides for the distribution and aging schedule for grandchildren as needed. Remember, if all of your children are living as of the date of the second death, then 100 percent goes to those children and the grandchildren are beneficiaries of your children's Wills rather than your own. Moreover, if you or your spouse have lived long enough, then your children/grandchildren should be over age 35 at the second death and therefore they will receive 100 percent at that death.

SIXTH: In addition to all powers now or hereafter conferred upon an Executor or Trustee of a (Your State) resident decedent under the law of (Your State), I confer upon my Executor and Trustees the following powers to be exercised by them as in their discretion they may deem for the best interests of my estate or the Trusts created by this Will and without authorization by any Court.

(a) To retain any and all investments and property, real and personal, that I may own at my decease or that thereafter shall become part of my estate or Trusts, without regard to any principle of diversification and notwithstanding the same may be of a wasting nature or may not be recognized by law as legal investments for Trust funds;

Paragraph SIXTH deals with the powers of an executor and a trustee. The role of the executor is to accumulate all of the assets of the estate, hire the attorney, hire the accountant, and file the appropriate tax returns. The executor is then responsible for making distribution of the assets to the beneficiaries as per the Will.

The executor should be a family member who knows where the assets are and who has a good relationship with the beneficiaries of the estate. The executor does not have to be an attorney or an accountant, but merely has to be someone with sufficient intelligence and insight to hire the appropriate professionals and fulfill the mandates of the Testamentary Will. Because the executor is entitled to a fee, I normally recommend against anyone other than a family member being executor. In most cases I recommend the surviving spouse, who can waive the fee and take the assets on a tax-free rather than taxable basis.

With respect to item (a), I have allowed the estate and/or trust to retain both wasting assets and assets that may not be recognized as legal investments for trust funds. A wasting asset is one such as an oil well or a coal mine in which the assets are depleted over time. Many state laws do not allow such assets to be held by a trust. It is my intent with these documents to give maximum flexibility to all parties concerned. If you felt at the time that it was appropriate for you to own an interest in an oil well, you may want your executor and trustee to have the legal authority to retain those investments if they feel that they are appropriate and proper. Moreover, your principal residence is not a legal investment for trust funds because it is not an income-producing investment. However, your principal residence may be the most appropriate asset to put into your credit shelter equivalent trust for the benefit of your surviving spouse.

(b) To invest and reinvest my estate or Trust funds in stocks, bonds, or other securities, notes, mortgages, units of participation in any common Trust fund maintained by my Trustee, or in any other property, real or personal, without regard to decisional or statutory law, rules of court, or principles concerning the investment of Trust funds, or to the amount which shall be invested in any one investment or type of investment and even though all, or substantially all, of the Trust fund may be invested in common stocks or other so-called "equities";

(c) To sell and dispose of any and all property, real or personal, of which I may die seized or possessed or which may become part of my estate or the Trusts created by this Will, either at public or private sale and upon such terms and conditions as they deem for the best interests of my estate and to make good and sufficient conveyances in the law therefor;

The preceding paragraphs expand the flexibility of your executor and trustee with respect to the type of property that they may own and how they may dispose of any property that they acquire.

(d) To use Executor's commissions, attorneys' fees, and other administration expenses, or part thereof, as deductions for estate tax purposes or income tax purposes and to use date of death values or optional values for estate tax purposes, without regard to the effect thereof on any of the interests or shares under this Will, and I direct that there shall be no adjustment of such interests or shares by reason of any action taken by my Executor in respect to the foregoing and all action shall be final, conclusive, and binding upon all beneficiaries;

This paragraph is important. The executor has the option of deducting certain fees either on the estate tax or the income tax. At the first death, there will be no estate tax, and therefore you want to deduct the expenses on your income tax return. At the second death, you have to weigh the marginal tax rate on your income tax return against the marginal tax rate on your estate tax return, and deduct wherever you would get the biggest bang for your buck.

This paragraph also allows you to use date of death values or optional values for estate tax purposes. Optional value is the fair market value of your assets six months from the date of death. If this is the first death, then there will be no estate tax and you will want to use the higher values in order to grant to your beneficiaries the higher basis under Internal Revenue Code Section 1014. If this is the second death, and an estate tax is due, you probably will want to use the lower values to reduce your estate tax. Remember, the first dollar of estate tax is imposed at a rate of 37 percent and has to be paid within nine months of death. The maximum capital gains rate is currently only 20 percent, and that only applies to gains rather than the total fair market value of the property. Moreover, here there's no tax until the asset is sold.

(e) To borrow, in order to invest, to pay taxes, debts, or other proper liabilities, such sum or sums of money from time to time and for such periods of time and upon such terms and conditions as my Executor and Trustee shall deem advisable, and to secure the same by mortgage or pledge of any part of my estate, real or personal, and to execute and deliver bonds, notes, mortgages, agreements, and other instruments necessary or proper to evidence and secure the loans so made;

(f) To exercise any stock options that I may own at my death and in connection therewith to borrow funds to exercise said options;

(g) *To make division, partition, and distribution of my estate or Trusts in cash or kind, or partly in each, and for the purpose of making such division, partition, and distribution in kind, the assets selected by my Executor and Trustees shall be valued at their respective values on the date or dates of division, partition, or distribution;*

(h) *To employ such accountants, custodians, attorneys, investment counsel, and other persons as they may deem advisable in the administration of my estate or any Trust created hereunder and to pay them such compensation as they may deem proper;*

(i) *To allocate to principal all stock dividends and cash in lieu of fractional shares paid as a result of a stock dividend received on any stock held in my estate or any Trust created hereunder;*

(j) *To exercise generally with respect to any and all stocks, securities, or other property held hereunder all rights, powers, and privileges that may be lawfully exercised by persons owning similar property in their own individual right.*

What you have done in the preceding paragraphs is to grant as much flexibility with specificity as possible with respect to the assets of the estate. In paragraph (j), you have covered all assets not specifically identified in any other paragraphs of this Will.

SEVENTH: If I shall not be survived by said spouse, or any issue, all of my estate shall be devised and bequeathed in fee simple as follows:

50% equally to my siblings, and 50% equally to the siblings of my said spouse, or to their estates.

SEVENTH is the maximum disaster clause. It determines what will happen to your assets if you are not survived by any spouse or issue. If there is a common disaster in which all of your immediate family is killed, you want a Will that dots all of the i's and crosses all of the t's to include a provision for what happens in that instance.

EIGHTH: I direct that all inheritance, succession, legacy, and estate taxes and duties, state, federal, or otherwise, which may be assessed property taxable as, or as if, a part of my estate, be paid out of that credit shelter equivalent portion of my estate (SHARE A) hereinbefore given by Paragraph FOURTH of this Will as expenses of administration and not as a charge on the beneficiary or beneficiaries of such property. Regardless, however, of anything contained herein above, said SHARE A shall be increased by any payment required by this Paragraph EIGHTH, so that my estate shall not be liable for any federal estate taxes.

The preceding paragraph deals with the payment of any state inheritance, succession, legacy, or estate taxes. We want all taxes to be paid as expenses of administration and not as a charge on any beneficiary. Note that when I say, "so that my estate shall not be liable for any federal estate taxes," I am *only* referring to the first estate.

NINTH: If any legatee, devisee, or beneficiary under this Will shall in any way directly or indirectly contest or object to the probate of this Will, or dispute any clause or provision hereof, or exercise or attempt to exercise any right of election or other right to take any part or share of my estate against the provisions of this Will, or institute or prosecute, or be in any way directly or indirectly interested or instrumental in the institution or prosecution of, any action, proceeding, contest, or objection, or give any notice, for the purpose of setting aside or invalidating this Will, or any clause or provision hereof, then and in each such case all provisions for such legatee, devisee, or beneficiary or for his or her descendants above contained in this Will shall be wholly void and ineffectual, and my estate shall be disposed of in like manner as though such legatee, devisee, or beneficiary, if an individual, had predeceased me leaving no descendants who survive me or, if a Trust or other entity, had ceased to exist prior to my death.

Paragraph NINTH is the in terreorum clause. Basically it says that if anybody contests the Will, he or she gets nothing. It is not so much directed against your children as to protect your children. For example, in my experience I have seen the spouse of a decedent's child complain that that child should have gotten more because, for example, the child took care of the aging parent in the last months before the parent's death. The existence of this in terreorum clause allows the child of the decedent to deflect a spouse's pressure to initiate litigation because, if the child were to contest the Will, he or she would get nothing. And since he or she would be entitled to nothing as a beneficiary of the Will, he or she would lack the standing (the legal right) to even contest the Will.

TENTH: In the event that any beneficiary of any Trust estate, by reason of illness, age, incapacity, or any other cause shall, in the Trustees' opinion, be unable properly to receive and disburse the income and principal to which he or she may be entitled, or during the minority of any beneficiary, the Trustees, in their sole discretion, shall pay and apply the income and principal due such beneficiary to his or her comfortable maintenance and support, without the intervention of any guardian and without being required to apply to any Court for leave to make such payments.

This paragraph says that if your beneficiary is either too young, or too old and feeble, to handle his or her assets, then the trustees are directed to use those assets directly for the comfortable maintenance and support of the beneficiary without being required to go to court. You never, ever want to go to court if you can avoid it.

ELEVENTH: I direct that all legacies and all shares and interests in my estate, whether principal or income while in the hands of my Executors or Trustees, shall not be subject to attachment, execution, or sequestration for any debt, contract, obligation, or liability of any legatee or beneficiary and shall not be subject to pledge, assignment, conveyance, or anticipation.

This paragraph protects the assets against any claims of creditors of the beneficiaries while those assets are held in trust. Once the assets are out of trust and in the hands of the beneficiaries, at that point creditors can go after those assets.

This paragraph also protects against a 17-year-old beneficiary going into an auto dealership to pick up a Corvette based upon his or her "anticipation" of receiving income or principal distributions in the future.

TWELFTH: Notwithstanding the foregoing, if my spouse shall die prior to the expiration of six (6) months from the date of my death, then the amount referred to in Article THIRD (SHARE B) shall be reduced to an amount which shall obtain for my estate a marital deduction which would result in the lowest combined federal estate tax in both my estate and the estate of my said spouse, on the assumption that my spouse died after me, but on the date of my death, and that the estate of said spouse was valued as of the date on, and in the manner which, my estate is valued for federal estate tax purposes. My purpose is to equalize, insofar as possible, my estate and my spouse's estate for federal estate tax purposes, based upon said assumptions.

What we have done is to create a situation whereby there is no tax to be paid at the first death, but there is a potential tax at the second death. However, there is a special provision in the Tax Code that says that if both husband and wife die within six months of each other, their estates can be equalized so that the sum of the two taxes is less than the single tax based upon our progressive tax system. That's what paragraph TWELFTH does. It allows you to equalize the two taxes so that you pay a lower total combined tax than you would have paid if the first spouse paid zero and the second spouse was subject to the higher progressive tax rate.

THIRTEENTH: I nominate, constitute, and appoint my spouse, (SPOUSE'S NAME), if said spouse be living, as Executrix of this my Last Will and Testament and, if said spouse be not living, my children, age 18 or older, jointly, or, until there be any, (NAME), or, if he can not serve, (NAME), as Executor of this my Last Will and Testament. I nominate, constitute, and appoint (NAME), or if he can not serve, (NAME), as Trustee for all Trusts created under this Will the beneficiaries of which are my spouse or issue, or the issue of my or my said spouse's siblings. I further direct that no bond shall be required of said Executrix or Trustees for the administration of my estate or any Trust created hereunder in any jurisdiction. If my spouse does not survive me, I nominate, constitute, and appoint (NAME), or if he can not serve, (NAME), as Guardians of my minor children without the need for any bond in any jurisdiction.

For most people, this is probably the most important paragraph. You are first selecting the person who will be your executor (a female executor is known as an executrix). You should always have secondary and potentially tertiary executors available if your first choice cannot serve. You then are selecting your trustees. You can have successor trustees or joint trustees if you desire. The role of the trustee is different from the role of the executor. The trustee must take control of the trust assets and interpret the trust terms. The trustee establishes an investment strategy and makes distribution of income and principal as required. The trustee files an annual tax return and is liable for all investment decisions.

Here an attorney or an accountant may be an appropriate selection for a trustee. Can the trustee be a family member? Absolutely. However, the trustee should be a family member who is comfortable with investment and one with whom you have a good personal relationship. Remember, the trustee is the person your beneficiaries are going to depend upon in order to get their money.

Should a trustee be a bank or a financial institution? My normal answer to this question is no. This is because most banks and financial institutions are impersonal; they rarely know who you really are and the intimate needs of your beneficiaries. A really good trust officer will be promoted and you might have someone else handling your account. Moreover, institutional trustees are normally paid on the basis of income earned and the magnitude of assets in the account. Because of that, they will be hesitant to make generous distributions to your beneficiaries as those distributions will reduce their opportunity for fees and income. Layer on top of that the fact that such institutions may be more anxious than you would like to invest in their own internal instruments rather than those of outside entities—and that those instruments may be low yielding with little opportunity for appreciation—and you understand my hesitancy in recommending institutional trustees.

Again, if you are selecting individuals, make sure you delineate successor trustees if your primary trustee is not available.

The most important thing in many Wills for people with young children is the selection of guardians. Again here, if the first selection is not available, you should provide for a successor.

In all cases, I recommend that your selected representatives be able to serve without posting a bond. If you have any hesitancy about their ability, stability, or honesty, then perhaps you should look further for an alternative selection.

IN WITNESS WHEREOF, I have hereunto set my hand and seal this day of   , Two Thousand (2000).

_____

(YOUR NAME)

The foregoing Will, consisting of (number) typewritten pages, including this page, was signed, sealed, published, and declared by the said (YOUR NAME) as and for his Last Will and Testament, in the presence of us who were present at the same time, and who, thereupon, at his request, in his presence and in the presence of each other, have hereunto subscribed our names as Witnesses.

_____ _residing at_ _____

_____ _residing at_ _____

_____ _residing at_ _____

You then date the Will, sign the Will, and have the Will witnessed. Normally you need two non-beneficiary witnesses. I always use three just to make sure.

Once you have signed your Will and that Will has been appropriately witnessed, you have a good Will.

However, many states have instituted the concept of a self-proving Will. If your Will is signed twice by you, and signed twice by your witnesses, and the second signatures are notarized, that creates a self-proving Will. With a self-proving Will, you never have to bring the witnesses in to establish the legitimacy of the Will itself. In many states, if you have a self-proving Will, all you need to do is bring the Will and the death certificate to a court of competent jurisdiction, and you are done with probate.

Qualified Terminable Interest Property

There may be circumstances where you would be hesitant to bequeath the remainder of your estate to your spouse outright. Your spouse may have children from a prior marriage or you may be concerned about a subsequent remarriage after your death. In those circumstances, in order to preserve your estate for your children rather than laying it bare for a subsequent spouse, a special kind of trust is created. This trust, known as a QTIP Trust, mandates that your surviving spouse receive all of the income of the trust, allows limited ascertainable distributions from principal, and requires all assets, after any and all estate or inheritance taxes due are paid from those assets, to go to your specified children.

The trust will not be taxable in your estate, but will potentially be includable in the estate of your surviving spouse.

An example of a Testamentary Will with a QTIP provision follows. It is the same as the prior Will except for paragraph THIRD.

LAST WILL AND TESTAMENT
OF
(YOUR NAME)

I, (YOUR NAME), domiciled and residing at (Your Address), being of sound and disposing mind, memory, and understanding, do hereby make, publish, and declare this to be my Last Will and Testament, thereby revoking all Wills and codicils heretofore made by me.

FIRST: I direct the payment of all my just debts and funeral and testamentary expenses as soon as convenient after my decease.

SECOND: If my spouse, (SPOUSE'S NAME), shall survive me by 30 days (720 hours), then I direct my Executor to divide the remainder of my estate, both real and personal, of or to which I am now or may hereafter become seized, possessed, or entitled, into two parts, so that the first part, hereinafter designated as SHARE A, shall constitute an amount of my adjusted gross estate as defined by the Internal Revenue Code and finally determined for federal estate tax purposes, to be computed by my Executor to total the then CURRENT maximum credit equivalent amount allowed by law. This amount shall be reduced by any credit equivalent amount used during my lifetime for inter vivos gifts.

The second part, hereinafter designated as SHARE B, shall constitute the entire balance of my said residuary estate. In allocating property to SHARE B, my Executor shall not use any property in respect of which no marital deduction is allowed. To the extent that other property qualifying for the marital deduction is available, my Executor shall not allocate to SHARE B: (a) assets with respect to which a credit for foreign taxes paid is allowable under the Internal Revenue Code: (b) assets which may be subject to both income and estate taxes and which may be eligible for a credit or deduction. SHARE A and SHARE B shall be disposed of as provided in Paragraphs THIRD and FOURTH of this Will.

It is my primary intent that the marital deduction bequest in SHARE B and the property comprising that share shall qualify for the federal estate tax marital deduction, notwithstanding any provision in my Will that might be construed as compromising this objective. All questions regarding the marital deduction bequest and this share shall be resolved accordingly. The powers and discretions of the Executor and Trustee with respect to administration of my estate and of said share shall not be exercised or exercisable except in a manner consistent with my intent as expressed in this paragraph. To the extent that any other provision of my Will conflicts with my primary intent as expressed in this paragraph, giving rise to an ambiguity, the ambiguity shall be resolved as directed in this paragraph. Should there be an ambiguity as to whether any provision necessary for qualification for the marital deduction is included in my Will, the ambiguity shall be resolved as directed in this paragraph. As regards the marital deduction, all other provisions of my Will are subordinate to this provision.

THIRD: I give, devise, and bequeath SHARE B, my residuary estate, to my hereinafter named TRUSTEE, IN TRUST, NEVERTHELESS, for the sole benefit of my surviving spouse during said spouse's lifetime, and said Trustee shall from the date of my death pay said spouse all the income at least semiannually, and so much of the principal as may be necessary or appropriate for the educational needs, medical care, and in order to maintain the then standard of living of said spouse, taking into account any other means of support said spouse may have to the knowledge of my Trustee. Upon the death of my surviving spouse, my Trustee shall distribute any accrued but unpaid income to my surviving spouse's estate. All other assets held in such Trust shall, after paying any and all estate or inheritance taxes which may be due from my surviving spouse's estate on account of this Trust, be held, administrated, and distributed as set forth in Item FOURTH of this Will.

This Item is intended to give my estate maximum tax saving flexibility by creating a "qualified terminable interest trust," and same shall be so construed.

If my spouse shall fail to survive me, then the bequest for the benefit of said spouse shall lapse and shall pass as part of SHARE A hereinafter disposed of.

FOURTH: I give, devise, and bequeath SHARE A to my hereinafter named TRUSTEE, IN TRUST, NEVERTHELESS, for the following uses and purposes:

(a) To invest in high-yield issues to the extent possible and reinvest the income and profits therefrom;

(b) Commencing with the date of my death, to pay to or apply for the benefit of my said spouse, at the request of said spouse, during the lifetime of said spouse, all the net income in convenient installments, at least as frequently as quarter-annually;

(c) In addition to the payment of such income, to pay to or apply for benefit of my said spouse during the whole lifetime, all or none of the principal of the Trust fund as my Trustee, in the Trustee's uncontrolled judgment and discretion, shall consider necessary or advisable for my said spouse's medical and educational needs and in order to maintain said spouse's current standard of living as of the date of my death. In addition, my spouse, (SPOUSE'S NAME), during the lifetime of said spouse, shall have the noncumulative right to withdraw each year from the principal of the Trust estate the sum of five thousand dollars ($5,000) or five percent (5%) of the then principal of the Trust estate, whichever amount shall be greater;

(d) Upon the death of my said spouse, to divide the then remaining principal of the Trust as follows:

The remaining principal of the Trust shall be divided into so many equal shares that there shall be one of said equal shares for each child of mine then living and one for the then surviving issue, per stirpes, collectively of each child of mine who shall not be then living, and to set aside one of said shares for each child of mine then living and one of said shares for the then surviving issue, per stirpes, collectively of each child of mine who shall not be then living, and to hold, administer, and distribute each of said shares as provided in the following sections (e) and (f);

(e) As to the one share so set aside for the benefit of each child above living, each share is hereby given to my hereinafter TRUSTEE, IN TRUST, NEVERTHELESS, to hold and administer the same and to pay to or apply for the benefit of said children, equally, per stirpes, all the net income in convenient installments, at least as frequently as quarter-annually. In addition to the payment of such income, to pay to or apply for the benefit of said children, so much, all or none, of the principal of said equal share as my Trustee, in his or her uncontrolled judgment and discretion, shall consider necessary or advisable for the support, maintenance, and education of such children, and in order to maintain his or her current standard of living, said payments to be made subject to the schedule below, at which time the remainder of his or her respective share of my estate, with the accumulations, if any, shall be paid and distributed to him or her, or if he or she shall die before that time, shall be paid and distributed upon his or her death to his or her Executors or administrators, to be administered and distributed as part of his or her estate.

Age	Per Stirpes Share of Principal
18	5%
21	10%
25	25%
30	25%
35	35% (REMAINDER)

(f) As to the one share so set aside for the benefit of the then surviving issue, per stirpes, collectively of each child of mine who shall not be then living, to pay and distribute the same to the said then surviving issue of said children, per stirpes, for whom said share was so set aside, subject to the provisions of Paragraph FIFTH hereof, if any of such issue be then not yet 35 years of age;

FIFTH: If any part of my estate shall become payable or distributable at any time to the issue of my children who shall not yet be 35 years of age, then I give, devise, and bequeath his or her respective share of my estate to my hereinafter named TRUSTEE, IN TRUST, NEVERTHELESS, to hold and administer the same and to pay to or for the benefit of each such issue, so much, all or none, of said share, both income and principal, as my Trustee, in said Trustee's uncontrolled judgment and discretion, shall consider necessary or advisable for the support, maintenance, and education of such issue as per the schedule below, at which time the remainder of his or her respective share of my estate, with the accumulations, if any, shall be paid and distributed to him or her, or if he or she dies before that time, shall be paid and distributed upon his or her death to his or her Executors and administrators, to be administered and distributed as part of his or her estate.

Age	Per Stirpes Share of Principal
18	5%
21	10%
25	25%
30	25%
35	35% (REMAINDER)

SIXTH: In addition to all powers now or hereafter conferred upon an Executor or Trustee of a (Your State) resident decedent under the law of (Your State), I confer upon my Executor and Trustees the following powers to be exercised by them as in their discretion they may deem for the best interests of my estate or the Trusts created by this Will and without authorization by any Court.

(a) To retain any and all investments and property, real and personal, that I may own at my decease or that thereafter shall become part of my estate or Trusts, without regard to any principle of diversification and notwithstanding the same may be of a wasting nature or may not be recognized by law as legal investments for Trust funds;

(b) To invest and reinvest my estate or Trust funds in stocks, bonds, or other securities, notes, mortgages, units of participation in any common Trust fund maintained by my Trustee, or in any other property, real or personal, without regard to decisional or statutory law, rules of court, or principles concerning the investment of Trust funds, or to the amount which shall be invested in any one investment or type of investment and even though all, or substantially all, of the Trust fund may be invested in common stocks or other so-called "equities";

(c) To sell and dispose of any and all property, real or personal, of which I may die seized or possessed or which may become part of my estate or the Trusts created by this Will, either at public or private sale and upon such terms and conditions as they deem for the best interests of my estate and to make good and sufficient conveyances in the law therefor;

(d) To use Executor's commissions, attorney's fees, and other administration expenses, or part thereof, as deductions for estate tax purposes or income tax purposes and to use date of death values or optional values for estate tax purposes, without regard to the effect thereof on any of the interests or shares under this Will, and I direct that there shall be no adjustment of such interests or shares by reason of any action taken by my Executor in respect to the foregoing and all action shall be final, conclusive, and binding upon all beneficiaries;

(e) To borrow, in order to invest, to pay taxes, debts, or other proper liabilities, such sum or sums of money from time to time and for such periods of time and upon such terms and conditions as my Executor and Trustee shall deem advisable, and to secure the same by mortgage or pledge of any part of my estate, real or personal, and to execute and deliver bonds, notes, mortgages, agreements, and other instruments necessary or proper to evidence and secure the loans so made;

(f) To exercise any stock options that I may own at my death and in connection therewith to borrow funds to exercise said options;

(g) To make division, partition, and distribution of my estate or Trusts in cash or kind, or partly in each, and for the purpose of making such division, partition, and distribution in kind, the assets selected by my Executor and Trustees shall be valued at their respective values on the date or dates of division, partition, or distribution;

(h) To employ such accountants, custodians, attorneys, investment counsel, and other persons as they may deem advisable in the administration of my estate or any Trust created hereunder and to pay them such compensation as they may deem proper;

(i) To allocate to principal all stock dividends and cash in lieu of fractional shares paid as a result of a stock dividend received on any stock held in my estate or any Trust created hereunder;

(j) To exercise generally with respect to any and all stocks, securities, or other property held hereunder all rights, powers, and privileges that may be lawfully exercised by persons owning similar property in their own individual right.

SEVENTH: If I shall not be survived by said spouse, or any issue, all of my estate shall be devised and bequeathed in fee simple as follows:

50% equally to my siblings, and 50% equally to the siblings of my said spouse, or to their estates.

EIGHTH: I direct that all inheritance, succession, legacy, and estate taxes and duties, state, federal, or otherwise, which may be assessed property taxable as, or as if, a part of my estate, be paid out of that credit shelter equivalent portion of my estate (SHARE A) hereinbefore given by Paragraph FOURTH of this Will as expenses of administration and not as a charge on the beneficiary or beneficiaries of such property. Regardless, however, of anything contained herein above, said SHARE A shall be increased by any payment required by this Paragraph EIGHTH, so that my estate shall not be liable for any federal estate taxes.

NINTH: If any legatee, devisee, or beneficiary under this Will shall in any way directly or indirectly contest or object to the probate of this Will, or dispute any clause or provision hereof, or exercise or attempt to exercise any right of election or other right to take any part or share of my estate against the provisions of this Will, or institute or prosecute, or be in any way directly or indirectly interested or instrumental in the institution or prosecution of, any action, proceeding, contest, or objection, or give any notice, for the purpose of setting aside or invalidating this Will, or any clause or provision hereof, then and in each such case all provisions for such legatee, devisee, or beneficiary or for his or her descendants above contained in this Will shall be wholly void and ineffectual, and my estate shall be disposed of in like manner as though such legatee, devisee, or beneficiary, if an individual, had predeceased me leaving no descendants who survive me or, if a Trust or other entity, had ceased to exist prior to my death.

TENTH: In the event that any beneficiary of any Trust estate, by reason of illness, age, incapacity, or any other cause shall, in the Trustees' opinion, be unable properly to receive and disburse the income and principal to which he or she may be entitled, or during the minority of any beneficiary, the Trustees, in their sole discretion, shall pay and apply the income and principal due such beneficiary to his or her comfortable maintenance and support, without the intervention of any guardian and without being required to apply to any Court for leave to make such payments.

ELEVENTH: I direct that all legacies and all shares and interests in my estate, whether principal or income while in the hands of my Executors or Trustees, shall not be subject to attachment, execution, or sequestration for any debt, contract, obligation, or liability of any legatee or beneficiary and shall not be subject to pledge, assignment, conveyance, or anticipation.

TWELFTH: Notwithstanding the foregoing, if my spouse shall die prior to the expiration of six (6) months from the date of my death, then the amount referred to in Article THIRD (SHARE B) shall be reduced to an amount which shall obtain for my estate a marital deduction which would result in the lowest combined federal estate tax in both my estate and the estate of my said spouse, on the assumption that my spouse died after me, but on the date of my death, and that the estate of said spouse was valued as of the date on, and in the manner which, my estate is valued for federal estate tax purposes. My purpose is to equalize, insofar as possible, my estate and my spouse's estate for federal estate tax purposes, based upon said assumptions.

THIRTEENTH: I nominate, constitute, and appoint my spouse, (SPOUSE'S NAME), if said spouse be living, as Executrix of this my Last Will and Testament and, if said spouse be not living, my children, age 18 or older, jointly, or, until there be any, (NAME), or, if he can not serve, (NAME), as Executor of this my Last Will and Testament. I nominate, constitute, and appoint (NAME), or if he can not serve, (NAME), as Trustee for all Trusts created under this Will the beneficiaries of which are my spouse or issue, or the issue of my or my said spouse's siblings. I further direct that no bond shall be required of said Executrix or Trustees for the administration of my estate or any Trust created hereunder in any jurisdiction. If my spouse does not survive me, I nominate, constitute, and appoint (NAME), or if he can not serve, (NAME), as Guardians of my minor children without the need for any bond in any jurisdiction.

IN WITNESS WHEREOF, I have hereunto set my hand and seal this day of   , Two Thousand (2000).

_____

(YOUR NAME)

The foregoing Will, consisting of (number) typewritten pages, including this page, was signed, sealed, published, and declared by the said (YOUR NAME) as and for his Last Will and Testament, in the presence of us who were present at the same time, and who, thereupon, at his request, in his presence and in the presence of each other, have hereunto subscribed our names as Witnesses.

_____ residing at _____

_____ residing at _____

_____ residing at _____

STATE OF (YOUR STATE)

SS:

COUNTY OF (YOUR COUNTY)

We, (Name), (Name), (Name), and (YOUR NAME), the Witnesses and Testator, respectively, whose names are signed to the foregoing instrument, being duly sworn, do hereby declare to the undersigned authority that the Testator signed and executed the instrument as his Last Will, and that he executed it as his free and voluntary act for the purposes therein expressed, and that each of the Witnesses, in the presence and hearing of the Testator, signed the Will as Witness and that to the best of his or her knowledge, the Testator was at that time eighteen (18) years of age or older, of sound mind, and under no constraint or undue influence.

_____
Testator

_____

Witness

_____

Witness

_____

Witness

    SUBSCRIBED, SWORN TO, AND ACKNOWLEDGED before me by (YOUR NAME), the Testator, and subscribed and sworn before me by the above Witnesses, Witness this _____ day of _____ , 2000.

_____

Notary Public

Adult Children

There may be a situation where you have all adult children and do not see the need to have an aging schedule for them. If that's the case, then simply substitute the following for paragraph FOURTH in the original Will.

    FOURTH: I give, devise, and bequeath SHARE A to my hereinafter named TRUSTEE, IN TRUST, NEVERTHELESS, for the following uses and purposes:

(a) To invest in high-yield issues to the extent possible and reinvest the income and profits therefrom;

(b) Commencing with the date of my death, to pay to or apply for the benefit of my said spouse, at the request of said spouse, during the lifetime of said spouse, all the net income in convenient installments, at least as frequently as quarter-annually;

(c) In addition to the payment of such income, to pay to or apply for the benefit of my said spouse during the whole lifetime, all or none of the principal of the Trust fund as my Trustee, in the Trustee's uncontrolled judgment and discretion, shall consider necessary or advisable for my said spouse's medical and educational needs and in order to maintain said spouse's current standard of living as of the date of my death. In addition, my spouse, (SPOUSE'S NAME), during the lifetime of said spouse, shall have the noncumulative right to withdraw each year from the principal of the Trust estate the sum of five thousand dollars ($5,000) or five percent (5%) of the then principal of the Trust estate, whichever amount shall be greater;

(d) Upon the death of my said spouse, to divide the then remaining principal of the Trust as follows:

The remaining principal of the Trust shall be divided into so many equal shares that there shall be one of said equal shares for each child of mine then living and one for the then surviving issue, per stirpes, collectively of each child of mine who shall not be then living, and to set aside one of said shares for each child of mine then living and one of said shares for the then surviving issue, per stirpes, collectively of each child of mine who shall not be then living, and to hold, administer, and distribute each of said shares as provided in the following sections (e) and (f);

(e) *As to the one share so set aside for the benefit of each child above living, each share is hereby given in fee simple absolute;*

(f) As to the one share so set aside for the benefit of the then surviving issue, per stirpes, collectively of each child of mine who shall not be then living, to pay and distribute the same to the said then surviving issue of said children, per stirpes, for whom said share was so set aside, subject to the provisions of Paragraph FIFTH hereof, if any of such issue be then not yet 35 years of age;

Pour Over Wills

In certain states, and under certain circumstances, it is suggested that you use a revocable trust (also known as a living trust or a Living Will) and a Pour Over Will rather than the traditional Wills discussed previously. All Wills are made public record. That means that if you are concerned with privacy issues, you may want to use the Pour Over Will into a revocable trust rather than the standard Testamentary Will.

Alternatively, you may be in a state where attorneys charge a percentage of the probate estate (your probate estate is the estate that passes exclusively through your Will) as their fee to take you through probate. In those cases, you can significantly reduce your legal fees by minimizing the size of your probate estate. This is how it's done.

Rather than owning all of your assets directly, you would own all of your assets through a revocable trust. A revocable trust is a trust that you can change and/or revoke at any time. Since you can change or revoke the trust any time, from a federal estate tax point of view and from a federal income tax point of view, the trust is ignored. However, from a state law point of view, those assets in the trust do not pass as part of your probate estate. They pass as per the specific directions contained in the trust.

To do this, you title all of your assets in the name of the revocable trust. Your beneficiaries are as beneficiaries not of your estate, but of your trust. Those assets therefore are not subject to potential exposure as a Testamentary Will, nor will those assets be subject to legal fees as part of your probate estate.

In states where attorneys charge a percentage of the probate estate as their legal fee, this is the route to elect.

Let's take a look at the revocable trust.

THE (YOUR NAME) REVOCABLE TRUST

  On   , this Trust was created by (YOUR NAME), hereinafter referred to as the "Grantor," and sometimes as the "Trustee," domiciled and residing at (Your Address), who declared that said person holds and administers the Trust funds as follows:

  The Grantor holds, as Trustee, the property listed in Schedule A attached hereto and made an integral part hereof, to be held and administered according to the terms of this Trust. The Grantor and anyone else may transfer additional property to the then Trustee at any time, whether during the Grantor's life or after the Grantor's death, including life insurance proceeds, to be held and administered according to the terms of this Trust.

  The Grantor can revoke or amend all or any part of this Trust at any time, without the consent of anyone, by delivering to the Trustee a written instrument specifying the character and date of the intended amendment or revocation, or by specific reference to this Trust in the Grantor's Last Will. During the lifetime of the Grantor, the power to revoke or amend all or any part of this Trust shall be exercisable by the Grantor's legally authorized attorney-in-fact, in the same manner and under the same conditions as the Grantor could have exercised them. However, the Trustee's duties, powers, or liabilities can not be changed without the Trustee's prior written consent. Upon the Grantor's death, this Trust shall become irrevocable and shall be administered as per the provisions below.

The first three paragraphs establish the trust, detail the property of the trust, provide that the trust can be changed by you as grantor at any time during your lifetime, and mandate that the trust become irrevocable upon your death. Notice that all of the assets of the trust can be listed on Schedule A and can be constantly updated as more assets are transferred into the trust.

  The trust is then used as a substitute for your Testamentary Will. Each of the subsequent paragraphs are the equivalent of the same paragraphs in the original Testamentary Will provided earlier. Note that instead of there being both an executor and trustee, the trustee here serves the same purpose as the executor did in the original Testamentary Will. To transfer an asset into the revocable trust, you merely have to change the title of the asset. For example, if I had a brokerage account under the name of Jeff Schnepper, I would change the account to be titled the Jeff Schnepper Revocable Trust. Any property that I owned would be redeeded from me to the Jeff Schnepper Revocable Trust.

Just because you have a revocable trust doesn't mean that you don't need a Testamentary Will. There are going to be things that you have not transferred into your revocable trust. Your last Social Security check and the cash in your pocket when you die will probably not be part of your revocable trust. How then do you get these assets into your revocable trust? That's where the Pour Over Will comes into play. Your Last Will and Testament will be structured to "pour over" all of the assets into your revocable trust. Following is an example of a Pour Over Will for someone who has adult children. Note the need for an aging schedule for grandchildren, but not for children, since the youngest child in this case was over age 35.

LAST WILL AND TESTAMENT
OF
(YOUR NAME)

I, (YOUR NAME), domiciled and residing at (Your Address), being of sound and disposing mind, memory, and understanding, do hereby make, publish, and declare this to be my Last Will and Testament, thereby revoking all Wills and codicils heretofore made by me.

FIRST: I direct the payment of all my just debts and funeral and testamentary expenses as soon as convenient after my decease.

SECOND: I direct my Executor to pour over the remainder of my estate, both real and personal, of or to which I am now or may hereafter become seized, possessed, or entitled, into the (YOUR NAME) REVOCABLE TRUST dated .

THIRD: In addition to all powers now or hereafter conferred upon an Executor of a (Your State) resident decedent under the law of (Your State), I confer upon my Executors the following powers to be exercised by them as in their discretion they may deem for the best interests of my estate created by this Will and without authorization by any Court.

(a) To retain any and all investments and property, real and personal, that I may own at my decease or that thereafter shall become part of my estate, without regard to any principle of diversification and notwithstanding the same may be of a wasting nature or may not be recognized by law as legal investments for estate funds;

(b) To invest and reinvest my estate funds in stocks, bonds, or other securities, notes, mortgages, units of participation in any common Trust fund maintained by my Executor, or in any other property, real or personal, without regard to decisional or statutory law, rules of court, or principles concerning the investment of estate funds, or to the amount which shall be invested in any one investment or type of investment and even though all, or substantially all, of the estate fund may be invested in common stocks or other so-called "equities";

(c) To sell and dispose of any and all property, real or personal, of which I may die seized or possessed or which may become part of my estate created by this Will, either at public or private sale and upon such terms and conditions as they deem for the best interests of my estate and to make good and sufficient conveyances in the law therefor;

(d) To use Executor's commissions, attorneys' fees, and other administration expenses, or part thereof, as deductions for estate tax purposes or income tax purposes and to use date of death values or optional values for estate tax purposes, without regard to the effect thereof on any of the interests or shares under this Will, and I direct that there shall be no adjustment of such interests or shares by reason of any action taken by my Executor in respect to the foregoing and all action shall be final, conclusive, and binding upon all beneficiaries;

(e) To borrow, in order to invest, to pay taxes, debts, or other proper liabilities, such sum or sums of money from time to time and for such periods of time and upon such terms and conditions as my Executor shall deem advisable, and to secure the same by mortgage or pledge of any part of my estate, real or personal, and to execute and deliver bonds, notes, mortgages, agreements, and other instruments necessary or proper to evidence and secure the loans so made;

(f) To exercise any stock options that I may own at my death and in connection therewith to borrow funds to exercise said options;

(g) To make division, partition, and distribution of my estate in cash or kind, or partly in each, and for the purpose of making such division, partition, and distribution in kind, the assets selected by my Executor shall be valued at their respective values on the date or dates of division, partition, or distribution;

(h) To employ such accountants, custodians, attorneys, investment counsel, and other persons as they may deem advisable in the administration of my estate or created hereunder and to pay them such compensation as they may deem proper;

(i) To allocate to principal all stock dividends and cash in lieu of fractional shares paid as a result of a stock dividend received on any stock held in my estate created hereunder;

(j) To exercise generally with respect to any and all stocks, securities, or other property held hereunder all rights, powers, and privileges that may be lawfully exercised by persons owning similar property in their own individual right.

FOURTH: If any legatee, devisee, or beneficiary under this Will shall in any way directly or indirectly contest or object to the probate of this Will, or dispute any clause or provision hereof, or exercise or attempt to exercise any right of election or other right to take any part or share of my estate against the provisions of this Will, or institute or prosecute, or be in any way directly or indirectly interested or instrumental in the institution or prosecution of, any action, proceeding, contest, or objection, or give any notice, for the purpose of setting aside or invalidating this Will, or any clause or provision hereof, then and in each such case all provisions for such legatee, devisee, or beneficiary or for his or her descendants above contained in this Will shall be wholly void and ineffectual, and my estate shall be disposed of in like manner as though such legatee, devisee, or beneficiary, if an individual, had predeceased me leaving no descendants who survive me or, if a Trust or other entity, had ceased to exist prior to my death.

FIFTH: I direct that all legacies and all shares and interests in my estate, whether principal or income while in the hands of my Executors, shall not be subject to attachment, execution, or sequestration for any debt, contract, obligation, or liability of any legatee or beneficiary and shall not be subject to pledge, assignment, conveyance, or anticipation.

SIXTH: I nominate, constitute, and appoint my spouse, (SPOUSE'S NAME), if said spouse be living, as Executrix of this my Last Will and Testament and, if said spouse be not living, my children, jointly, as Executor of this my Last Will and Testament. I further direct that no bond shall be required of said Executrix for the administration of my estate created hereunder in any jurisdiction.

IN WITNESS WHEREOF, I have hereunto set my hand and seal this day of   , Two Thousand (2000).

_____
(YOUR NAME)

The foregoing Will, consisting of (number) typewritten pages, including this page, was signed, sealed, published, and declared by the said (YOUR NAME) as and for his Last Will and Testament, in the presence of us who were present at the same time, and who, thereupon, at his request, in his presence and in the presence of each other, have hereunto subscribed our names as Witnesses.

_____ residing at _____

_____ residing at _____

_____ residing at _____

STATE OF (YOUR STATE)

SS:

COUNTY OF (YOUR COUNTY)

We, (Name), (Name), (Name), and (YOUR NAME), the Witnesses and Testator, respectively, whose names are signed to the foregoing instrument, being duly sworn, do hereby declare to the undersigned authority that the Testator signed and executed the instrument as his Last Will, and that he executed it as his free and voluntary act for the purposes therein expressed, and that each of the Witnesses, in the presence and hearing of the Testator, signed the Will as Witness and that to the best of his or her knowledge, the Testator was at that time eighteen (18) years of age or older, of sound mind, and under no constraint or undue influence.

_____
Testator

_____
Witness

_____
Witness

_____
Witness

SUBSCRIBED, SWORN TO, AND ACKNOWLEDGED before me by (YOUR NAME), the Testator, and subscribed and sworn before me by the above Witnesses, Witness this   day of   , 2000.

_____
Notary Public

EXAMPLES

LAST WILL AND TESTAMENT
OF
(YOUR NAME)

I, (YOUR NAME), domiciled and residing at (Your Address), being of sound and disposing mind, memory, and understanding, do hereby make, publish, and declare this to be my Last Will and Testament, thereby revoking all Wills and codicils heretofore made by me.

FIRST: I direct the payment of all my just debts and funeral and testamentary expenses as soon as convenient after my decease.

SECOND: If my spouse, (SPOUSE'S NAME), shall survive me by 30 days (720 hours), then I direct my Executor to divide the remainder of my estate, both real and personal, of or to which I am now or may hereafter become seized, possessed, or entitled, into two parts, so that the first part, hereinafter designated as SHARE A, shall constitute an amount of my adjusted gross estate as defined by the Internal Revenue Code and finally determined for federal estate tax purposes, to be computed by my Executor to total the then CURRENT maximum credit equivalent amount allowed by law. This amount shall be reduced by any credit equivalent amount used during my lifetime for inter vivos gifts.

The second part, hereinafter designated as SHARE B, shall constitute the entire balance of my said residuary estate. In allocating property to SHARE B, my Executor shall not use any property in respect of which no marital deduction is allowed. To the extent that other property qualifying for the marital deduction is available, my Executor shall not allocate to SHARE B: (a) assets with respect to which a credit for foreign taxes paid is allowable under the Internal Revenue Code: (b) assets which may be subject to both income and estate taxes and which may be eligible for a credit or deduction. SHARE A and SHARE B shall be disposed of as provided in Paragraphs THIRD and FOURTH of this Will.

It is my primary intent that the marital deduction bequest in SHARE B and the property comprising that share shall qualify for the federal estate tax marital deduction, notwithstanding any provision in my Will that might be construed as compromising this objective. All questions regarding the marital deduction bequest and this share shall be resolved accordingly. The powers and discretions of the Executor and Trustee with respect to administration of my estate and of said share shall not be exercised or exercisable except in a manner consistent with my intent as expressed in this paragraph. To the extent that any other provision of my Will conflicts with my primary intent as expressed in this paragraph, giving rise to an ambiguity, the ambiguity shall be resolved as directed in this paragraph. Should there be an ambiguity as to whether any provision necessary for qualification for the marital deduction is included in my Will, the ambiguity shall be resolved as directed in this paragraph. As regards the marital deduction, all other provisions of my Will are subordinate to this provision.

THIRD: I give, devise and bequeath SHARE B, my residuary estate, to my said spouse in fee simple without any restrictions whatsoever. It shall consist of, to the extent possible, my cash and liquid assets.

If my said spouse shall fail to survive me, then the bequest for the benefit of said spouse shall lapse and shall pass as part of SHARE A hereinafter disposed of.

FOURTH: I give, devise, and bequeath SHARE A to my hereinafter named TRUSTEE, IN TRUST, NEVERTHELESS, for the following uses and purposes:

(a) To invest in high-yield issues to the extent possible and reinvest the income and profits therefrom;

(b) Commencing with the date of my death, to pay to or apply for the benefit of my said spouse, at the request of said spouse, during the lifetime of said spouse, all the net income in convenient installments, at least as frequently as quarter-annually;

(c) In addition to the payment of such income, to pay to or apply for benefit of my said spouse during the whole lifetime, all or none of the principal of the Trust fund as my Trustee, in the Trustee's uncontrolled judgment and discretion, shall consider necessary or advisable for my said spouse's medical and educational needs and in order to maintain said spouse's current standard of living as of the date of my death. In addition, my spouse, (SPOUSE'S NAME), during the lifetime of said spouse, shall have the non-cumulative right to withdraw each year from the principal of the Trust estate the sum of five thousand dollars ($5,000) or five percent (5%) of the then principal of the Trust estate, whichever amount shall be greater;

(d) Upon the death of my said spouse, to divide the then remaining principal of the Trust as follows:

The remaining principal of the Trust shall be divided into so many equal shares that there shall be one of said equal shares for each child of mine then living and one for the then surviving issue, per stirpes, collectively of each child of mine who shall not be then living, and to set aside one of said shares for each child of mine then living and one of said shares for the then surviving issue, per stirpes, collectively of each child of mine who shall not be then living, and to hold, administer, and distribute each of said shares as provided in the following sections (e) and (f);

(e) As to the one share so set aside for the benefit of each child above living, each share is hereby given to my hereinafter TRUSTEE, IN TRUST, NEVERTHELESS, to hold and administer the same and to pay to or apply for the benefit of said children, equally, per stirpes, all the net income in convenient installments, at least as frequently as quarter-annually. In addition to the payment of such income, to pay to or apply for the benefit of said children, so much, all or none, of the principal of said equal share as my Trustee, in his or her uncontrolled judgment and discretion, shall consider necessary or advisable for the support, maintenance, and education of such children, and in order to maintain his or her current standard of living, said payments to be made subject to the schedule below, at which time the remainder of his or her respective share of my estate, with the accumulations, if any, shall be paid and distributed to him or her, or if he or she shall die before that time, shall be paid and distributed upon his or her death to his or her Executors or administrators, to be administered and distributed as part of his or her estate.

Age	Per Stirpes Share of Principal
18	5%
21	10%
25	25%
30	25%
35	35% (REMAINDER)

(f) As to the one share so set aside for the benefit of the then surviving issue, per stirpes, collectively of each child of mine who shall not be then living, to pay and distribute the same to the said then surviving issue of said children, per stirpes, for whom said share was so set aside, subject to the provisions of Paragraph FIFTH hereof, if any of such issue be then not yet 35 years of age;

FIFTH: If any part of my estate shall become payable or distributable at any time to the issue of my children who shall not yet be 35 years of age, then I give, devise, and bequeath his or her respective share of my estate to my hereinafter named TRUSTEE, IN TRUST, NEVERTHELESS, to hold and administer the same and to pay to or for the benefit of each such issue, so much, all or none, of said share, both income and principal, as my Trustee, in said Trustee's uncontrolled judgment and discretion, shall consider necessary or advisable for the support, maintenance, and education of such issue as per the schedule below, at which time the remainder of his or her respective share of my estate, with the accumulations, if any, shall be paid and distributed to him or her, or if he or she dies before that time, shall be paid and distributed upon his or her death to his or her Executors and administrators, to be administered and distributed as part of his or her estate.

Age	Per Stirpes Share of Principal
18	5%
21	10%
25	25%
30	25%
35	35% (REMAINDER)

SIXTH: In addition to all powers now or hereafter conferred upon an Executor or Trustee of a (Your State) resident decedent under the law of (Your State), I confer upon my Executor and Trustees the following powers to be exercised by them as in their discretion they may deem for the best interests of my estate or the Trusts created by this Will and without authorization by any Court.

(a) To retain any and all investments and property, real and personal, that I may own at my decease or that thereafter shall become part of my estate or Trusts, without regard to any principle of diversification and notwithstanding the same may be of a wasting nature or may not be recognized by law as legal investments for Trust funds;

(b) To invest and reinvest my estate or Trust funds in stocks, bonds, or other securities, notes, mortgages, units of participation in any common Trust fund maintained by my Trustee, or in any other property, real or personal, without regard to decisional or statutory law, rules of court, or principles concerning the investment of Trust funds, or to the amount which shall be invested in any one investment or type of investment and even though all, or substantially all, of the Trust fund may be invested in common stocks or other so-called "equities";

(c) To sell and dispose of any and all property, real or personal, of which I may die seized or possessed or which may become part of my estate or the Trusts created by this Will, either at public or private sale and upon such terms and conditions as they deem for the best interests of my estate and to make good and sufficient conveyances in the law therefor;

(d) To use Executor's commissions, attorneys' fees, and other administration expenses, or part thereof, as deductions for estate tax purposes or income tax purposes and to use date of death values or optional values for estate tax purposes, without regard to the effect thereof on any of the interests or shares under this Will, and I direct that there shall be no adjustment of such interests or shares by reason of any action taken by my Executor in respect to the foregoing and all action shall be final, conclusive, and binding upon all beneficiaries;

(e) To borrow, in order to invest, to pay taxes, debts, or other proper liabilities, such sum or sums of money from time to time and for such periods of time and upon such terms and conditions as my Executor and Trustee shall deem advisable, and to secure the same by mortgage or pledge of any part of my estate, real or personal, and to execute and deliver bonds, notes, mortgages, agreements, and other instruments necessary or proper to evidence and secure the loans so made;

(f) To exercise any stock options that I may own at my death and in connection therewith to borrow funds to exercise said options;

(g) To make division, partition, and distribution of my estate or Trusts in cash or kind, or partly in each, and for the purpose of making such division, partition, and distribution in kind, the assets selected by my Executor and Trustees shall be valued at their respective values on the date or dates of division, partition, or distribution;

(h) To employ such accountants, custodians, attorneys, investment counsel, and other persons as they may deem advisable in the administration of my estate or any Trust created hereunder and to pay them such compensation as they may deem proper;

(i) To allocate to principal all stock dividends and cash in lieu of fractional shares paid as a result of a stock dividend received on any stock held in my estate or any Trust created hereunder;

(j) To exercise generally with respect to any and all stocks, securities, or other property held hereunder all rights, powers, and privileges that may be lawfully exercised by persons owning similar property in their own individual right.

SEVENTH: If I shall not be survived by said spouse, or any issue, all of my estate shall be devised and bequeathed in fee simple as follows:

50% equally to my siblings, and 50% equally to the siblings of my said spouse, or to their estates.

EIGHTH: I direct that all inheritance, succession, legacy, and estate taxes and duties, state, federal, or otherwise, which may be assessed property taxable as, or as if, a part of my estate, be paid out of that credit shelter equivalent portion of my estate (SHARE A) hereinbefore given by Paragraph FOURTH of this Will as expenses of administration and not as a charge on the beneficiary or beneficiaries of such property. Regardless, however, of anything contained herein above, said SHARE A shall be increased by any payment required by this Paragraph EIGHTH, so that my estate shall not be liable for any federal estate taxes.

NINTH: If any legatee, devisee, or beneficiary under this Will shall in any way directly or indirectly contest or object to the probate of this Will, or dispute any clause or provision hereof, or exercise or attempt to exercise any right of election or other right to take any part or share of my estate against the provisions of this Will, or institute or prosecute, or be in any way directly or indirectly interested or instrumental in the institution or prosecution of, any action, proceeding, contest, or objection, or give any notice, for the purpose of setting aside or invalidating this Will, or any clause or provision hereof, then and in each such case all provisions for such legatee, devisee, or beneficiary or for his or her descendants above contained in this Will shall be wholly void and ineffectual, and my estate shall be disposed of in like manner as though such legatee, devisee, or beneficiary, if an individual, had predeceased me leaving no descendants who survive me, or, if a Trust or other entity, had ceased to exist prior to my death.

TENTH: In the event that any beneficiary of any Trust estate, by reason of illness, age, incapacity, or any other cause shall, in the Trustees' opinion, be unable properly to receive and disburse the income and principal to which he or she may be entitled, or during the minority of any beneficiary, the Trustees, in their sole discretion, shall pay and apply the income and principal due such beneficiary to his or her comfortable maintenance and support, without the intervention of any guardian and without being required to apply to any Court for leave to make such payments.

ELEVENTH: I direct that all legacies and all shares and interests in my estate, whether principal or income while in the hands of my Executors or Trustees, shall not be subject to attachment, execution, or sequestration for any debt, contract, obligation, or liability of any legatee or beneficiary and shall not be subject to pledge, assignment, conveyance, or anticipation.

TWELFTH: Notwithstanding the foregoing, if my spouse shall die prior to the expiration of six (6) months from the date of my death, then the amount referred to in Article THIRD (SHARE B) shall be reduced to an amount which shall obtain for my estate a marital deduction which would result in the lowest combined federal estate tax in both my estate and the estate of my said spouse, on the assumption that my spouse died after me, but on the date of my death, and that the estate of said spouse was valued as of the date on, and in the manner which, my estate is valued for federal estate tax purposes. My purpose is to equalize, insofar as possible, my estate and my spouse's estate for federal estate tax purposes, based upon said assumptions.

THIRTEENTH: I nominate, constitute, and appoint my spouse, (SPOUSE'S NAME), if said spouse be living, as Executrix of this my Last Will and Testament and, if said spouse be not living, my children, age 18 or older, jointly, or, until there be any, (NAME), or, if he can not serve, (NAME), as Executor of this my Last Will and Testament. I nominate, constitute, and appoint (NAME), or if he can not serve, (NAME), as Trustee for all Trusts created under this Will the beneficiaries of which are my spouse or issue, or the issue of my or my said spouse's siblings. I further direct that no bond shall be required of said Executrix or Trustees for the administration of my estate or any Trust created hereunder in any jurisdiction. If my spouse does not survive me, I nominate, constitute, and appoint (NAME), or if he can not serve, (NAME), as Guardians of my minor children without the need for any bond in any jurisdiction.

IN WITNESS WHEREOF, I have hereunto set my hand and seal this day of   , Two Thousand (2000).

_____
(YOUR NAME)

The foregoing Will, consisting of (number) typewritten pages, including this page, was signed, sealed, published, and declared by the said (YOUR NAME) as and for his Last Will and Testament, in the presence of us who were present at the same time, and who, thereupon, at his request, in his presence and in the presence of each other, have hereunto subscribed our names as Witnesses.

_____ residing at _____

_____ residing at _____

_____ residing at _____

STATE OF (YOUR STATE)

SS:

COUNTY OF (YOUR COUNTY)

We, (Name), (Name), (Name), and (YOUR NAME), the Witnesses and Testator, respectively, whose names are signed to the foregoing instrument, being duly sworn, do hereby declare to the undersigned authority that the Testator signed and executed the instrument as his Last Will, and that he executed it as his free and voluntary act for the purposes therein expressed, and that each of the Witnesses, in the presence and hearing of the Testator, signed the Will as Witness and that to the best of his or her knowledge, the Testator was at that time eighteen (18) years of age or older, of sound mind, and under no constraint or undue influence.

_____

Testator

_____

Witness

_____

Witness

_____

Witness

SUBSCRIBED, SWORN TO, AND ACKNOWLEDGED before me by (YOUR NAME), the Testator, and subscribed and sworn before me by the above Witnesses, Witness this _____ day of _____, 2000.

_____

Notary Public

(QTIP) LAST WILL AND TESTAMENT
OF
(YOUR NAME)

I, (YOUR NAME), domiciled and residing at (Your Address), being of sound and disposing mind, memory, and understanding, do hereby make, publish, and declare this to be my Last Will and Testament, thereby revoking all Wills and codicils heretofore made by me.

FIRST: I direct the payment of all my just debts and funeral and testamentary expenses as soon as convenient after my decease.

SECOND: If my spouse, (SPOUSE'S NAME), shall survive me by 30 days (720 hours), then I direct my Executor to divide the remainder of my estate, both real and personal, of or to which I am now or may hereafter become seized, possessed, or entitled, into two parts, so that the first part, hereinafter designated as SHARE A, shall constitute an amount of my adjusted gross estate as defined by the Internal Revenue Code and finally determined for federal estate tax purposes, to be computed by my Executor to total the then CURRENT maximum credit equivalent amount allowed by law. This amount shall be reduced by any credit equivalent amount used during my lifetime for inter vivos gifts.

The second part, hereinafter designated as SHARE B, shall constitute the entire balance of my said residuary estate. In allocating property to SHARE B, my Executor shall not use any property in respect of which no marital deduction is allowed. To the extent that other property qualifying for the marital deduction is available, my Executor shall not allocate to SHARE B: (a) assets with respect to which a credit for foreign taxes paid is allowable under the Internal Revenue Code: (b) assets which may be subject to both income and estate taxes and which may be eligible for a credit or deduction. SHARE A and SHARE B shall be disposed of as provided in Paragraphs THIRD and FOURTH of this Will.

It is my primary intent that the marital deduction bequest in SHARE B and the property comprising that share shall qualify for the federal estate tax marital deduction, notwithstanding any provision in my Will that might be construed as compromising this objective. All questions regarding the marital deduction bequest and this share shall be resolved accordingly. The powers and discretions of the Executor and Trustee with respect to administration of my estate and of said share shall not be exercised or exercisable except in a manner consistent with my intent as expressed in this paragraph. To the extent that any other provision of my Will conflicts with my primary intent as expressed in this paragraph, giving rise to an ambiguity, the ambiguity shall be resolved as directed in this paragraph. Should there be an ambiguity as to whether any provision necessary for qualification for the marital deduction is included in my Will, the ambiguity shall be resolved as directed in this paragraph. As regards the marital deduction, all other provisions of my Will are subordinate to this provision.

THIRD: I give, devise, and bequeath SHARE B, my residuary estate, to my hereinafter named TRUSTEE, IN TRUST, NEVERTHELESS, for the sole benefit of my surviving spouse during said spouse's lifetime, and said Trustee shall from the date of my death pay said spouse all the income at least semiannually, and so much of the principal as may be necessary or appropriate for the educational needs, medical care, and in order to maintain the then standard of living of said spouse, taking into account any other means of support said spouse may have to the knowledge of my Trustee. Upon the death of my surviving spouse, my Trustee shall distribute any accrued but unpaid income to my surviving spouse's estate. All other assets held in such Trust shall, after paying any and all estate or inheritance taxes which may be due from my surviving spouse's estate on account of this Trust, be held, administered, and distributed as set forth in Item FOURTH of this Will.

This Item is intended to give my estate maximum tax saving flexibility by creating a "qualified terminable interest trust," and same shall be so construed.

If my spouse shall fail to survive me, then the bequest for the benefit of said spouse shall lapse and shall pass as part of SHARE A hereinafter disposed of.

FOURTH: I give, devise, and bequeath SHARE A to my hereinafter named TRUSTEE, IN TRUST, NEVERTHELESS, for the following uses and purposes:

(a) To invest in high-yield issues to the extent possible and reinvest the income and profits therefrom;

(b) Commencing with the date of my death, to pay to or apply for the benefit of my said spouse, at the request of said spouse, during the lifetime of said spouse, all the net income in convenient installments, at least as frequently as quarter-annually;

(c) In addition to the payment of such income, to pay to or apply for benefit of my said spouse during the whole lifetime, all or none of the principal of the Trust fund as my Trustee, in the Trustee's uncontrolled judgment and discretion, shall consider necessary or advisable for my said spouse's medical and educational needs and in order to maintain said spouse's current standard of living as of the date of my death. In addition, my spouse, (SPOUSE'S NAME), during the lifetime of said spouse, shall have the non-cumulative right to withdraw each year from the principal of the Trust estate the sum of five thousand dollars ($5,000) or five percent (5%) of the then principal of the Trust estate, whichever amount shall be greater;

(d) Upon the death of my said spouse, to divide the then remaining principal of the Trust as follows:

The remaining principal of the Trust shall be divided into so many equal shares that there shall be one of said equal shares for each child of mine then living and one for the then surviving issue, per stirpes, collectively of each child of mine who shall not be then living, and to set aside one of said shares for each child of mine then living and one of said shares for the then surviving issue, per stirpes, collectively of each child of mine who shall not be then living, and to hold, administer, and distribute each of said shares as provided in the following sections (e) and (f);

(e) As to the one share so set aside for the benefit of each child above living, each share is hereby given to my hereinafter TRUSTEE, IN TRUST, NEVERTHELESS, to hold and administer the same and to pay to or apply for the benefit of said children, equally, per stirpes, all the net income in convenient installments, at least as frequently as quarter-annually. In addition to the payment of such income, to pay to or apply for the benefit of said children, so much, all or none, of the principal of said equal share as my Trustee, in his or her uncontrolled judgment and discretion, shall consider necessary or advisable for the support, maintenance, and education of such children, and in order to maintain his or her current standard of living, said payments to be made subject to the schedule below, at which time the remainder of his or her respective share of my estate, with the accumulations, if any, shall be paid and distributed to him or her, or if he or she shall die before that time, shall be paid and distributed upon his or her death to his or her Executors or administrators, to be administered and distributed as part of his or her estate.

Age	Per Stirpes Share of Principal
18	5%
21	10%
25	25%
30	25%
35	35% (REMAINDER)

(f) As to the one share so set aside for the benefit of the then surviving issue, per stirpes, collectively of each child of mine who shall not be then living, to pay and distribute the same to the said then surviving issue of said children, per stirpes, for whom said share was so set aside, subject to the provisions of Paragraph FIFTH hereof, if any of such issue be then not yet 35 years of age;

FIFTH: If any part of my estate shall become payable or distributable at any time to the issue of my children who shall not yet be 35 years of age, then I give, devise, and bequeath his or her respective share of my estate to my hereinafter named TRUSTEE, IN TRUST, NEVERTHELESS, to hold and administer the same and to pay to or for the benefit of each such issue, so much, all or none, of said share, both income and principal, as my Trustee, in said Trustee's uncontrolled judgment and discretion, shall consider necessary or advisable for the support, maintenance, and education of such issue as per the schedule below, at which time the remainder of his or her respective share of my estate, with the accumulations, if any, shall be paid and distributed to him or her, or if he or she dies before that time, shall be paid and distributed upon his or her death to his or her Executors and administrators, to be administered and distributed as part of his or her estate.

Age	Per Stirpes Share of Principal
18	5%
21	10%
25	25%
30	25%
35	35% (REMAINDER)

SIXTH: In addition to all powers now or hereafter conferred upon an Executor or Trustee of a (Your State) resident decedent under the law of (Your State), I confer upon my Executor and Trustees the following powers to be exercised by them as in their discretion they may deem for the best interests of my estate or the Trusts created by this Will and without authorization by any Court.

(a) To retain any and all investments and property, real and personal, that I may own at my decease or that thereafter shall become part of my estate or Trusts, without regard to any principle of diversification and notwithstanding the same may be of a wasting nature or may not be recognized by law as legal investments for Trust funds;

(b) To invest and reinvest my estate or Trust funds in stocks, bonds, or other securities, notes, mortgages, units of participation in any common Trust fund maintained by my Trustee, or in any other property, real or personal, without regard to decisional or statutory law, rules of court, or principles concerning the investment of Trust funds, or to the amount which shall be invested in any one investment or type of investment and even though all, or substantially all, of the Trust fund may be invested in common stocks or other so-called "equities";

(c) To sell and dispose of any and all property, real or personal, of which I may die seized or possessed or which may become part of my estate or the Trusts created by this Will, either at public or private sale and upon such terms and conditions as they deem for the best interests of my estate and to make good and sufficient conveyances in the law therefor;

(d) To use Executor's commissions, Attorneys' fees, and other administration expenses, or part thereof, as deductions for estate tax purposes or income tax purposes and to use date of death values or optional values for estate tax purposes, without regard to the effect thereof on any of the interests or shares under this Will, and I direct that there shall be no adjustment of such interests or shares by reason of any action taken by my Executor in respect to the foregoing and all action shall be final, conclusive, and binding upon all beneficiaries;

(e) To borrow, in order to invest, to pay taxes, debts, or other proper liabilities, such sum or sums of money from time to time and for such periods of time and upon such terms and conditions as my Executor and Trustee shall deem advisable, and to secure the same by mortgage or pledge of any part of my estate, real or personal, and to execute and deliver bonds, notes, mortgages, agreements, and other instruments necessary or proper to evidence and secure the loans so made;

(f) To exercise any stock options that I may own at my death and in connection therewith to borrow funds to exercise said options;

(g) To make division, partition, and distribution of my estate or Trusts in cash or kind, or partly in each, and for the purpose of making such division, partition, and distribution in kind, the assets selected by my Executor and Trustees shall be valued at their respective values on the date or dates of division, partition, or distribution;

(h) To employ such accountants, custodians, attorneys, investment counsel, and other persons as they may deem advisable in the administration of my estate or any Trust created hereunder and to pay them such compensation as they may deem proper;

(i) To allocate to principal all stock dividends and cash in lieu of fractional shares paid as a result of a stock dividend received on any stock held in my estate or any Trust created hereunder;

(j) To exercise generally with respect to any and all stocks, securities, or other property held hereunder all rights, powers, and privileges that may be lawfully exercised by persons owning similar property in their own individual right.

SEVENTH: If I shall not be survived by said spouse, or any issue, all of my estate shall be devised and bequeathed in fee simple as follows:

50% equally to my siblings, and 50% equally to the siblings of my said spouse, or to their estates.

EIGHTH: I direct that all inheritance, succession, legacy, and estate taxes and duties, state, federal, or otherwise, which may be assessed property taxable as, or as if, a part of my estate, be paid out of that credit shelter equivalent portion of my estate (SHARE A) hereinbefore given by Paragraph FOURTH of this Will as expenses of administration and not as a charge on the beneficiary or beneficiaries of such property. Regardless, however, of anything contained herein above, said SHARE A shall be increased by any payment required by this Paragraph EIGHTH, so that my estate shall not be liable for any federal estate taxes.

NINTH: If any legatee, devisee, or beneficiary under this Will shall in any way directly or indirectly contest or object to the probate of this Will, or dispute any clause or provision hereof, or exercise or attempt to exercise any right of election or other right to take any part or share of my estate against the provisions of this Will, or institute or prosecute, or be in any way directly or indirectly interested or instrumental in the institution or prosecution of, any action, proceeding, contest, or objection, or give any notice, for the purpose of setting aside or invalidating this Will, or any clause or provision hereof, then and in each such case all provisions for such legatee, devisee, or beneficiary or for his or her descendants above contained in this Will shall be wholly void and ineffectual, and my estate shall be disposed of in like manner as though such legatee, devisee, or beneficiary, if an individual, had predeceased me leaving no descendants who survive me or, if a Trust or other entity, had ceased to exist prior to my death.

TENTH: In the event that any beneficiary of any Trust estate, by reason of illness, age, incapacity, or any other cause shall, in the Trustees' opinion, be unable properly to receive and disburse the income and principal to which he or she may be entitled, or during the minority of any beneficiary, the Trustees, in their sole discretion, shall pay and apply the income and principal due such beneficiary to his or her comfortable maintenance and support, without the intervention of any guardian and without being required to apply to any Court for leave to make such payments.

ELEVENTH: I direct that all legacies and all shares and interests in my estate, whether principal or income while in the hands of my Executors or Trustees, shall not be subject to attachment, execution, or sequestration for any debt, contract, obligation, or liability of any legatee or beneficiary and shall not be subject to pledge, assignment, conveyance, or anticipation.

TWELFTH: Notwithstanding the foregoing, if my spouse shall die prior to the expiration of six (6) months from the date of my death, then the amount referred to in Article THIRD (SHARE B) shall be reduced to an amount which shall obtain for my estate a marital deduction which would result in the lowest combined federal estate tax in both my estate and the estate of my said spouse, on the assumption that my spouse died after me, but on the date of my death, and that the estate of said spouse was valued as of the date on, and in the manner which, my estate is valued for federal estate tax purposes. My purpose is to equalize, insofar as possible, my estate and my spouse's estate for federal estate tax purposes, based upon said assumptions.

THIRTEENTH: I nominate, constitute, and appoint my spouse, (SPOUSE'S NAME), if said spouse be living, as Executrix of this my Last Will and Testament and, if said spouse be not living, my children, age 18 or older, jointly, or, until there be any, (NAME), or, if he can not serve, (NAME), as Executor of this my Last Will and Testament. I nominate, constitute, and appoint (NAME), or if he can not serve, (NAME), as Trustee for all Trusts created under this Will the beneficiaries of which are my spouse or issue, or the issue of my or my said spouse's siblings. I further direct that no bond shall be required of said Executrix or Trustees for the administration of my estate or any Trust created hereunder in any jurisdiction. If my spouse does not survive me, I nominate, constitute, and appoint (NAME), or if he can not serve, (NAME), as Guardians of my minor children without the need for any bond in any jurisdiction.

IN WITNESS WHEREOF, I have hereunto set my hand and seal this day of   , Two Thousand (2000).

_____
(YOUR NAME)

The foregoing Will, consisting of (number) typewritten pages, including this page, was signed, sealed, published, and declared by the said (YOUR NAME) as and for his Last Will and Testament, in the presence of us who were present at the same time, and who, thereupon, at his request, in his presence and in the presence of each other, have hereunto subscribed our names as Witnesses.

_____ residing at _____

_____ residing at _____

_____ residing at _____

STATE OF (YOUR STATE)

                                        SS:

COUNTY OF (YOUR COUNTY)

We, (Name), (Name), (Name), and (YOUR NAME), the Witnesses and Testator, respectively, whose names are signed to the foregoing instrument, being duly sworn, do hereby declare to the undersigned authority that the Testator signed and executed the instrument as his Last Will, and that he executed it as his free and voluntary act for the purposes therein expressed, and that each of the Witnesses, in the presence and hearing of the Testator, signed the Will as Witness and that to the best of his or her knowledge, the Testator was at that time eighteen (18) years of age or older, of sound mind, and under no constraint or undue influence.

                                        _____
                                        Testator

_____

Witness

_____

Witness

_____

Witness

    SUBSCRIBED, SWORN TO, AND ACKNOWLEDGED before me by (YOUR NAME), the Testator, and subscribed and sworn before me by the above Witnesses, Witness this   day of   , 2000.

_____

Notary Public

(ADULT CHILDREN) LAST WILL AND TESTAMENT
OF
(YOUR NAME)

I, (YOUR NAME), domiciled and residing at (Your Address), being of sound and disposing mind, memory, and understanding, do hereby make, publish, and declare this to be my Last Will and Testament, thereby revoking all Wills and codicils heretofore made by me.

FIRST: I direct the payment of all my just debts and funeral and testamentary expenses as soon as convenient after my decease.

SECOND: If my spouse, (SPOUSE'S NAME), shall survive me by 30 days (720 hours), then I direct my Executor to divide the remainder of my estate, both real and personal, of or to which I am now or may hereafter become seized, possessed, or entitled, into two parts, so that the first part, hereinafter designated as SHARE A, shall constitute an amount of my adjusted gross estate as defined by the Internal Revenue Code and finally determined for federal estate tax purposes, to be computed by my Executor to total the then CURRENT maximum credit equivalent amount allowed by law. This amount shall be reduced by any credit equivalent amount used during my lifetime for inter vivos gifts.

The second part, hereinafter designated as SHARE B, shall constitute the entire balance of my said residuary estate. In allocating property to SHARE B, my Executor shall not use any property in respect of which no marital deduction is allowed. To the extent that other property qualifying for the marital deduction is available, my Executor shall not allocate to SHARE B: (a) assets with respect to which a credit for foreign taxes paid is allowable under the Internal Revenue Code: (b) assets which may be subject to both income and estate taxes and which may be eligible for a credit or deduction. SHARE A and SHARE B shall be disposed of as provided in Paragraphs THIRD and FOURTH of this Will.

It is my primary intent that the marital deduction bequest in SHARE B and the property comprising that share shall qualify for the federal estate tax marital deduction, notwithstanding any provision in my Will that might be construed as compromising this objective. All questions regarding the marital deduction bequest and this share shall be resolved accordingly. The powers and discretions of the Executor and Trustee with respect to administration of my estate and of said share shall not be exercised or exercisable except in a manner consistent with my intent as expressed in this paragraph. To the extent that any other provision of my Will conflicts with my primary intent as expressed in this paragraph, giving rise to an ambiguity, the ambiguity shall be resolved as directed in this paragraph. Should there be an ambiguity as to whether any provision necessary for qualification for the marital deduction is included in my Will, the ambiguity shall be resolved as directed in this paragraph. As regards the marital deduction, all other provisions of my Will are subordinate to this provision.

THIRD: I give, devise, and bequeath SHARE B, my residuary estate, to my said spouse in fee simple without any restrictions whatsoever. It shall consist of, to the extent possible, my cash and liquid assets.

If my said spouse shall fail to survive me, then the bequest for the benefit of said spouse shall lapse and shall pass as part of SHARE A hereinafter disposed of.

FOURTH: I give, devise, and bequeath SHARE A to my hereinafter named TRUSTEE, IN TRUST, NEVERTHELESS, for the following uses and purposes:

(a) To invest in high-yield issues to the extent possible and reinvest the income and profits therefrom;

(b) Commencing with the date of my death, to pay to or apply for the benefit of my said spouse, at the request of said spouse, during the lifetime of said spouse, all the net income in convenient installments, at least as frequently as quarter-annually;

(c) In addition to the payment of such income, to pay to or apply for benefit of my said spouse during the whole lifetime, all or none of the principal of the Trust fund as my Trustee, in the Trustee's uncontrolled judgment and discretion, shall consider necessary or advisable for my said spouse's medical and educational needs and in order to maintain said spouse's current standard of living as of the date of my death. In addition, my spouse, (SPOUSE'S NAME), during the lifetime of said spouse, shall have the noncumulative right to withdraw each year from the principal of the Trust estate the sum of five thousand dollars ($5,000) or five percent (5%) of the then principal of the Trust estate, whichever amount shall be greater;

(d) Upon the death of my said spouse, to divide the then remaining principal of the Trust as follows:

The remaining principal of the Trust shall be divided into so many equal shares that there shall be one of said equal shares for each child of mine then living and one for the then surviving issue, per stirpes, collectively of each child of mine who shall not be then living, and to set aside one of said shares for each child of mine then living and one of said shares for the then surviving issue, per stirpes, collectively of each child of mine who shall not be then living, and to hold, administer, and distribute each of said shares as provided in the following sections (e) and (f);

(e) As to the one share so set aside for the benefit of each child above living, each share is hereby given in fee simple absolute;

(f) As to the one share so set aside for the benefit of the then surviving issue, per stirpes, collectively of each child of mine who shall not be then living, to pay and distribute the same to the said then surviving issue of said children, per stirpes, for whom said share was so set aside, subject to the provisions of Paragraph FIFTH hereof, if any of such issue be then not yet 35 years of age;

FIFTH: If any part of my estate shall become payable or distributable at any time to the issue of my children who shall not yet be 35 years of age, then I give, devise, and bequeath his or her respective share of my estate to my hereinafter named TRUSTEE, IN TRUST, NEVERTHELESS, to hold and administer the same and to pay to or for the benefit of each such issue, so much, all or none, of said share, both income and principal, as my Trustee, in said Trustee's uncontrolled judgment and discretion, shall consider necessary or advisable for the support, maintenance, and education of such issue as per the schedule below, at which time the remainder of his or her respective share of my estate, with the accumulations, if any, shall be paid and distributed to him or her, or if he or she dies before that time, shall be paid and distributed upon his or her death to his or her Executors and administrators, to be administered and distributed as part of his or her estate.

Age	Per Stirpes Share of Principal
18	5%
21	10%
25	25%
30	25%
35	35% (REMAINDER)

SIXTH: In addition to all powers now or hereafter conferred upon an Executor or Trustee of a (Your State) resident decedent under the law of (Your State), I confer upon my Executor and Trustees the following powers to be exercised by them as in their discretion they may deem for the best interests of my estate or the Trusts created by this Will and without authorization by any Court.

(a) To retain any and all investments and property, real and personal, that I may own at my decease or that thereafter shall become part of my estate or Trusts, without regard to any principle of diversification and notwithstanding the same may be of a wasting nature or may not be recognized by law as legal investments for Trust funds;

(b) To invest and reinvest my estate or Trust funds in stocks, bonds, or other securities, notes, mortgages, units of participation in any common Trust fund maintained by my Trustee, or in any other property, real or personal, without regard to decisional or statutory law, rules of court, or principles concerning the investment of Trust funds, or to the amount which shall be invested in any one investment or type of investment and even though all, or substantially all, of the Trust fund may be invested in common stocks or other so-called "equities";

(c) To sell and dispose of any and all property, real or personal, of which I may die seized or possessed or which may become part of my estate or the Trusts created by this Will, either at public or private sale and upon such terms and conditions as they deem for the best interests of my estate and to make good and sufficient conveyances in the law therefor;

(d) To use Executor's commissions, attorneys' fees, and other administration expenses, or part thereof, as deductions for estate tax purposes or income tax purposes and to use date of death values or optional values for estate tax purposes, without regard to the effect thereof on any of the interests or shares under this Will, and I direct that there shall be no adjustment of such interests or shares by reason of any action taken by my Executor in respect to the foregoing and all action shall be final, conclusive, and binding upon all beneficiaries;

(e) To borrow, in order to invest, to pay taxes, debts, or other proper liabilities, such sum or sums of money from time to time and for such periods of time and upon such terms and conditions as my Executor and Trustee shall deem advisable, and to secure the same by mortgage or pledge of any part of my estate, real or personal, and to execute and deliver bonds, notes, mortgages, agreements, and other instruments necessary or proper to evidence and secure the loans so made;

(f) To exercise any stock options that I may own at my death and in connection therewith to borrow funds to exercise said options;

(g) To make division, partition, and distribution of my estate or Trusts in cash or kind, or partly in each, and for the purpose of making such division, partition, and distribution in kind, the assets selected by my Executor and

Trustees shall be valued at their respective values on the date or dates of division, partition, or distribution;

(h) To employ such accountants, custodians, attorneys, investment counsel, and other persons as they may deem advisable in the administration of my estate or any Trust created hereunder and to pay them such compensation as they may deem proper;

(i) To allocate to principal all stock dividends and cash in lieu of fractional shares paid as a result of a stock dividend received on any stock held in my estate or any Trust created hereunder;

(j) To exercise generally with respect to any and all stocks, securities, or other property held hereunder all rights, powers, and privileges that may be lawfully exercised by persons owning similar property in their own individual right.

SEVENTH: If I shall not be survived by said spouse, or any issue, all of my estate shall be devised and bequeathed in fee simple as follows:

50% equally to my siblings, and 50% equally to the siblings of my said spouse, or to their estates.

EIGHTH: I direct that all inheritance, succession, legacy, and estate taxes and duties, state, federal, or otherwise, which may be assessed property taxable as, or as if, a part of my estate, be paid out of that credit shelter equivalent portion of my estate (SHARE A) hereinbefore given by Paragraph FOURTH of this Will as expenses of administration and not as a charge on the beneficiary or beneficiaries of such property. Regardless, however, of anything contained herein above, said SHARE A shall be increased by any payment required by this Paragraph EIGHTH, so that my estate shall not be liable for any federal estate taxes:

NINTH: If any legatee, devisee, or beneficiary under this Will shall in any way directly or indirectly contest or object to the probate of this Will, or dispute any clause or provision hereof, or exercise or attempt to exercise any right of election or other right to take any part or share of my estate against the provisions of this Will, or institute or prosecute, or be in any way directly or indirectly interested or instrumental in the institution or prosecution of, any action, proceeding, contest, or objection, or give any notice, for the purpose of setting aside or invalidating this Will, or any clause or provision hereof, then and in each such case all provisions for such legatee, devisee, or beneficiary or for his or her descendants above contained in this Will shall be wholly void and ineffectual, and my estate shall be disposed of in like manner as though such legatee, devisee, or beneficiary, if an individual, had predeceased me leaving no descendants who survive me or, if a Trust or other entity, had ceased to exist prior to my death.

TENTH: In the event that any beneficiary of any Trust estate, by reason of illness, age, incapacity, or any other cause shall, in the Trustees' opinion, be unable properly to receive and disburse the income and principal to which he or she may be entitled, or during the minority of any beneficiary, the Trustees, in their sole discretion, shall pay and apply the income and principal due such beneficiary to his or her comfortable maintenance and support, without the intervention of any guardian and without being required to apply to any Court for leave to make such payments.

ELEVENTH: I direct that all legacies and all shares and interests in my estate, whether principal or income while in the hands of my Executors or Trustees, shall not be subject to attachment, execution, or sequestration for any debt, contract, obligation, or liability of any legatee or beneficiary and shall not be subject to pledge, assignment, conveyance, or anticipation.

TWELFTH: Notwithstanding the foregoing, if my spouse shall die prior to the expiration of six (6) months from the date of my death, then the amount referred to in Article THIRD (SHARE B) shall be reduced to an amount which shall obtain for my estate a marital deduction which would result in the lowest combined federal estate tax in both my estate and the estate of my said spouse, on the assumption that my spouse died after me, but on the date of my death, and that the estate of said spouse was valued as of the date on, and in the manner which, my estate is valued for federal estate tax purposes. My purpose is to equalize, insofar as possible, my estate and my spouse's estate for federal estate tax purposes, based upon said assumptions.

THIRTEENTH: I nominate, constitute, and appoint my spouse, (SPOUSE'S NAME), if said spouse be living, as Executrix of this my Last Will and Testament and, if said spouse be not living, my children, age 18 or older, jointly, or, until there be any, (NAME), or, if he can not serve, (NAME), as Executor of this my Last Will and Testament. I nominate, constitute, and appoint (NAME), or if he can not serve, (NAME), as Trustee for all Trusts created under this Will the beneficiaries of which are my spouse or issue, or the issue of my or my said spouse's siblings. I further direct that no bond shall be required of said Executrix or Trustees for the administration of my estate or any Trust created hereunder in any jurisdiction. If my spouse does not survive me, I nominate, constitute, and appoint (NAME), or if he can not serve, (NAME), as Guardians of my minor children without the need for any bond in any jurisdiction.

IN WITNESS WHEREOF, I have hereunto set my hand and seal this day of   , Two Thousand (2000).

_____

(YOUR NAME)

The foregoing Will, consisting of (number) typewritten pages, including this page, was signed, sealed, published, and declared by the said (YOUR NAME) as and for his Last Will and Testament, in the presence of us who were present at the same time, and who, thereupon, at his request, in his presence and in the presence of each other, have hereunto subscribed our names as Witnesses.

_____ residing at _____

_____ residing at _____

_____ residing at _____

STATE OF (YOUR STATE)

SS:

COUNTY OF (YOUR COUNTY)

We, (Name), (Name), (Name), and (YOUR NAME), the Witnesses and Testator, respectively, whose names are signed to the foregoing instrument, being duly sworn, do hereby declare to the undersigned authority that the Testator signed and executed the instrument as his Last Will, and that he executed it as his free and voluntary act for the purposes therein expressed, and that each of the Witnesses, in the presence and hearing of the Testator, signed the Will as Witness and that to the best of his or her knowledge, the Testator was at that time eighteen (18) years of age or older, of sound mind, and under no constraint or undue influence.

_____

Testator

_____
Witness

_____
Witness

_____
Witness

SUBSCRIBED, SWORN TO, AND ACKNOWLEDGED before me by (YOUR NAME), the Testator, and subscribed and sworn before me by the above Witnesses, Witness this   day of   , 2000.

_____
Notary Public

THE (YOUR NAME) REVOCABLE TRUST

On   , this Trust was created by (YOUR NAME), hereinafter referred to as the "Grantor," and sometimes as the "Trustee," domiciled and residing at (Your Address), who declared that said person holds and administers the Trust funds as follows:

The Grantor holds, as Trustee, the property listed in Schedule A attached hereto and made an integral part hereof, to be held and administered according to the terms of this Trust. The Grantor and anyone else may transfer additional property to the then Trustee at any time, whether during the Grantor's life or after the Grantor's death, including life insurance proceeds, to be held and administered according to the terms of this Trust.

The Grantor can revoke or amend all or any part of this Trust at any time, without the consent of anyone, by delivering to the Trustee a written instrument specifying the character and date of the intended amendment or revocation, or by specific reference to this Trust in the Grantor's Last Will. During the lifetime of the Grantor, the power to revoke or amend all or any part of this Trust shall be exercisable by the Grantor's legally authorized attorney-in-fact, in the same manner and under the same conditions as the Grantor could have exercised them. However, the Trustee's duties, powers, or liabilities can not be changed without the Trustee's prior written consent. Upon the Grantor's death, this Trust shall become irrevocable and shall be administered as per the provisions below.

FIRST: The then Trustee shall pay off all of the Grantor's just debts, including any and all taxes and funeral and testamentary expenses, as soon as convenient after the death of said Grantor.

SECOND: If the spouse of said Grantor, (SPOUSE'S NAME), shall survive said Grantor by 30 days (720 hours), then the Trustee is directed to divide the remainder of this Trust, both real and personal, including any property of or to which this Trust is now or may hereafter become seized, possessed, or entitled, and including any Pour Over from the Will of said Grantor, into two parts, so that the first part, hereinafter designated as SHARE A, shall constitute an amount of said Grantor's adjusted gross estate as defined by the Internal Revenue Code and finally determined for federal estate tax purposes, to be computed by the below said Trustee to total the then current maximum credit equivalent amount allowed by law. This amount shall be reduced by any credit equivalent amount used during the lifetime of said Grantor for inter vivos gifts.

The second part, hereinafter designated as SHARE B, shall constitute the entire balance of this Trust. In allocating property to SHARE B, the Trustee shall not use any property in respect of which no marital deduction is allowed. To the extent that other property qualifying for the marital deduction is available, the Trustee shall not allocate to SHARE B: (a) assets with respect to which a credit for foreign taxes paid is allowable under the Internal Revenue Code; (b) assets which may be subject to both income and estate taxes and which may be eligible for a credit or deduction. SHARE A and SHARE B shall be disposed of as provided in Paragraphs THIRD and FOURTH of this Trust.

It is the primary intent of this Trust that the marital deduction bequest in SHARE B and the property comprising that share shall qualify for the federal estate tax marital deduction, notwithstanding any provision herein that might be construed as compromising this objective. All questions regarding the marital deduction bequest and this share shall be resolved accordingly. The powers and discretions of the Trustee with respect to administration of this Trust and of said share shall not be exercised or exercisable except in a manner consistent with the intent as expressed in this paragraph. To the extent that any other provision of this Trust conflicts with the primary intent as expressed in this paragraph, giving rise to an ambiguity, the ambiguity shall be resolved as directed in this paragraph. Should there be an ambiguity as to whether any provision necessary for qualification for the marital deduction is included in this Trust, the ambiguity shall be resolved as directed in this paragraph. As regards the marital deduction, all other provisions of this Trust are subordinate to this provision.

THIRD: SHARE B, the residuary of this Trust, is hereby given to the said spouse of the Grantor in fee simple without any restrictions whatsoever. It shall consist of, to the extent possible, cash and liquid assets.

If the said spouse shall fail to survive the Grantor, then the disposition for the benefit of said spouse shall lapse and shall pass as part of SHARE A hereinafter disposed of.

FOURTH: SHARE A is hereby given to my hereinafter named TRUSTEE, IN TRUST, NEVERTHELESS, for the following uses and purposes:

(a) To invest in high-yield issues to the extent possible and reinvest the income and profits therefrom;

(b) Commencing with the date of the death of the Grantor, to pay to or apply for the benefit of said spouse, at the request of said spouse, during the lifetime of said spouse, all the net income in convenient installments, at least as frequently as quarter-annually;

(c) In addition to the payment of such income, to pay to or apply for the benefit of said spouse during the whole lifetime, all or none of the principal of the Trust fund as the Trustee, in the Trustee's uncontrolled judgment and discretion, shall consider necessary or advisable for said spouse's medical and educational needs and in order to maintain said spouse's current standard of living as of the date of the death of the Grantor. In addition, said spouse, (SPOUSE'S NAME), during the lifetime of said spouse, shall have the noncumulative right to withdraw each year from the principal of the Trust estate the sum of five thousand dollars ($5,000) or five percent (5%) of the then principal of the Trust estate, whichever amount shall be greater;

(d) Upon the death of the said spouse, to divide the then remaining principal of the Trust as follows:

    The remaining principal of the Trust shall be divided into so many equal shares that there shall be one of said equal shares for each child of the Grantor then living and one for the then surviving issue, per stirpes, collectively of each child of the Grantor who shall not be then living, and to set aside one of said shares for each child of the Grantor then living and one of said shares for the then surviving issue, per stirpes, collectively of each child of the Grantor who shall not be then living, and to hold, administer, and distribute each of said shares as provided in the following sections (e) and (f);

(e) As to the one share so set aside for the benefit of each child above living, said share shall be distributed in fee simple absolute;

(f) As to the one share so set aside for the benefit of the then surviving issue, per stirpes, collectively of each child of the Grantor who shall not be then living, to pay and distribute the same to the said then surviving issue of said children, per stirpes, for whom said share was so set aside, subject to the provisions of Paragraph FIFTH hereof, if any of such issue be then not yet 35 years of age;

    FIFTH: If any part of this Trust shall become payable or distributable at any time to the issue of the Grantor's children who shall not yet be 35 years of age, then said share shall be held by the hereinafter named TRUSTEE, IN TRUST, NEVERTHELESS, to hold and administer the same and to pay to or for the benefit of each such issue, so much, all or none, of said share, both income and principal, as the Trustee, in said Trustee's uncontrolled judgment and discretion, shall consider necessary or advisable for the support, maintenance, and education of such issue as per the schedule below, at which time the remainder of his or her respective share of the Trust, with the accumulations, if any, shall be paid and distributed to him or her, or if he or she dies before that time, shall be paid and distributed upon his or her death to his or her Executors and administrators, to be administered and distributed as part of his or her estate.

Age	Per Stirpes Share of Principal
18	5%
21	10%
25	25%
30	25%
35	35% (REMAINDER)

SIXTH: In addition to all powers now or hereafter conferred upon a Trustee under the law of (Your State), the Trustees herein shall have the following powers to be exercised by them as in their discretion they may deem for the best interests of the Trust created herein and without authorization by any Court.

(a) To retain any and all investments and property, real and personal, that the Trust may own at the decease of the Grantor or that thereafter shall become part of this Trust, without regard to any principle of diversification and notwithstanding the same may be of a wasting nature or may not be recognized by law as legal investments for Trust funds;

(b) To invest and reinvest Trust funds in stocks, bonds, or other securities, notes, mortgages, units of participation in any common Trust fund maintained by the Trustee, or in any other property, real or personal, without regard to decisional or statutory law, rules of court, or principles concerning the investment of Trust funds, or to the amount which shall be invested in any one investment or type of investment and even though all, or substantially all, of the Trust fund may be invested in common stocks or other so-called "equities";

(c) To sell and dispose of any and all property, real or personal, of which the Trust is seized or possessed or which may become part of the Trust created herein, either at public or private sale and upon such terms and conditions as they deem for the best interests of this Trust and to make good and sufficient conveyances in the law therefor;

(d) To borrow, in order to invest, to pay taxes, debts, or other proper liabilities, such sum or sums of money from time to time and for such periods of time and upon such terms and conditions as the Trustee shall deem advisable, and to secure the same by mortgage or pledge of any part of the Trust, real or personal, and to execute and deliver bonds, notes, mortgages, agreements, and other instruments necessary or proper to evidence and secure the loans so made;

(e) To exercise any stock options that the Trust may own at or after the death of the Grantor and in connection therewith to borrow funds to exercise said options;

(f) To make division, partition, and distribution of the Trust in cash or kind, or partly in each, and for the purpose of making such division, partition, and distribution in kind, the assets selected by the Trustees shall be valued at their respective values on the date or dates of division, partition, or distribution;

(g) To employ such accountants, custodians, attorneys, investment counsel, and other persons as they may deem advisable in the administration of the Trust created hereunder and to pay them such compensation as they may deem proper;

(h) To allocate to principal all stock dividends and cash in lieu of fractional shares paid as a result of a stock dividend received on any stock held in the Trust created hereunder;

(i) To exercise generally with respect to any and all stocks, securities, or other property held hereunder all rights, powers, and privileges that may be lawfully exercised by persons owning similar property in their own individual right.

SEVENTH: If the Grantor shall not be survived by said spouse, or any issue, all of this Trust shall be devised and bequeathed in fee simple as follows:

Equally to the surviving spouses of the children of the Grantor.

EIGHTH: It is hereby directed that all inheritance, succession, legacy, and estate taxes and duties, state, federal, or otherwise, which may be assessed property taxable as, or as if, a part of the estate of the Grantor, be paid out of that credit shelter equivalent portion of this Trust (SHARE A) hereinbefore given by Paragraph FOURTH of this Will as expenses of administration of the Grantor's estate and not as a charge on the beneficiary or beneficiaries of such property. Regardless, however, of anything contained herein above, said SHARE A shall be increased by any payment required by this Paragraph EIGHTH, so that the estate of the Grantor shall not be liable for any federal estate taxes.

NINTH: If any beneficiary under this Trust shall in any way directly or indirectly contest or object to the probate of the Will of the Grantor, or dispute any clause or provision hereof or of said Will, or exercise or attempt to exercise any right of election or other right to take any part or share of the estate of said Grantor against the provisions of the Will of said Grantor, or institute or prosecute, or be in any way directly or indirectly interested or instrumental in the institution or prosecution of any action, proceeding, contest, or objection, or give any notice, for the purpose of setting aside or invalidating this Trust or said Will, or any clause or provision hereof, then and in each such case all provisions for such beneficiary or for his or her descendants above contained in this Trust shall be wholly void and ineffectual, and the Trust shall be disposed of in like manner as though such legatee, devisee, or beneficiary, if an individual, had predeceased the Grantor leaving no descendants who survive the Grantor or, if a Trust or other entity, had ceased to exist prior to the death of the Grantor.

TENTH: In the event that any beneficiary of any Trust estate, by reason of illness, age, incapacity, or any other cause shall, in the Trustees' opinion, be unable properly to receive and disburse the income and principal to which he or she may be entitled, or during the minority of any beneficiary, the Trustees, in their sole discretion, shall pay and apply the income and principal due such beneficiary to his or her comfortable maintenance and support, without the intervention of any guardian and without being required to apply to any Court for leave to make such payments.

ELEVENTH: I direct that all legacies and all shares and interests in this Trust, whether principal or income while in the hands of the Trustees, shall not be subject to attachment, execution, or sequestration for any debt, contract, obligation, or liability of any beneficiary and shall not be subject to pledge, assignment, conveyance, or anticipation.

TWELFTH: Notwithstanding the foregoing, if the spouse of the Grantor shall die prior to the expiration of six (6) months from the date of the Grantor's death, then the amount referred to in Article THIRD (SHARE B) shall be reduced to an amount which shall obtain for the estate of the Grantor a marital deduction which would result in the lowest combined federal estate tax in both the Grantor's estate and the estate of the Grantor's spouse, on the assumption that said spouse died after the Grantor, but on the date of the Grantor's death, and that the estate of said spouse was valued as of the date on, and in the manner which, the estate of the Grantor is valued for federal estate tax purposes. The purpose here is to equalize, insofar as possible, the estate of the Grantor and the spouse's estate for federal estate tax purposes, based upon said assumptions.

THIRTEENTH: At any time, should the Grantor be unable to serve, the said spouse of the Grantor shall serve as Trustee. If said spouse can not serve, the children of the Grantor, jointly, with any individual being able to make decisions independently, shall be the Trustee of this Trust. No bond shall be required of any Trustees for the administration of this Trust created hereunder in any jurisdiction.

IN WITNESS WHEREOF, I have hereunto set my hand and seal this day of   , Two Thousand (2000).

_____

(YOUR NAME)

In token of the acceptance of this Trust and to acknowledge receipt of the property herein described, the Trustee has set his hand and affixed his seal this day of   , Two Thousand (2000).

_____

(YOUR NAME)

SCHEDULE A

Schedule of property transferred pursuant to the foregoing Trust Agreement:

Asset	Date of Transfer	Basis of Asset	Value of Asset

(POUR OVER) LAST WILL AND TESTAMENT
OF
(YOUR NAME)

I, (YOUR NAME), domiciled and residing at (Your Address), being of sound and disposing mind, memory, and understanding, do hereby make, publish, and declare this to be my Last Will and Testament, thereby revoking all Wills and codicils heretofore made by me.

FIRST: I direct the payment of all my just debts and funeral and testamentary expenses as soon as convenient after my decease.

SECOND: I direct my Executor to pour over the remainder of my estate, both real and personal, of or to which I am now or may hereafter become seized, possessed, or entitled, into the (YOUR NAME) REVOCABLE TRUST dated   .

THIRD: In addition to all powers now or hereafter conferred upon an Executor of a (Your State) resident decedent under the law of (Your State), I confer upon my Executors the following powers to be exercised by them as in their discretion they may deem for the best interests of my estate created by this Will and without authorization by any Court.

(a) To retain any and all investments and property, real and personal, that I may own at my decease or that thereafter shall become part of my estate, without regard to any principle of diversification and notwithstanding the same may be of a wasting nature or may not be recognized by law as legal investments for estate funds;

(b) To invest and reinvest my estate funds in stocks, bonds, or other securities, notes, mortgages, units of participation in any common Trust fund maintained by my Executor, or in any other property, real or personal, without regard to decisional or statutory law, rules of court, or principles concerning the investment of estate funds, or to the amount which shall be invested in any one investment or type of investment and even though all, or substantially all, of the estate fund may be invested in common stocks or other so-called "equities";

(c) To sell and dispose of any and all property, real or personal, of which I may die seized or possessed or which may become part of my estate created by this Will, either at public or private sale and upon such terms and conditions as they deem for the best interests of my estate and to make good and sufficient conveyances in the law therefor;

(d) To use Executor's commissions, attorneys' fees, and other administration expenses, or part thereof, as deductions for estate tax purposes or income tax purposes and to use date of death values or optional values for estate tax purposes, without regard to the effect thereof on any of the interests or shares under this Will, and I direct that there shall be no adjustment of such interests or shares by reason of any action taken by my Executor in respect to the foregoing and all action shall be final, conclusive, and binding upon all beneficiaries;

(e) To borrow, in order to invest, to pay taxes, debts, or other proper liabilities, such sum or sums of money from time to time and for such periods of time and upon such terms and conditions as my Executor shall deem advisable, and to secure the same by mortgage or pledge of any part of my estate, real or personal, and to execute and deliver bonds, notes, mortgages, agreements, and other instruments necessary or proper to evidence and secure the loans so made;

(f) To exercise any stock options that I may own at my death and in connection therewith to borrow funds to exercise said options;

(g) To make division, partition, and distribution of my estate in cash or kind, or partly in each, and for the purpose of making such division, partition, and distribution in kind, the assets selected by my Executor shall be valued at their respective values on the date or dates of division, partition, or distribution;

(h) To employ such accountants, custodians, attorneys, investment counsel, and other persons as they may deem advisable in the administration of my estate or created hereunder and to pay them such compensation as they may deem proper;

(i) To allocate to principal all stock dividends and cash in lieu of fractional shares paid as a result of a stock dividend received on any stock held in my estate created hereunder;

(j) To exercise generally with respect to any and all stocks, securities, or other property held hereunder all rights, powers, and privileges that may be lawfully exercised by persons owning similar property in their own individual right.

FOURTH: If any legatee, devisee, or beneficiary under this Will shall in any way directly or indirectly contest or object to the probate of this Will, or dispute any clause or provision hereof, or exercise or attempt to exercise any right of election or other right to take any part or share of my estate against the provisions of this Will, or institute or prosecute, or be in any way directly or indirectly interested or instrumental in the institution or prosecution of, any action, proceeding, contest, or objection, or give any notice, for the purpose of setting aside or invalidating this Will, or any clause or provision hereof, then and in each such case all provisions for such legatee, devisee, or beneficiary or for his or her descendants above contained in this Will shall be wholly void and ineffectual, and my estate shall be disposed of in like manner as though such legatee, devisee, or beneficiary, if an individual, had predeceased me leaving no descendants who survive me or, if a Trust or other entity, had ceased to exist prior to my death.

FIFTH: I direct that all legacies and all shares and interests in my estate, whether principal or income while in the hands of my Executors, shall not be subject to attachment, execution, or sequestration for any debt, contract, obligation, or liability of any legatee or beneficiary and shall not be subject to pledge, assignment, conveyance, or anticipation.

SIXTH: I nominate, constitute, and appoint my spouse, (SPOUSE'S NAME), if said spouse be living, as Executrix of this my Last Will and Testament and, if said spouse be not living, my children, jointly, as Executor of this my Last Will and Testament. I further direct that no bond shall be required of said Executrix for the administration of my estate created hereunder in any jurisdiction.

IN WITNESS WHEREOF, I have hereunto set my hand and seal this day of   , Two Thousand (2000).

(YOUR NAME)

The foregoing Will, consisting of (number) typewritten pages, including this page, was signed, sealed, published, and declared by the said (YOUR NAME) as and for his Last Will and Testament, in the presence of us who were present at the same time, and who, thereupon, at his request, in his presence and in the presence of each other, have hereunto subscribed our names as Witnesses.

_____ residing at _____

_____ residing at _____

_____ residing at _____

STATE OF (YOUR STATE)

                                        SS:

COUNTY OF (YOUR COUNTY)

        We, (Name), (Name), (Name), and (YOUR NAME), the Witnesses and
Testator, respectively, whose names are signed to the foregoing instrument,
being duly sworn, do hereby declare to the undersigned authority that the Testator signed and executed the instrument as his Last Will, and that he executed
it as his free and voluntary act for the purposes therein expressed, and that each
of the Witnesses, in the presence and hearing of the Testator, signed the Will as
Witness and that to the best of his or her knowledge, the Testator was at that
time eighteen (18) years of age or older, of sound mind, and under no constraint or undue influence.

                                        _____
                                        Testator

                                        _____
                                        Witness

_____

Witness

_____

Witness

    SUBSCRIBED, SWORN TO, AND ACKNOWLEDGED before me by (YOUR NAME), the Testator, and subscribed and sworn before me by the above Witnesses, Witness this   day of   , 2000.

_____

Notary Public

CHAPTER 6

Irrevocable Life Insurance Trusts

Life insurance is not a probate asset. What that means is that even if your Will says that you want your life insurance to go to your children, if the policy specifically has your spouse named as beneficiary, then your spouse gets the proceeds.

Remember, *probate* only means passing through your Will. Even though life insurance is not part of your probate estate, it may be part of your taxable estate.

Most people think that life insurance is tax free. What they are thinking about is the income tax, not the estate tax. Any life insurance over which you have sufficient control to constitute what is technically referred to as *incidents of ownership* will be includable and taxable in your estate. If you can change beneficiaries, if you can change the proportions among beneficiaries, if you can control who owns the policy, then you are deemed to have sufficient incidents of ownership to have that policy includable in your estate.

This means that if you're in the 50 percent estate tax bracket, a $500,000 insurance policy will only yield your beneficiaries $250,000. This is another trap for the unwary.

There is a way to exclude all life insurance proceeds from your estate. If you have no incidents of ownership, then none of the proceeds will be includable in

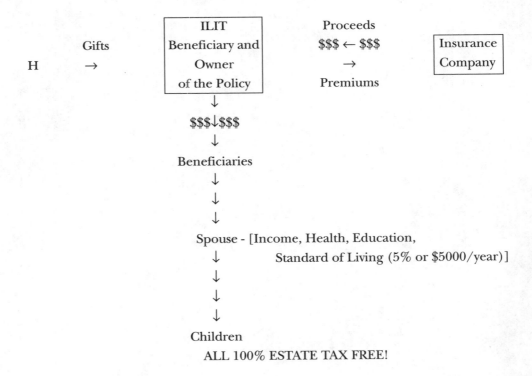

your estate. To accomplish this, you create and fund an Irrevocable Life Insurance Trust (ILIT).

Here's how it works. You set up an irrevocable trust with an independent trustee. The trust will be both the beneficiary and the owner of the policy. However, the beneficiary of the trust will be first your spouse and then your children. Because the proceeds are filtered through the trust, those assets completely escape estate taxation.

Procedurally, this is what you would do. First, set up an irrevocable trust. The form at the end of this chapter will enable you to do that. Then select a trustee to run the trust. That trustee should be someone you have confidence in, but someone who is independent of your beneficiaries. We want to avoid any possibility of the IRS alleging that the trustee was under your control and therefore making all of the proceeds taxable in your estate.

Each year you will make gifts into the trust for the trustee to invest. With a life insurance trust, the trustee will invest in a policy of life insurance on your life. You can't make the life insurance mandatory, but it is understood by all parties that that is your desire.

The trustee uses these gifts to pay the premiums for the life insurance. Because the beneficiaries of the trust are your spouse and issue, the gifts are really gifts to your spouse and issue. We will come back to this later.

When you die, the insurance company will pay the proceeds to the trust. These proceeds now become assets of the trust, either to be invested or to be distributed as per your directions.

If an Irrevocable Life Insurance Trust is properly executed and followed, all proceeds will be out of your estate. There are, however, three more issues that should be discussed before we go through the document itself. The first is the three-year rule.

This is the three-year rule: if the trust purchases the life insurance initially, then the life insurance is out of your estate immediately. However, if the life insurance policy is one that has been transferred into the trust, then you must live at least three years after the date of transfer for that insurance to be tax free. If nothing else, it gives you a good reason to hang on.

The second thing I want to discuss before we look at the document itself is the concept of *Crummey powers*. Here's where they are important.

Remember I told you that in order to fund the trust, you make annual gifts into the trust. Most people would think that, to the extent of $10,000 per year (or $20,000 with a split gift between spouses), these gifts would be tax free—that is, not subject to the gift tax. What most people fail to recognize, however, is that the $10,000/$20,000 annual exclusion only applies to gifts of what is known as a *present interest*. In other words, the recipient of the gift must have an immediate benefit, now, from the gift. If these gifts of cash are to be used to pay premiums on a life insurance policy, they are gifts of a *future interest*—one that grants the beneficiaries a future benefit to be realized later. The $10,000/$20,000 annual exclusion does not apply to such gifts.

Present Interest	→	Future Interest
Immediate Benefit		Future Benefit
Now		Later

In 1969, a creative attorney, whose client's name was Mr. Crummey, came up with a brilliant idea. Every time a contribution was made into the trust, the trust document required the trustee to send the following letter to each of the beneficiaries:

Dear Beneficiary:
A gift of $ has been made into your trust. You have thirty (30) days in which to withdraw your appropriate share or the terms of the trust will apply.
Please advise.

By sending this letter to each of the beneficiaries, the attorney was able to create a 30-day window of opportunity which in and of itself created the present interest that would allow the gift to come to the trust free of gift tax. Through this legal fiction, even though there is no expectation that the proportionate shares of the premium will be taken, the present interest is created.

While this may appear to be legal trickery, it has been good law since 1969. If the "Crummey letters" are sent, then the gifts qualify for the $10,000/$20,000 annual exclusion. The courts have even validated exclusions for contingent remainder beneficiaries and for newborn infants so long as someone of age and competence is designated with the authority to make the withdrawals.

If you currently own or plan to own life insurance, and your estate potentially will ever exceed the exclusion amount, then that life insurance should be owned by an Irrevocable Life Insurance Trust. In the lowest estate tax bracket, 37 percent, an inclusion of even $100,000 worth of life insurance in your estate will cost your beneficiaries $37,000 in unnecessary taxation.

There is one last thing I want to talk about before we get to the actual document itself. It is what I call the Schnepper Pension Rollover. With appropriate structuring, it is possible to buy life insurance through your pension with both an income tax deduction for the premiums and an estate tax exclusion for the proceeds. This is how it works.

I am going to use simple numbers so you'll understand the concept. Assume you have $200,000 in your qualified pension plan. You can take as many as 100,000 of those dollars and purchase a single premium life insurance policy. But what you want your life insurance agent to do is to find you a policy that really is the equivalent of a paid-up term policy. In other words, you want whatever cash values have built up inside the policy from your immediate one-payment overfunding to be used to pay all of your premiums in the future.

Appropriately structured, this $100,000 premium may buy you a $1 million life insurance policy with little to no current cash value. You then immediately transfer the policy out of the qualified pension to yourself, and then you immediately roll that policy over into an Irrevocable Life Insurance Trust.

Let's see what you have accomplished. You have taken $100,000 out of your pension and used it to pay the premiums on a life insurance policy. Because pension contributions were tax deductible, you in effect used tax-deductible money to pay for your life insurance.

Next, when you roll the policy out of the pension to yourself, you are taxed not on the value of the policy, but only on its *cash* value. Because the policy has been structured to be a paid-up policy, the equivalent of almost a term policy, its cash value is little to none. You have then therefore taken $100,000 out of your pension and paid little to no income tax on that distribution.

When you finally roll the policy over into an Irrevocable Life Insurance Trust, you make those proceeds potentially free of estate tax. To complete the triple play, all you have to do is live three years after the date of transfer. If you do so, the insurance—$1 million—comes to your beneficiaries tax free. Had you not done this, the $100,000 pension money would have been both taxable income when it was received, and includable and taxable in your estate when you died.

If you were in the 30 percent income tax bracket when you received the money, you would have been left with only $70,000. If you were in the 50 percent estate tax bracket, your beneficiaries would be left with only $35,000. If you use the Schnepper Pension Rollover, your beneficiaries may have as much as $1 million tax free.

Now let's look at the document itself.

The trust I have given you is completely appropriate to hold life insurance, but has been structured to hold other assets as well. Under current law, there may not be any compelling reason to have an irrevocable trust to hold assets other than life insurance. However, the only constant in our tax law is its changeability. It may be appropriate for you, some time in the future, to have an irrevocable trust to hold assets other than life insurance. By adding several small changes and additional paragraphs, you can make this trust work both for life insurance and any other assets that may be appropriate to put into it.

(YOUR NAME)
IRREVOCABLE LIFE INSURANCE TRUST

THIS AGREEMENT is entered into by and between (YOUR NAME), as Donor, and (NAME), hereinafter referred to as my "Trustee."

This paragraph declares this to be your trust and identifies your trustee.

WITNESSETH:
ITEM ONE

I hereby irrevocably transfer, set over, assign, and convey unto my Trustee those assets as per SCHEDULE A attached hereto, the receipt of which by my Trustee is hereby acknowledged. I contemplate that I, or others, including the below said beneficiaries, directly or by his or her representative, will also transfer, set over, convey, or assign additional property to be held in trust in conformity with this instrument; and upon any such transfer, conveyance, or assignment from time to time made, my Trustee shall have all the interests, rights, powers, options, incidents of ownership, advantages, titles, benefits, and privileges which I, or said other transferors, now have or hereafter may have in and to said property.

Item One introduces the assets that will go into your trust. These assets are to be put onto a schedule that can be added to at any time.

ITEM TWO

My Trustee may receive any other property (provided said property is acceptable to my Trustee), real or personal, transferred, set over, conveyed, or assigned to said Trustee by me, by others, or by my personal representative to constitute a part of the Trust fund hereby created and to be held, invested, managed, and distributed by my Trustee in accordance with the provisions hereof. Notwithstanding any other provisions of this Trust or any statute or rule of law, unless the principal of this Trust (exclusive of sums described in Paragraph B of ITEM FOUR and Paragraph B of ITEM EIGHT) exceeds the sum of five hundred dollars ($500.00), my Trustee shall be under no obligation to invest such principal held by it in this Trust.

Item Two allows the trustee to receive any additional property at any other time from any other donor. It also provides the first of what I call our de

---

minimus clauses. These are clauses that say that if the magnitude of the assets is so small, either the trustee is not required to invest those assets or the trustee has the discretion to distribute all of those assets.

ITEM THREE

This Trust shall be irrevocable, and I shall have no right to alter, amend, revoke, or terminate this Trust or any provision hereof. After the execution of this Trust, I shall have no right, title, or interest in the income or principal of this Trust, and I shall have no interest, right, power, option, incident of ownership, advantage, title, benefit, or privilege in any property constituting a part of this Trust fund. In no event shall I or my estate have any reversionary or similar type interest in this Trust or in the property contained herein.

Item Three is what keeps the assets of the trust out of your estate. The trust is declared to be irrevocable and you relinquish any and all incidents of ownership with respect to the trust.

ITEM FOUR

My Trustee shall hold said property and all income therefrom, and shall manage, invest, and reinvest same upon the following uses and Trusts:

A. Subject to the provisions of Paragraphs B.2 and B.4 of ITEM EIGHT, during my lifetime my Trustee shall pay out, equally to my below said beneficiaries, or accumulate all of the Trust net income and add same to principal.

Item Four allows the trustee to either accumulate or distribute income or principal in the discretion of the trustee. It also introduces your beneficiaries.

B. During my lifetime, each of my children (including those conceived prior to my death) and my spouse, (SPOUSE'S NAME), shall, during each calendar year, have the power to withdraw from this Trust, by giving written notice to my Trustee, an amount not to exceed the lesser of (1) his or her pro rata share of the amount which I have contributed to this Trust during such calendar year, or (2) an amount equal to the maximum annual gift tax exclusion allowable under Section 2503(b) of the Internal

Revenue Code, or any corresponding provision of any subsequent federal tax laws (if the contributor of the property is married at the time of the gift, a demand beneficiary may request from his or her pro rata share of the transferred property an amount not to exceed twice that annual exclusion if the spouse of the contributor elects to split the gift on a timely filed federal gift tax return; this noncumulative right applies only to inter vivos transfers and not to testamentary dispositions, but otherwise applies notwithstanding any provision of this Agreement to the contrary), or (3) an amount equal to the maximum annual amount allowable under Section 2514(e) of the Internal Revenue Code, or any corresponding provision of any subsequent federal tax laws, as to which the lapse of a Power of Appointment shall not be considered a release of such power. The aforesaid powers of my said spouse and children shall be exercisable in any calendar year for a period of thirty (30) days after my Trustee gives the notice required in Paragraph B.3 of ITEM EIGHT. Each and all of the aforesaid powers shall be noncumulative and to the extent any such power is unexercised (either in whole or in part) in any calendar year, said power (or unexercised part thereof) shall lapse as to such beneficiary and shall not be added to the sums available for withdrawal by any beneficiary under this paragraph in any other calendar year.

Each above withdrawal right shall be exercisable only by a written instrument executed by the demand beneficiary (if such beneficiary shall be under any legal disability of any kind, execution may be by his or her legal, natural, or general guardian, other than the Donor, or, if there be none, by (NAME)) followed by delivery to the Trustee. Upon receipt of a written request, my Trustee shall make distribution within thirty (30) days.

The Trustee, in his, her, their, or its discretion, may fund such withdrawals by distributing cash or other property, including insurance policies, or by borrowing. The Trustee's election as to form and source of payment shall be final and binding on any beneficiary.

If such a demand request is not timely made within the thirty (30)-day period following the receipt of notice of any contribution, it will be fully released by the demand beneficiary to the extent provided in Paragraph C of this ITEM FOUR.

The withdrawal powers held by a demand beneficiary in any one calendar year will be fully released on a cumulative annual basis only to the extent of the greater of (a) $5,000; or (b) 5% of the aggregate value of the assets out of which the powers to withdraw could have been exercised prior to the lapse of any such powers. The amounts not released under this provision can be appointed by the demand beneficiary solely under provisions of Paragraph C of this ITEM FOUR below.

C. *A demand beneficiary may appoint the portion of the share created for him or her corresponding to the sum of all withdrawal powers that were not fully released under the provisions of Paragraph B above of this ITEM FOUR to such of those persons who would be his or her heirs at law as he or she directs by specific reference to this Power of Appointment in his or her valid Last Will, but in no event are those assets to be paid to a demand beneficiary's estate, his or her creditors, or the creditors of his or her estate. My Trustee may rely upon an instrument admitted to probate in any jurisdiction as the Last Will of a deceased beneficiary, but if said Trustee has not received written notice of such an instrument within six (6) months after a demand beneficiary's death, it is to be presumed that the demand beneficiary died intestate and said Trustee will not be liable for acting in accordance with that presumption. If a deceased demand beneficiary does not effectively exercise the foregoing Power of Appointment with respect to any portion of the share created for him or her, said Trustee shall add the proceeds to this Trust to be administered under the terms of this Trust as specified herein.*

D. *In creating this power it is the intent of the Donor to create a noncumulative power of invasion which will qualify any transfer or deemed contribution of property to the Trust as transfer or contribution of a present interest under Section 2503(b) of the Internal Revenue Code. The failure of any beneficiary to exercise such power will not be treated as release of such power as that term is defined in Section 2514(e) of the Internal Revenue Code.*

Now in English—what you have just attempted to read are the Crummey clauses. These are the clauses that mandate a letter to the beneficiaries upon each receipt of dollars into the trust. These clauses allow those gifts to be present interest contributions and therefore eligible for the annual exclusion. Note that the reason for these clauses is specified in paragraph D: "In creating this power it is the intent . . ." to create a "present interest . . ."

ITEM FIVE

After my death, my Trustee is authorized to receive from whatever source additional property (as part of the principal of this Trust) and shall hold, manage, invest, reinvest, and distribute same and any property of the Trust held by my Trustee at the time of my death, for the benefit of my spouse, (SPOUSE'S NAME), and my children, as hereinafter set out:

The preceding paragraph authorizes your trustee to receive additional property after your death.

A. *My Trustee shall pay all of the Trust net income to or for my spouse (SPOUSE'S NAME), at least quarter-annually, but only if so requested. In addition, my said spouse, during the lifetime of said spouse, shall have the noncumulative right to withdraw each year from the principal of this Trust the sum of five thousand dollars ($5,000), or five percent (5%) of the principal of this Trust estate, whichever amount shall be greater.*

B. *My Trustee shall also be directed to encroach upon the principal of this Trust, at any time and from time to time, in such amounts as my Trustee may deem necessary or appropriate in said Trustee's judgment to provide for the proper support, maintenance, and medical care of my said spouse and to provide for the proper support, maintenance, medical care, and education (including college, postgraduate, and vocational education) of any one or more of my children, taking into account any other means of support they or any of them may have to the knowledge of my Trustee. Encroachments pursuant to this paragraph for such children need not be made in equal amounts during my said spouse's lifetime.*

> Note that these paragraphs are really mirror images of your Will. Your spouse is given the income from the trust plus access to the principal as per the ascertainable standards discussed, with the remainder to be distributed equally to your children.

C. *Upon the death of my said spouse (or upon my death if my said spouse predeceases me), my Trustee shall continue this Trust for the benefit of my children as per Paragraph D below.*

D. *Upon the death of my said spouse (or upon my death if my said spouse predeceases me), my Trustee shall divide the then remaining principal of the Trust into so many shares so that there shall be one share for each child of mine then living and one for the then surviving issue, per stirpes, collectively of each child of mine who shall not be then living, and to set aside one of said shares for each child of mine then living and one of said shares for the then surviving issue, per stirpes, collectively of each child of mine who shall not be then living, and to hold, administer, and distribute each of said shares as provided in the following sections (i) and (ii);*

   (i) *As to the one share so set aside for the benefit of each child of mine living, then I give, devise, and bequeath his or her respective share of this Trust to my hereinafter named TRUSTEE, IN TRUST, NEVERTHELESS, to hold and administer the same and to pay to or for the benefit of each such child, so much, all or none, of said share, both income and principal, as my Trustee, in his, her, their, or its uncontrolled judgment and discretion, shall consider necessary or advisable for the support, maintenance, and education of such issue as per the schedule below, at which time the remainder of his or her respective share of my estate, with the accumulations, if any, shall be paid and distributed to him or her, upon notice and request, or if he or she die before that time, shall be paid and distributed upon his or her death to his or her executors or administrators, to be administered and distributed as part of his or her estate.*

Age	*Per Stirpes Share of Principal*
18	*5%*
21	*10%*
25	*25%*
30	*25%*
35	*35% (REMAINDER)*

(ii) As to the one share so set aside for the benefit of the then surviving issue, per stirpes, collectively of each child of mine who shall not be then living, to pay and distribute the same to the said then surviving issue of said children, per stirpes, for whom said share was so set aside, subject to the provisions of Paragraph E hereof, if any of such issue be then not yet 35 years of age;

E. *If any part of this Trust shall become payable or distributable at any time to the issue of my children who shall not yet be 35 years of age, then I give, devise, and bequeath his or her respective share of this Trust to my hereinafter named TRUSTEE, IN TRUST, NEVERTHELESS, to hold and administer the same and to pay to or for the benefit of each such issue, so much, all or none, of said share, both income and principal, as my Trustee, in his, her, their, or its uncontrolled judgment and discretion, shall consider necessary or advisable for the support, maintenance, and education of such issue as per the schedule below, at which time the remainder of his or her respective share of my estate, with the accumulations, if any, shall be paid and distributed to him or her, or if he or she dies before that time, shall be paid and distributed upon his or her death to his or her executors or administrators, to be administered and distributed as part of his or her estate.*

Age	*Per Stirpes Share of Principal*
18	*5%*
21	*10%*
25	*25%*
30	*25%*
35	*35% (REMAINDER)*

Note again that these provisions are the mirror image of what is contained in your Will. However, by allowing these dollars to flow through as insurance dollars rather than as assets probatable under your Will, you ensure that they escape all federal taxation.

F. *If I shall not be survived by said spouse or any issue, then the property remaining in the hands of my Trustee shall vest in and be distributed as follows:*

IN TRUST, NEVERTHELESS, for the benefit of the issue of my siblings and the issue of the siblings of my said spouse, to be used exclusively for the payment of 50% of the college and graduate school tuition of said beneficiaries.

In no event shall I or my estate have any reversionary or similar type interest in this Trust or in the property contained herein.

The preceding paragraphs constitute the maximum disaster clause for assets received by your trust. If you are not survived by your spouse or any issue, it details where you want the dollars to go.

G. *Regardless of the foregoing provisions, however, in the event the assets in this Trust at any time after my death but before the division of the Trust property into shares pursuant to Paragraph D of this Item have a value of less than $50,000.00, then I authorize (but I do not direct) my Trustee to terminate this Trust and to distribute said assets to my said spouse if said spouse is then living, and if not, then equally among my children, with the then living descendants of any deceased child to take the share of such decedent as per Paragraphs D and E above. In addition, in the event (at any time after said division of Trust property into shares) the assets in any share have a value of less than $50,000.00, then I authorize (but I do not direct) my Trustee to terminate this Trust as to such share and to turn over the assets then held in such share to the issue of mine for whose benefit such share was being held. My Trustee shall have no liability in respect to such termination of this Trust and delivery of such assets, and my Trustee's discretion in this regard shall be absolute.*

The preceding paragraph is another de minimus clause. It allows the trustee to minimize trust costs by distributing the principal of the trust should that principal ever fall to a level that you designate.

ITEM SIX

A. *Wherever in this Trust the terms "children" or "descendants" (or similar terms denoting class for purposes of inheritance) are used, the same shall be deemed to include children by adoption and descendants by adoption, regardless of whether the adopting parent was a natural born member of the class referred to or whether such adopting parent was, himself or herself, a member of such class by adoption.*

This paragraph defines the terms "children" and "descendants" to include adopted children and descendants by adoption.

B. *Whenever my Trustee is directed or authorized to deliver any notice, money, or property (whether income, principal, or upon Trust termination) to any person who has not attained age twenty-one (21), or to use the same for the benefit of any such person, my Trustee need not, in his, her, their, or its discretion, require the appointment of a guardian but shall be authorized to deliver the same to the person having custody of such beneficiary, to deliver the same to such beneficiary without the intervention of a guardian, to deliver the same to a legal guardian for such beneficiary if one has already been appointed, or to use the same for the benefit of such beneficiary. My Trustee shall have no duty to see to the proper application of such assets by any such recipient.*

This paragraph allows the trustee to retain control of the assets even when directed to give assets to a beneficiary under the age of 21. The trustee is directed to spend the assets for the benefit of that beneficiary rather than giving the assets to that beneficiary directly.

C. *In addition to the above, whenever my Trustee is directed to distribute any money or property in partial or final liquidation or termination of a Trust to a person who has not attained age twenty-one (21), my Trustee may, in his, her, their, or its discretion, continue to hold the share of such beneficiary in trust for such beneficiary until he or she attains age twenty-one (21), and in the meantime shall use such part of the income or principal (or both) of the share of such beneficiary as my Trustee may deem necessary to provide for the proper support and education of such beneficiary.*

The preceding paragraph provides the same protection until age 21 for any assets that the trust may have directed to be distributed as partial liquidation to a youthful beneficiary.

ITEM SEVEN

A. *Anything in this Trust Agreement to the contrary notwithstanding, if (1) my death occurs within three years from the date of any funding of this Trust by me, so that any or all of the assets which comprise this Trust are includible in my gross estate for federal estate tax purposes, and (2) if I have any surviving spouse, then and in that event, my Trustee shall hold the assets which are so includible as a separate Trust for the sole benefit of my surviving spouse during said spouse's lifetime, and shall from the date of my death pay said spouse all the income at least semiannually and so much of the principal as may be necessary or appropriate for the support, maintenance, and medical care of said spouse, taking into account any other means of support said spouse may have to the knowledge of my Trustee; provided, however, that if the assets in such separate Trust shall at any time have a value of less than $50,000.00, then I authorize (but I do not direct) my Trustee to terminate such Trust and to distribute the assets to my surviving spouse. Upon the death of my surviving spouse, my Trustee shall distribute any accrued but unpaid income to my surviving spouse's estate. All other assets then held in such separate Trust shall, after paying any and all estate or inheritance taxes which may be due from my surviving spouse's estate on account of this Trust, be held, administered, and distributed, as set forth in ITEM FIVE of this Trust Agreement.*

B. *This Item is intended to give my estate maximum tax savings flexibility by creating a "qualified terminable interest trust" in the event any or all of the assets in this Trust are included in my estate for federal estate tax purposes, and same shall be so construed.*

Item Seven is a fail-safe provision in case you should die within three years of transferring a life insurance policy into the trust. If that does happen, the trust provides for the proceeds of that policy to be put into a QTIP trust for the benefit of the surviving spouse. While those dollars will be included in the estate of the surviving spouse, they will not be taxable in your estate and the QTIP restrictions provide a measure of insurance that your secondary beneficiaries (your children) will receive the assets of the trust upon your spouse's death.

ITEM EIGHT

A. *My Trustee (and his, her, their, or its successor or successors in office) shall have the following privileges and exemptions and shall, without order of any Court, have the power to:*

1. *Sell or exchange Trust property, at public or private sale, for cash or upon terms with or without advertisement;*

2. *Improve or repair or lease (as lessor or lessee) any real estate and grant or receive options to purchase property; and a lease or option may be made for a term that may extend beyond the period of the Trust;*

3. *Retain any property conveyed to this Trust, including any stock and securities; invest in stocks, bonds, loans, securities, mutual funds, money market funds, or other property, buy securities from or sell securities to a fiduciary as principal or as agent, and pay reasonable compensation therefor, all without regard to any statute or rule of law now or hereafter in force limiting the class of investments for Trustees, and register any of same in the name of a nominee without indicating that such are held in a fiduciary capacity, maintaining, however, accurate records showing such as Trust assets; and to do all of same without obligation to diversify investments or liability for failure to diversify investments. The foregoing power shall include the power to purchase or invest in assets of my estate after my death, irrespective of whether my Trustee may also be serving as a personal representative of my estate, provided that my estate receives full and adequate consideration in money or money's worth; and provided that any such purchase or investment shall not contravene the provisions of Paragraph 14 of this ITEM EIGHT;*

4. *Borrow or lend money for any purpose that the Trustee may deem proper, including the power to borrow from or lend to my fiduciary, upon reasonable terms, and to secure such indebtedness by Trust or loan deed, or otherwise;*

5. *Employ real estate brokers, attorneys, accountants, or other expert assistants, including any who may be affiliates or subsidiaries of the fiduciary, and to pay reasonable compensation from Trust funds for their services;*

6. *Compromise or settle any and all claims for or against the Trust; and rescind or modify any contract affecting the Trust, all in such manner and upon such terms as my Trustee deems best;*

7. *Make division or distribution in kind or in money, or partly in kind and partly in money; and any asset distributed in kind need not be distributed pro rata or in fractional shares among beneficiaries;*

8. *Vote any stock by itself or by proxy; enter into any plan or agreement for the sale, merger, consolidation, liquidation, recapitalization, or other disposition of any Trust property or of any corporation issuing securities held as part of the Trust; and accept in such transaction any cash, securities, or property that my Trustee deems proper;*

9. *Determine the allocation of dividends, distributions, profits resulting from the maturity or sale of any asset, and any other receipts and the allocation of payments and expenses as between income and principal; provide (or not provide) reserves from income otherwise distributable for depreciation, obsolescence, or other prospective loss, reduction in value, or casualty; amortize (or not amortize) premiums, and accumulate (or not accumulate) discounts, at which securities or other assets were acquired; provided that all such determinations, allocations, and other actions are reasonable;*

10. *Exercise any and all options, whether such be options to purchase stock (qualified, nonqualified, restricted, or other), or whether such shall be options to purchase other types or kinds of property;*

11. *Make, fail to make, or terminate any election permitted under the Internal Revenue Code (including any election under Subchapter S of said Code, and my Trustee is hereby authorized to amend this Trust so to qualify to hold said Subchapter S stock);*

12. *Do all things which may be necessary or proper to protect and preserve the Trust estate or any part thereof, and my Trustee hereunder shall be liable only for the use of ordinary care in his, her, their, or its execution of this Trust;*

13. *This Trust may consist from time to time in whole or in large part of stock in a single corporation, of stock in only a few corporations, or of a substantial concentration in some other investment. I do not desire that my Trustee sell or otherwise dispose of such stock, stocks, or other investment, if such sale or disposition is made solely for purposes of diversification, or solely because there appears to be a limited market for such stock, stocks, or other investment, or for both of such reasons. Accordingly, I hereby relieve my Trustee from any duty to diversify the investments in this Trust and from any duty to sell or dispose of such stock, stocks, or other investment for any one or more of the foregoing reasons; and my Trustee shall have no liability in respect to any such failure to diversify the investments of this Trust or for failure to sell or dispose of such stock, stocks, or other investment;*

14. *Notwithstanding anything herein contained to the contrary, my Trustee shall not have the power to use any assets of this Trust "for the benefit of my estate" in the manner contemplated by Title 26 of the Code of Federal Regulations Section 20.2042-1(b);*

15. *My Trustee shall have the power to amend this Trust to qualify as a Qualified Subchapter S Trust should said Trustee hold S corporate stock and desire to continue the "S election."*

The preceding provisions detail the trustee's duties, obligations, responsibilities, and powers with respect to the trust assets. They are relatively self-explanatory. The key is Paragraph 14, in which the trustee is prohibited from using any of the assets of the trust for the benefit of your estate.

B. *During my lifetime, my Trustee's duties in respect to any policy or policies of insurance on my life which are at any time owned by the Trust shall consist solely of the following:*

1. *To safeguard such policies;*

2. *To retain any sum contributed by me to this Trust for the period during which such contribution is subject to right of withdrawal as specified in Paragraph B of ITEM FOUR;*

3. *To give written notice, in a form and manner as my Trustee deems appropriate under the circumstances, to each person who has exercisable withdrawal rights under Paragraph B of ITEM FOUR promptly upon each receipt of funds into this Trust, including the initial funding of this Trust;*

4. *To pay premiums due on any such policies, when, and only when, (a) cash sums are held by or deposited with my Trustee sufficient to pay the same, and (b) such sums are not withdrawn from this Trust pursuant to the powers set forth in Paragraph B of ITEM FOUR. My Trustee may, however, in his, her, their, or its sole discretion, exercise any other options available under such policies including, but not limited to, borrowing upon such policies for the payment of premiums thereon, applying cash values of such policies to the purchase of paid-up insurance, and accepting the cash surrender values of such policies;*

5. *To make reasonable efforts to notify the Donor of any life insurance premiums which my Trustee does not have adequate funds to pay; and*

6. *To receive any sum or sums which may be paid to my Trustee by the insurance company issuing such policy and to hold the same subject to the provisions of this Trust Agreement.*

The preceding paragraphs detail the trustee's duties with respect to any policy or policies of insurance on your life that are owned by the trust. Note that the policies must be safeguarded and that the Crummey notices must be sent.

C. *Upon being advised that any sum is payable to this Trust by reason of my death, my Trustee shall make reasonable effort to collect the same, including the duty to bring suit therefor if necessary and in the opinion of its counsel advisable; provided, however, that my Trust shall be under no duty to bring suit unless the expenses of such suit, including counsel fees and costs, shall have been advanced or guaranteed in an amount and in a manner reasonably satisfactory to said Trustee. My Trustee may repay any advances out of the Trust assets and be reimbursed for any advances made for expenses incurred in collecting or attempting to collect any sum from any insurance company by suit or otherwise for the benefit of this Trust.*

The preceding paragraph instructs the trustee to litigate, if necessary, to receive the proceeds of the policy.

D. *No insurance company under any policy of insurance deposited with my Trustee hereunder shall be responsible for the application or disposition of the proceeds of such policy by my Trustee. Payment to and receipt by my Trustee of such proceeds shall be a full discharge of the liability of such insurance company under such policy and shall be binding upon every beneficiary of this Trust.*

This paragraph eliminates any need for the trustee to sue. It grants a full and complete release and discharge to every insurance company if they pay the proceeds to the trustee. Based upon that release, the insurance company should have no hesitation to make payment when due.

E. *My Trustee hereunder is relieved from any obligation to file or make any bond, inventory, appraisement, return, or report to any Court, but shall render semiannually a statement to income beneficiaries and beneficiaries with vested remainder interests showing the condition of the estate and the receipts and disbursements during the preceding six (6) months.*

This paragraph relieves the trustee from making any reports to any judicial body, but does require the trustee to notify beneficiaries of receipts and disbursements on a semiannual basis.

ITEM NINE

A. *During my lifetime, (NAME), hereinbefore designated as "my Trustee," shall be the sole "Trustee" of this Trust, with the full powers, duties, and responsibilities as set forth in this Trust Agreement. In the event my said Trustee shall die or for any reason cease to act as Trustee hereunder prior to my death, then (NAME) shall serve as Trustee. If he can not then serve, the beneficiaries shall elect a successor Trustee.*

B. *Upon my death, (NAME), or his successor as per above, shall continue to be Trustee of this Trust, and shall have full powers, duties, and responsibilities as set forth herein.*

The preceding paragraphs name the current and successor trustees both during and after your lifetime.

ITEM TEN

If my Trustee, in his, her, their, or its sole discretion, invests in a policy or policies of life insurance on my life, I agree to submit to whatever examinations are required by the issuing insurance company and to sign whatever documents are required in my capacity as insured.

This paragraph mandates your cooperation if the trustee does decide to buy life insurance.

ITEM ELEVEN

I direct that all shares and interests in this Trust, whether principal or income while in the hands of my Trustee, shall not be subject to attachment, execution, or sequestration for any debt, contract, obligation, or liability of any beneficiary and shall not be subject to pledge, assignment, conveyance, or anticipation.

This item is also identical to that in your Testamentary Will and provides beneficiary protection against creditors and against anticipation.

IN WITNESS WHEREOF, I have hereunto set my hand and affixed my seal, this day of   , Two Thousand (2000).

_____(SEAL)

(YOUR NAME)

In token of the acceptance of this Trust and to acknowledge receipt of the property herein described, (NAME) has set his hand and affixed his seal, this   day of   , Two Thousand (2000).

_____(SEAL)

(NAME)

SCHEDULE A

Schedule of property transferred pursuant to the foregoing Trust Agreement between (YOUR NAME), as Donor, and (NAME), as Trustee.

Asset	Date of Transfer	Basis of Asset	Value of Asset

You then sign the document as grantor and your trustee then accepts the document and the assets by signing as trustee. Schedule A is a listing of the assets put into the trust. This listing can be updated manually—it does not have to be typed. However, make sure that any assets owned by the trust are in the name of the trust.

For example, if a life insurance policy is purchased by the trust, the application should have the name of the trust as the owner. The application should always have the name of the trust as beneficiary.

If a life insurance policy is transferred into the trust, make sure it is done correctly and quickly. Go to your life insurance agent. Request a change of ownership and a change of beneficiary form. These are very easy forms to fill out. They will ask you who is the current owner and who is the new owner, who is the current beneficiary and who is the new beneficiary. The forms will always be signed by the current owner.

Remember, if you are transferring policies into an Irrevocable Life Insurance Trust, you must live three years for that transfer to be effective to shield those dollars from the estate tax. The three-year period does not begin until that transfer is made. Do not hesitate to notify your insurance agent and make sure that transfer is done as expeditiously as possible.

EXAMPLE

(YOUR NAME)
IRREVOCABLE LIFE INSURANCE TRUST

THIS AGREEMENT is entered into by and between (YOUR NAME), as Donor, and (NAME), hereinafter referred to as my "Trustee."

WITNESSETH:
ITEM ONE

I hereby irrevocably transfer, set over, assign, and convey unto my Trustee those assets as per SCHEDULE A attached hereto, the receipt of which by my Trustee is hereby acknowledged. I contemplate that I, or others, including the below said beneficiaries, directly or by his or her representative, will also transfer, set over, convey, or assign additional property to be held in trust in conformity with this instrument; and upon any such transfer, conveyance, or assignment from time to time made, my Trustee shall have all the interests, rights, powers, options, incidents of ownership, advantages, titles, benefits, and privileges which I, or said other transferors, now have or hereafter may have in and to said property.

ITEM TWO

My Trustee may receive any other property (provided said property is acceptable to my Trustee), real or personal, transferred, set over, conveyed, or assigned to said Trustee by me, by others, or by my personal representative to constitute a part of the Trust fund hereby created and to be held, invested, managed, and distributed by my Trustee in accordance with the provisions hereof. Notwithstanding any other provisions of this Trust or any statute or rule of law, unless the principal of this Trust (exclusive of sums described in Paragraph B of ITEM FOUR and Paragraph B of ITEM EIGHT) exceeds the sum of five hundred dollars ($500.00), my Trustee shall be under no obligation to invest such principal held by it in this Trust.

ITEM THREE

This Trust shall be irrevocable, and I shall have no right to alter, amend, revoke, or terminate this Trust or any provision hereof. After the execution of this Trust, I shall have no right, title, or interest in the income or principal of this Trust, and I shall have no interest, right, power, option, incident of ownership, advantage, title, benefit, or privilege in any property constituting a part of this Trust fund. In no event shall I or my estate have any reversionary or similar type interest in this Trust or in the property contained herein.

ITEM FOUR

My Trustee shall hold said property and all income therefrom, and shall manage, invest, and reinvest same upon the following uses and Trusts:

A. Subject to the provisions of Paragraphs B.2 and B.4 of ITEM EIGHT, during my lifetime my Trustee shall pay out, equally to my below said beneficiaries, or accumulate all of the Trust net income and add same to principal.

B. During my lifetime, each of my children (including those conceived prior to my death) and my spouse, (SPOUSE'S NAME), shall, during each calendar year, have the power to withdraw from this Trust, by giving written notice to my Trustee, an amount not to exceed the lesser of (1) his or her pro rata share of the amount which I have contributed to this Trust during such calendar year, or (2) an amount equal to the maximum annual gift tax exclusion allowable under Section 2503(b) of the Internal Revenue Code, or any corresponding provision of any subsequent federal tax laws (if the contributor of the property is married at the time of the gift, a demand beneficiary may request from his or her pro rata share of the transferred property an amount not to exceed twice that annual exclusion if the spouse of the contributor elects to split the gift on a timely filed federal gift tax return; this noncumulative right applies only to inter vivos transfers and not to testamentary dispositions, but otherwise applies notwithstanding any provision of this Agreement to the contrary), or (3) an amount equal to the maximum annual amount allowable under Section 2514(e) of the Internal Revenue Code, or any corresponding provision of any subsequent federal tax laws, as to which the lapse of a Power of Appointment shall not be considered a release of such power. The aforesaid powers of my said spouse and children shall be exercisable in any calendar year for a period of thirty (30) days after my Trustee gives the notice required in Paragraph B.3 of ITEM EIGHT. Each and all of the aforesaid powers shall be noncumulative and to the extent any such power is unexercised (either in whole or in part) in any calendar year, said power (or unexercised part thereof) shall lapse as to such beneficiary and shall not be added to the sums available for withdrawal by any beneficiary under this paragraph in any other calendar year.

Each above withdrawal right shall be exercisable only by a written instrument executed by the demand beneficiary (if such beneficiary shall be under any legal disability of any kind, execution may be by his or her legal, natural, or general guardian, other than the Donor, or, if there be none, by (NAME)) followed by delivery to the Trustee. Upon receipt of a written request, my Trustee shall make distribution within thirty (30) days.

The Trustee, in his, her, their, or its discretion, may fund such withdrawals by distributing cash or other property, including insurance policies, or by borrowing. The Trustee's election as to form and source of payment shall be final and binding on any beneficiary.

If such a demand request is not timely made within the thirty (30)-day period following the receipt of notice of any contribution, it will be fully released by the demand beneficiary to the extent provided in Paragraph C of this ITEM FOUR.

The withdrawal powers held by a demand beneficiary in any one calendar year will be fully released on a cumulative annual basis only to the extent of the greater of (a) $5,000; or (b) 5% of the aggregate value of the assets out of which the powers to withdraw could have been exercised prior to the lapse of any such powers. The amounts not released under this provision can be appointed by the demand beneficiary solely under provisions of Paragraph C of this ITEM FOUR below.

C. A demand beneficiary may appoint the portion of the share created for him or her corresponding to the sum of all withdrawal powers that were not fully released under the provisions of Paragraph B above of this ITEM FOUR to such of those persons who would be his or her heirs at law as he or she directs by specific reference to this Power of Appointment in his or her valid Last Will, but in no event are those assets to be paid to a demand beneficiary's estate, his or her creditors, or the creditors of his or her estate. My Trustee may rely upon an instrument admitted to probate in any jurisdiction as the Last Will of a deceased beneficiary, but if said Trustee has not received written notice of such an instrument within six (6) months after a demand beneficiary's death, it is to be presumed that the demand beneficiary died intestate and said Trustee will not be liable for acting in accordance with that presumption. If a deceased demand beneficiary does not effectively exercise the foregoing Power of Appointment with respect to any portion of the share created for him or her, said Trustee shall add the proceeds to this Trust to be administered under the terms of this Trust as specified herein.

D. In creating this power it is the intent of the Donor to create a noncumulative power of invasion which will qualify any transfer or deemed contribution of property to the Trust as transfer or contribution of a present interest under Section 2503(b) of the Internal Revenue Code. The failure of any beneficiary to exercise such power will not be treated as release of such power as that term is defined in Section 2514(e) of the Internal Revenue Code.

ITEM FIVE

After my death, my Trustee is authorized to receive from whatever source additional property (as part of the principal of this Trust) and shall hold, manage, invest, reinvest, and distribute same and any property of the Trust held by my Trustee at the time of my death, for the benefit of my spouse (SPOUSE'S NAME), and my children, as hereinafter set out:

A. My Trustee shall pay all of the Trust net income to or for my spouse, (SPOUSE'S NAME), at least quarter-annually, but only if so requested. In addition, my said spouse, during the lifetime of said spouse, shall have the noncumulative right to withdraw each year from the principal of this Trust the sum of five thousand dollars ($5,000), or five percent (5%) of the principal of this Trust estate, whichever amount shall be greater.

B. My Trustee shall also be directed to encroach upon the principal of this Trust, at any time and from time to time, in such amounts as my Trustee may deem necessary or appropriate in said Trustee's judgment to provide for the proper support, maintenance, and medical care of my said spouse and to provide for the proper support, maintenance, medical care, and education (including college, postgraduate, and vocational education) of any one or more of my children, taking into account any other means of support they or any of them may have to the knowledge of my Trustee. Encroachments pursuant to this paragraph for such children need not be made in equal amounts during my said spouse's lifetime.

C. Upon the death of my said spouse (or upon my death if my said spouse predeceases me), my Trustee shall continue this Trust for the benefit of my children as per Paragraph D below.

D. Upon the death of my said spouse (or upon my death if my said spouse predeceases me), my Trustee shall divide the then remaining principal of the

Trust into so many shares so that there shall be one share for each child of mine then living and one for the then surviving issue, per stirpes, collectively of each child of mine who shall not be then living, and to set aside one of said shares for each child of mine then living and one of said shares for the then surviving issue, per stirpes, collectively of each child of mine who shall not be then living, and to hold, administer, and distribute each of said shares as provided in the following sections (i) and (ii);

(i) As to the one share so set aside for the benefit of each child of mine living, then I give, devise, and bequeath his or her respective share of this Trust to my hereinafter named TRUSTEE, IN TRUST, NEVERTHE-LESS, to hold and administer the same and to pay to or for the benefit of each such child, so much, all or none, of said share, both income and principal, as my Trustee, in his, her, their, or its uncontrolled judgment and discretion, shall consider necessary or advisable for the support, maintenance, and education of such issue as per the schedule below, at which time the remainder of his or her respective share of my estate, with the accumulations, if any, shall be paid and distributed to him or her, upon notice and request, or if he or she die before that time, shall be paid and distributed upon his or her death to his or her executors or administrators, to be administered and distributed as part of his or her estate.

Age	Per Stirpes Share of Principal
18	5%
21	10%
25	25%
30	25%
35	35% (REMAINDER)

(ii) As to the one share so set aside for the benefit of the then surviving issue, per stirpes, collectively of each child of mine who shall not be then living, to pay and distribute the same to the said then surviving issue of said children, per stirpes, for whom said share was so set aside, subject to the provisions of Paragraph E hereof, if any of such issue be then not yet 35 years of age;

E. If any part of this Trust shall become payable or distributable at any time to the issue of my children who shall not yet be 35 years of age, then I give, devise, and bequeath his or her respective share of this Trust to my hereinafter named TRUSTEE, IN TRUST, NEVERTHELESS, to hold and administer the same and to pay to or for the benefit of each such issue, so much, all or none, of said share, both income and principal, as my Trustee, in his, her, their, or its uncontrolled judgment and discretion, shall consider necessary or advisable for the support, maintenance, and education of such issue as per the schedule below, at which time the remainder of his or her respective share of my estate, with the accumulations, if any, shall be paid and distributed to him or her, or if he or she dies before that time, shall be paid and distributed upon his or her death to his or her executors or administrators, to be administered and distributed as part of his or her estate.

Age	Per Stirpes Share of Principal
18	5%
21	10%
25	25%
30	25%
35	35% (REMAINDER)

F. If I shall not be survived by said spouse or any issue, then the property remaining in the hands of my Trustee shall vest in and be distributed as follows:

IN TRUST, NEVERTHELESS, for the benefit of the issue of my siblings and the issue of the siblings of my said spouse, to be used exclusively for the payment of 50% of the college and graduate school tuition of said beneficiaries.

In no event shall I or my estate have any reversionary or similar type interest in this Trust or in the property contained herein.

G. Regardless of the foregoing provisions, however, in the event the assets in this Trust at any time after my death but before the division of the Trust property into shares pursuant to Paragraph D of this Item have a value of less than $50,000.00, then I authorize (but I do not direct) my Trustee to terminate this Trust and to distribute said assets to my said spouse if said spouse is then living, and if not, then equally among my children, with the then living descendants of any deceased child to take the share of such decedent as per Paragraphs D and E above. In addition, in the event (at any time after said division of Trust property into shares) the assets in any share have a value of less than $50,000.00, then I authorize (but I do not direct) my Trustee to terminate this Trust as to such share and to turn over the assets then held in such share to the issue of mine for whose benefit such share was being held. My Trustee shall have no liability in respect to such termination of this Trust and delivery of such assets, and my Trustee's discretion in this regard shall be absolute.

ITEM SIX

A. Wherever in this Trust the terms "children" or "descendants" (or similar terms denoting class for purposes of inheritance) are used, the same shall be deemed to include children by adoption and descendants by adoption, regardless of whether the adopting parent was a natural born member of the class referred to or whether such adopting parent was, himself or herself, a member of such class by adoption.

B. Whenever my Trustee is directed or authorized to deliver any notice, money, or property (whether income, principal, or upon Trust termination) to any person who has not attained age twenty-one (21), or to use the same for the benefit of any such person, my Trustee need not, in his, her, their, or its discretion, require the appointment of a guardian but shall be authorized to deliver the same to the person having custody of such beneficiary, to deliver the same to such beneficiary without the intervention of a guardian, to deliver the same to a legal guardian for such beneficiary if one has already been appointed, or to use the same for the benefit of such beneficiary. My Trustee shall have no duty to see to the proper application of such assets by any such recipient.

C. In addition to the above, whenever my Trustee is directed to distribute any money or property in partial or final liquidation or termination of a Trust to a person who has not attained age twenty-one (21), my Trustee may, in his, her, their, or its discretion, continue to hold the share of such beneficiary in trust for such beneficiary until he or she attains age twenty-one (21), and in the meantime shall use such part of the income or principal (or both) of the share of such beneficiary as my Trustee may deem necessary to provide for the proper support and education of such beneficiary.

ITEM SEVEN

A. Anything in this Trust Agreement to the contrary notwithstanding, if (1) my death occurs within three years from the date of any funding of this Trust by me, so that any or all of the assets which comprise this Trust are includible in my gross estate for federal estate tax purposes, and (2) if I have any surviving spouse, then and in that event, my Trustee shall hold the assets which are so includible as a separate Trust for the sole benefit of my surviving spouse during said spouse's lifetime, and shall from the date of my death pay said spouse all the income at least semiannually and so much of the principal as may be necessary or appropriate for the support, maintenance, and medical care of said spouse, taking into account any other means of support said spouse may have to the knowledge of my Trustee; provided, however, that if the assets in such separate Trust shall at any time have a value of less than $50,000.00, then I authorize (but I do not direct) my Trustee to terminate such Trust and to distribute the assets to my surviving spouse. Upon the death of my surviving spouse, my Trustee shall distribute any accrued but unpaid income to my surviving spouse's estate. All other assets then held in such separate Trust shall, after paying any and all estate or inheritance taxes which may be due from my surviving spouse's estate on account of this Trust, be held, administered, and distributed, as set forth in ITEM FIVE of this Trust Agreement.

B. This Item is intended to give my estate maximum tax savings flexibility by creating a "qualified terminable interest trust" in the event any or all of the assets in this Trust are included in my estate for federal estate tax purposes, and same shall be so construed.

ITEM EIGHT

A. My Trustee (and his, her, their, or its successor or successors in office) shall have the following privileges and exemptions and shall, without order of any Court, have the power to:

1. Sell or exchange Trust property, at public or private sale, for cash or upon terms with or without advertisement;

2. Improve or repair or lease (as lessor or lessee) any real estate and grant or receive options to purchase property; and a lease or option may be made for a term that may extend beyond the period of the Trust;

3. Retain any property conveyed to this Trust, including any stock and securities; invest in stocks, bonds, loans, securities, mutual funds, money market funds, or other property, buy securities from or sell securities to a fiduciary as principal or as agent, and pay reasonable compensation therefor, all without regard to any statute or rule of law

now or hereafter in force limiting the class of investments for Trustees, and register any of same in the name of a nominee without indicating that such are held in a fiduciary capacity, maintaining, however, accurate records showing such as Trust assets; and to do all of same without obligation to diversify investments or liability for failure to diversify investments. The foregoing power shall include the power to purchase or invest in assets of my estate after my death, irrespective of whether my Trustee may also be serving as a personal representative of my estate, provided that my estate receives full and adequate consideration in money or money's worth; and provided that any such purchase or investment shall not contravene the provisions of Paragraph 14 of this ITEM EIGHT;

4. Borrow or lend money for any purpose that the Trustee may deem proper, including the power to borrow from or lend to my fiduciary, upon reasonable terms, and to secure such indebtedness by Trust or loan deed, or otherwise;

5. Employ real estate brokers, attorneys, accountants, or other expert assistants, including any who may be affiliates or subsidiaries of the fiduciary, and to pay reasonable compensation from Trust funds for their services;

6. Compromise or settle any and all claims for or against the Trust; and rescind or modify any contract affecting the Trust, all in such manner and upon such terms as my Trustee deems best;

7. Make division or distribution in kind or in money, or partly in kind and partly in money; and any asset distributed in kind need not be distributed pro rata or in fractional shares among beneficiaries;

8. Vote any stock by itself or by proxy; enter into any plan or agreement for the sale, merger, consolidation, liquidation, recapitalization, or other disposition of any Trust property or of any corporation issuing securities held as part of the Trust; and accept in such transaction any cash, securities, or property that my Trustee deems proper;

9. Determine the allocation of dividends, distributions, profits resulting from the maturity or sale of any asset, and any other receipts and the allocation of payments and expenses as between income and principal; provide (or not provide) reserves from income otherwise distributable for depreciation, obsolescence, or other prospective loss, reduction in value, or casualty; amortize (or not amortize) premiums, and accumulate (or not accumulate) discounts, at which securities or

other assets were acquired; provided that all such determinations, allocations, and other actions are reasonable;

10. Exercise any and all options, whether such be options to purchase stock (qualified, nonqualified, restricted, or other), or whether such shall be options to purchase other types or kinds of property;

11. Make, fail to make, or terminate any election permitted under the Internal Revenue Code (including any election under Subchapter S of said Code, and my Trustee is hereby authorized to amend this Trust so to qualify to hold said Subchapter S stock);

12. Do all things which may be necessary or proper to protect and preserve the Trust estate or any part thereof, and my Trustee hereunder shall be liable only for the use of ordinary care in his, her, their, or its execution of this Trust;

13. This Trust may consist from time to time in whole or in large part of stock in a single corporation, of stock in only a few corporations, or of a substantial concentration in some other investment. I do not desire that my Trustee sell or otherwise dispose of such stock, stocks, or other investment, if such sale or disposition is made solely for purposes of diversification, or solely because there appears to be a limited market for such stock, stocks, or other investment, or for both of such reasons. Accordingly, I hereby relieve my Trustee from any duty to diversify the investments in this Trust and from any duty to sell or dispose of such stock, stocks, or other investment for any one or more of the foregoing reasons; and my Trustee shall have no liability in respect to any such failure to diversify the investments of this Trust or for failure to sell or dispose of such stock, stocks, or other investment;

14. Notwithstanding anything herein contained to the contrary, my Trustee shall not have the power to use any assets of this Trust "for the benefit of my estate" in the manner contemplated by Title 26 of the Code of Federal Regulations Section 20.2042-1(b);

15. My Trustee shall have the power to amend this Trust to qualify as a Qualified Subchapter S Trust should said Trustee hold S corporate stock and desire to continue the "S election."

B. During my lifetime, my Trustee's duties in respect to any policy or policies of insurance on my life which are at any time owned by the Trust shall consist solely of the following:

1. To safeguard such policies;

2. To retain any sum contributed by me to this Trust for the period during which such contribution is subject to right of withdrawal as specified in Paragraph B of ITEM FOUR;

3. To give written notice, in a form and manner as my Trustee deems appropriate under the circumstances, to each person who has exercisable withdrawal rights under Paragraph B of ITEM FOUR promptly upon each receipt of funds into this Trust, including the initial funding of this Trust;

4. To pay premiums due on any such policies, when, and only when, (a) cash sums are held by or deposited with my Trustee sufficient to pay the same, and (b) such sums are not withdrawn from this Trust pursuant to the powers set forth in Paragraph B of ITEM FOUR. My Trustee may, however, in his, her, their, or its sole discretion, exercise any other options available under such policies including, but not limited to, borrowing upon such policies for the payment of premiums thereon, applying cash values of such policies to the purchase of paid-up insurance, and accepting the cash surrender values of such policies;

5. To make reasonable efforts to notify the Donor of any life insurance premiums which my Trustee does not have adequate funds to pay; and

6. To receive any sum or sums which may be paid to my Trustee by the insurance company issuing such policy and to hold the same subject to the provisions of this Trust Agreement.

C. Upon being advised that any sum is payable to this Trust by reason of my death, my Trustee shall make reasonable effort to collect the same, including the duty to bring suit therefor if necessary and in the opinion of its counsel advisable; provided, however, that my Trust shall be under no duty to bring suit unless the expenses of such suit, including counsel fees and costs, shall have been advanced or guaranteed in an amount and in a manner reasonably satisfactory to said Trustee. My Trustee may repay any advances out of the Trust assets and be reimbursed for any advances made for expenses incurred in collecting or attempting to collect any sum from any insurance company by suit or otherwise for the benefit of this Trust.

D. No insurance company under any policy of insurance deposited with my Trustee hereunder shall be responsible for the application or disposition of the proceeds of such policy by my Trustee. Payment to and receipt by my Trustee of such proceeds shall be a full discharge of the liability of such insurance company under such policy and shall be binding upon every beneficiary of this Trust.

E. My Trustee hereunder is relieved from any obligation to file or make any bond, inventory, appraisement, return, or report to any Court, but shall render semiannually a statement to income beneficiaries and beneficiaries with vested remainder interests showing the condition of the estate and the receipts and disbursements during the preceding six (6) months.

ITEM NINE

A. During my lifetime, (NAME), hereinbefore designated as "my Trustee," shall be the sole "Trustee" of this Trust, with the full powers, duties, and responsibilities as set forth in this Trust Agreement. In the event my said Trustee shall die or for any reason cease to act as Trustee hereunder prior to my death, then (NAME) shall serve as Trustee. If he can not then serve, the beneficiaries shall elect a successor Trustee.

B. Upon my death, (NAME), or his successor as per above, shall continue to be Trustee of this Trust, and shall have full powers, duties, and responsibilities as set forth herein.

ITEM TEN

If my Trustee, in his, her, their, or its sole discretion, invests in a policy or policies of life insurance on my life, I agree to submit to whatever examinations are required by the issuing insurance company and to sign whatever documents are required in my capacity as insured.

ITEM ELEVEN

I direct that all shares and interests in this Trust, whether principal or income while in the hands of my Trustee, shall not be subject to attachment, execution, or sequestration for any debt, contract, obligation, or liability of any beneficiary and shall not be subject to pledge, assignment, conveyance, or anticipation.

IN WITNESS WHEREOF, I have hereunto set my hand and affixed my seal, this   day of   , Two Thousand (2000).

                            _____(SEAL)

                            (YOUR NAME)

In token of the acceptance of this Trust and to acknowledge receipt of the property herein described, (NAME) has set his hand and affixed his seal, this   day of   , Two Thousand (2000).

                                          _____(SEAL)

                                      (YOUR NAME)

SCHEDULE A

Schedule of property transferred pursuant to the foregoing Trust Agreement between (YOUR NAME), as Donor, and (NAME), as Trustee.

Asset	Date of Transfer	Basis of Asset	Value of Asset

CHAPTER 7

Family Limited Partnerships

Family Limited Partnerships (FLIPs) have been the hottest estate planning tool since 1993. In Revenue Ruling 93-12 (the twelfth ruling the IRS issued in 1993), the Internal Revenue Service ruled that it would now accept minority interest discounts within a family situation. Let's see how this relates to a Family Limited Partnership and to your estate planning.

A Family Limited Partnership is merely a limited partnership among family members. With a limited partnership, there is a general partner who controls all of the activities of the entity, and limited partners who, while they do have a liquidation interest in the partnership, have absolutely no voice or rights in the management of that partnership. The general partner has complete and absolute control over the operation of the partnership and can do anything that he or she deems appropriate. Anything that could have been done outside the partnership can be done inside the partnership. Anything that could be sold outside the partnership can be sold inside the partnership. The only difference is that the sales proceeds remain assets of the partnership. Think of the partnership as a giant umbrella covering and protecting your assets.

Here's the key. You set up a Family Limited Partnership, transfer your assets into that partnership, and then gift the limited partnership interests to your eventual beneficiaries (whom we will consider to be your children in this case).

There are two things that you need to focus on here. First is that as general partner, even though you have given away the assets, you still have absolute control over those assets until your death. The general partnership agreement provides that your spouse becomes general partner at your death. So, under the agreement, you and your spouse are able to control the assets for both of your lives. Even though those assets are no longer owned by you, you still have full and absolute control over them.

The second thing that you have to understand is that you are gifting not the assets, but the limited partnership shares themselves, to your children.

Here's where that Revenue Ruling 93-12 comes in. Assume you are transferring $1 million worth of assets into the partnership. For example's sake, we will ignore the general partner's 1 percent. Most people would then assume that since those assets are going to your limited partners, you have made a gift of $1 million to your children.

Fortunately, they would be wrong. Let's see why. Remember, limited partners have absolutely no control over the management of the assets. If they could buy the assets outside the partnership for $1 million and have complete control over those assets, then the limited partnership shares (which is what you are gifting to them), which have absolutely no control element, must be worth *less* than the $1 million.

That's that minority interest discount that the revenue ruling refers to. The IRS has allowed discounts of as much as 40 percent on transfers of limited partnership interests. The less liquid the assets in the partnership backing up those interests, the higher the discount.

So, with a 40 percent discount, a gift of $1 million into the limited partnership (remember we're still ignoring the 1 percent general partnership interest) is only a taxable transfer of $600,000. Let's look at the advantages of a Family Limited Partnership:

1. *You have control over the assets.* Even though you have given away the assets, you retain 100 percent control over those assets. Although you are no longer the owner of the assets, you have absolute control over those assets as general partner.

2. *Revenue Ruling 93-12 gives you an immediate tax savings.* Assume it is the year 2006 and you and your spouse both have $1 million exclusion amounts. Still ignoring the 1 percent general partnership interest, with a 40 percent discount, together you and your spouse can transfer $3,333,333 into the partnership ($3,333,333 × 60% = $2,000,000) without having to pay any estate or gift taxes. Without the minority interest discount, the maximum you could have transferred would have been $2 million ($1 million for you and $1 million for your spouse). Because of the discount, you can immediately transfer in excess of $1.3 million more to your children, saving, in the 50 percent tax bracket, $650,000 in tax immediately.

3. *All future appreciation is out of your estate.* The Rule of 72 says that dividing the number 72 by your rate of appreciation will tell you how long it will take for the value of your assets to double. So, for example, if you're earning 10 percent on your assets, those assets will double in 7.2 years. Let's be conservative and assume that the assets in the partnership appreciate at only 7.2 percent per year. That means that those assets will double every 10 years.

   Assume you are 40 years old when you make the transfer. Statistically, you and your spouse have a life expectancy of another 40 years. Assume you put $3 million into the Family Limited Partnership (and we're still ignoring the general partner's 1 percent). Let's see what happens.

   Remember, your assets will double every 10 years, so that in 10 years you will have $6 million in the partnership, in 20 years you will have $12 million in the partnership, in 30 years you will have $24 million in the partnership, and in 40 years you will have $48 million in the partnership.

Because that growth will occur while those assets are owned not by you but by the limited partners, all of that appreciation will be out of your estate. You will save, in the 50 percent tax bracket, as much as $24 million in estate taxes!

4. *You get income tax savings.*   Because the general partner owns 1 percent of the partnership and the limited partners own 99 percent, the general partner will pay tax on 1 percent of the income and the limited partners will pay tax on 99 percent of the income. Assume you have $1 million worth of assets in your Family Limited Partnership and that these assets earn 10 percent, or $100,000, each year. One thousand dollars ($1,000) will be taxed to you as general partner and $99,000 will be taxed to your kids. While this income will elevate your children's tax brackets, in no case should they be in a higher tax bracket than you. Because of that, there is the opportunity for some income tax savings. This is because some dollars that would have been taxed at your higher rates are now being taxed to your children at their lower rates.

5. *Your assets are protected.*   Prior to 1993, I was using Family Limited Partnerships for asset protection for my clients. If you are a doctor, an attorney, or any other successful individual who fears litigation and the potential loss of his or her assets through a simple mistake or unconscious negligence, then this is for you! Before you formed the Family Limited Partnership, 100 percent of your assets were vulnerable. Now only 1 percent of your assets are vulnerable.

If you place your assets in a Family Limited Partnership, you still retain complete and absolute control over those assets (as general partner rather than as owner) and have insulated 99 percent of those assets from any potential creditors. But what happens if someone sues your children?

Here's where a Family Limited Partnership really becomes fun. Under state law, the only thing a creditor can get against a limited partner is what is called a *charging order.* A charging order places the creditor in exactly the same shoes as the limited partner.

Let's see how that would work in reality. Assume you still have that same $1 million in the limited partnership earning 10 percent and that 99 percent or $99,000 is taxed to your children (limited partners). I would assume that, as general partner, you would distribute enough cash so that your children could at least pay the tax on that $99,000. However, as general partner, you have the option to distribute or not to distribute any or all of the assets of the partnership.

Assume a creditor has gotten a charging order against your children and now stands in their place as limited partner. Now, $99,000 is going to be taxable to the creditor! But here you do not distribute any dollars. The creditor now has what is technically known as "phantom income." The creditor is now being taxed on income that he or she will never, ever receive. Creditors never want to take a limited partnership interest. It represents a liability rather than an asset to them. Unless you, as general partner, are going to distribute cash, each year the creditor will be taxed on income that he or she never receives.

It's not a position that a creditor would want to be in. Limited partnership interests are not assets that a divorcing spouse would be interested in. In all cases, those limited partnership interests represent liabilities rather than assets to these individuals. Because of that, they too are sheltered and protected.

Based on the advantages just listed, the Family Limited Partnership Appears to be the best thing since the creation of sliced bread. However, there are two disadvantages:

1. It is a complete gift. Once the transfer has been made, those assets belong to your children. You and your spouse have full and absolute control over those assets for the rest of your life and for your spouse's lifetime as well. However, at the second death, those assets must go to your children.

2. The assets in the limited partnership should not be more than 80 percent marketable securities. If they are, then the limited partnership becomes an investment company and income must be distributed each year.

Marketable securities are stocks and bonds sold on nationally recognized stock exchanges. If you have a closely held corporation, that stock does not count as part of the 80 percent. We can turn this around and say that 20 percent of the assets in the partnership must either be closely held stock, real estate, art, investment gems, or some other form of investment asset other than marketable securities. If all you own are marketable securities, then I would suggest that you form a closely held corporation to hold those securities and put the stock of that closely held corporation into your Family Limited Partnership. You would then qualify under the 80/20 rules just discussed.

We have discussed the advantages and disadvantages of Family Limited Partnership, but we haven't discussed how you get money out of that partnership. There are three ways to accomplish this:

1. *The general partner can take compensation for services rendered.* I don't recommend this alternative because it makes those dollars taxable to the general partner.

2. *The general partner can take expense reimbursement for expenditures incurred in running the partnership.* However, this doesn't amount to a lot of dollars.

3. *You can borrow!* I strongly suggest that the best way to take money out of a Family Limited Partnership is to borrow it from the partnership. As general partner, you would have to sit down in front of a mirror and negotiate with yourself. I would suggest a demand note (a note that can be called at any time by the creditor). However, remember that you are the creditor—you are the general partner. I would provide for interest to be paid at least every 10 years. If the partnership is structured appropriately, the interest will be deductible by you and 99 percent taxable to your kids.

Let's see the *real* advantage of borrowing the money. Assume you borrow $100,000 each year for 10 years and then die. You die owing $1 million to the partnership. Ignoring the 1 percent general partnership interest, what you have really done is to transfer $1 million to your family at your death. However, because it is coming to them not as a bequest but as a repayment of a debt, this becomes a debt against your estate and you are able to deduct the $1 million dollars on your estate tax return. If you are in the 50 percent bracket, by borrowing the money from the Family Limited Partnership you have effectively saved as much as $500,000 in estate taxes!

What assets should and should not be in a Family Limited Partnership? We have discussed the role of marketable securities and how to get around the 80 percent limitation. Assets that should not be put into a Family Limited Partnership include your principal residence and any qualified pension money that you may have. You don't want to transfer your principal residence, because then you would lose your potential $250,000/$500,000 gain exclusion upon sale. And you don't want to include qualified pension plan assets, because those assets would then become income taxable to you upon transfer.

One more item should be discussed with respect to Family Limited Partnerships. A partnership agreement is a contract among the partners. In order to sign a partnership agreement, therefore, you must be at least 18 years old. What do you do if you have children under age 18 that you want to make limited partners? The solution to that problem is the creation of a separate trust to hold the limited partnership interests until your children hit age 18. At age 18, or later if you so desire, those limited partnership shares can be distributed to your children. It's important to remember, however, that regardless of who owns the limited partnership shares—be it the trust or your children directly—you, as general partner, will always have full and absolute control over the assets that are within the partnership itself.

Let's take a look at a Family Limited Partnership agreement.

FAMILY LIMITED PARTNERSHIPS

General partner—1%

Limited partners—99%

THE (LAST NAME) FAMILY LIMITED PARTNERSHIP AGREEMENT

On   , 2000, (YOUR NAME), (SPOUSE'S NAME), and (NAME), AS TRUSTEE OF THE (LAST NAME) TRUST, all living in or doing business in the State of (Your State), in order to centralize management, reduce costs, and minimize potential liability, entered into the following Limited Partnership Agreement:

The first paragraph details who the partners are going to be and the reason for the creation of the partnership. If you have any children over age 18, they will be named as individual partners. In this case, we will assume that all children are under age 18 and therefore a trust has to be created to be the limited partner and hold the limited partnership shares until the children reach age 18.

It is important to note that the reason for the partnership is not to gain tax savings, but to centralize management, reduce costs, and minimize potential liability. The courts have looked with disfavor at entities created exclusively for tax savings.

RECITALS:

A. *The Partners all desire to enter into an agreement (the "Agreement") to establish a Limited Partnership (the "Partnership") under the (Your State) Revised Uniform Limited Partnership Act; and*

B. *The Partners desire that the Partnership be able to do all things legal in the State of (Your State), including, but not limited to, owning certain policies of insurance on the life or lives of any or all of the Partners (the "Policy") described on Schedule B, and that they all share in the risks, benefits, profits, and losses of this investment.*

The preceding paragraphs define where the partnership is being created and the assets of the partnership. I have provided that the partnership here can own life insurance or any other asset it so chooses and that those assets will be included on a schedule. To add assets to the partnership, just manually create a schedule of those assets, but make sure that the assets themselves are retitled into the name of the partnership. For example, if real estate is transferred into the partnership, the real estate has to be deeded into the partnership name. If stocks and bonds are transferred into the partnership, a brokerage account in the name of the partnership must be opened.

AGREEMENTS:
SECTION 1
Definitions

1.1. *Agreement.*   The "Agreement" is THE (LAST NAME) FAMILY LIMITED PARTNERSHIP AGREEMENT, as amended from time to time. The Agreement includes Schedule A and Schedule B, as amended from time to time.

1.2. *Certificate.*   The "Certificate" is the certificate of Limited Partnership filed on behalf of THE (LAST NAME) FAMILY LIMITED PARTNERSHIP, as amended from time to time.

1.3. *General Partner.*   The "General Partner" shall refer to (YOUR NAME), or if he can not serve, (SPOUSE'S NAME), or any successor General Partner.

1.4. *Limited Partner.*   A "Limited Partner" and the "Limited Partners" shall refer to one (1) or more of the persons whose names are listed on Schedule A to the Agreement as being Limited Partners.

1.5. *Net Cash Flow.*   Net cash flow is the Partnership's taxable income, increased by (1) any depreciation or depletion deductions taken into account in computing taxable income, and (2) any nontaxable income or receipts (other than capital contributions and the proceeds of any Partnership); and reduced by (a) any principal payments on any Partnership debts, and (b) expenditures to acquire or improve Partnership assets.

1.6. *Partners.*   The "Partners" or a "Partner," when used without the words "General" or "Limited," shall refer to both the General and Limited Partners.

1.7. *Partnership.*   The "Partnership" is THE (LAST NAME) FAMILY LIMITED PARTNERSHIP.

1.8. *Partnership Capital.*   The "Partnership Capital" is the total of the Partners' capital contributions.

1.9. *Partnership Interests.*   The "Partnership Interests" are the relative interests of the individual Partners in the Partnership, as indicated in Schedule A.

Section 1 is your definitional section. It defines the individual components of the partnership and details who will serve as general partner. In each state you will have to file a certificate with the secretary of state of that state detailing the name of the partnership, the address of the partnership, the name and address of the general partner, and the name of the registered agent—for instance, who represents the partnership for all legal matters in the state. Blank certificates for each state can be obtained by calling the secretary of state for your state.

SECTION 2
Name

The Partnership's name is THE (LAST NAME) FAMILY LIMITED PARTNERSHIP.

SECTION 3
Place of Business and Registered Agent

3.1. Place of Business.   The Partnership's principal place of business is at (Your Address). The General Partner may from time to time change the Partnership's principal place of business to another location and add additional places of business.

3.2. Registered Agent.   (YOUR NAME), the GENERAL PARTNER for the Partnership, residing and doing business in the State of (Your State), shall be the Partnership's registered agent. The registered agent's business address is and shall be within the State of (Your State) and is currently (Your Address).

Section 2 reiterates the name of the partnership, and Section 3 details the partnership's address and registered agent.

SECTION 4
Business

The Partnership's purposes are owning the Policy and any other investments and the conduct of any other business that shall be legal for a Limited Partnership to conduct in the State of (Your State).

Section 4 describes the business of the partnership. In all cases I would prefer the business to be more expansive than limited—for instance, all things legal for a partnership in your state.

SECTION 5
Term

5.1. _Initial Term._   The Partnership begins on the date of this Agreement and ends on December 31, 2070, unless terminated earlier.

5.2. _Extension._   The Partnership may be continued beyond its scheduled termination date by an affirmative vote of the Partners holding a majority of the Partnership Interests. However, at any time after the scheduled termination date, any Partner may withdraw his or her capital account by written request to the General Partner, who shall cause the Partnership to distribute such capital account within thirty (30) calendar days of the receipt of such written request.

Section 5 details when the partnership will begin and end and the procedure for extending the partnership if so desired.

SECTION 6
Capital and Partnership Interests

6.1. _Each Partner's Share._   Each Partner owns that share of the total Partnership Capital in proportion to his or her Partnership Interest.

6.2. _Initial Capital Contribution._   The amount of each Partner's capital contribution is set forth in Schedule A.

6.3. _Additions._   No Partner will be required to make any additional capital contributions without his or her consent.

6.4. _Adjustments._   Each Partner's capital account shall be adjusted whenever necessary to reflect (1) his or her distributive share of Partnership profits and losses, including capital gains and losses; (2) his or her additional contributions to the Partnership; and (3) distributions made by the Partnership to the Partner. A Partner's loans to the Partnership are not to be added to his or her capital account.

6.5. _No Interest Paid._   No Partner shall receive any interest on his or her capital contributions or Partnership Interest.

Section 6 deals with capital and partnership interests of each partner. It is primarily an accounting section and specifies that no interest shall be paid on a partner's capital contributions or partnership interest.

SECTION 7
Profits, Losses, and Cash Flow

7.1. <u>*Profits and Losses.*</u>   *The Partnership's net profits and losses shall be computed in accordance with generally accepted accounting principles, consistently applied. The Partnership's net profits and losses, and every section of income, deduction, gain, loss, and credit therein, shall be allocated proportionately among the Partners according to their Partnership Interests. No Partner has priority over any other Partner as to Partnership profits. Notwithstanding any other provision of this section, income, gain, loss, and deductions with respect to property contributed to the Partnership by a Partner shall be shared among the Partners so as to take account of any variation between the basis of the property so contributed and its fair market value at the time of contribution, in accordance with any applicable Treasury regulations.*

7.2. <u>*Assignment or Death.*</u>   *In the event of an assignment of a Partnership Interest or of a Partner's death, retirement, or expulsion, profits and losses shall be allocated based on the number of days in the particular year during which each Partner owned his or her Partnership Interest, or on any other reasonable basis consistent with applicable United States tax laws and regulations.*

7.3. <u>*Cash Flow.*</u>   *The General Partner shall have the discretion to cause the Partnership to distribute any or all of its net cash flow to the Partners at least annually. All distributions of Partnership net cash flow shall be distributed to the Partners in proportion to their Partnership Interests.*

Section 7 deals with the profits, losses, and cash flow of the partnership. It is important to note that the general partner here is given the full discretion to distribute or not to distribute any or all of the partnership's net cash flow.

SECTION 8
Management and Operations

8.1. <u>*Limited Partners.*</u>   *The Limited Partners (not including a Limited Partner who is also the General Partner) shall take no part in and have no vote respecting the Partnership's management and operations.*

8.2. <u>*General Partner.*</u>   *The General Partner has the full and exclusive power on the Partnership's behalf, in its name, to manage, control, administer, and operate its business and affairs and to do or cause to be done anything he or she deems necessary or appropriate for the Partnership's business.*

8.3. Compensation.   The General Partner shall be entitled to compensation for managing the Partnership's business.

8.4. Expenses.   All reasonable expenses incurred by the General Partner in managing and conducting the Partnership's business, including (but not limited to) overhead, rent, administrative and travel expenses, and professional, technical, administrative and other services, will be reimbursed by the Partnership.

8.5. Tax Matters Partner.   The General Partner shall also be the Tax Matters Partner and, as such, shall be solely responsible for representing the Partnership in all dealings with the Internal Revenue Service and any state, local, and foreign tax authorities, but the General Partner shall keep the other Partners reasonably informed of any Partnership dealings with any tax agency.

Section 8 deals with the management and operations of the partnership. Note that the general partner has full and exclusive power to control, administer, and operate the partnership's business and affairs and that the general partner is entitled to both compensation for managing the partnership's business and reimbursement for any partnership expenses. Limited partners have absolutely no vote respecting the partnership's management and operations. That's what creates that discount with respect to transfers of limited partnership shares.

SECTION 9
Books and Records

9.1. General.   The Partnership's books and records will be kept on the cash method of accounting and in accordance with other comprehensive basis of accounting, tax basis, consistently applied, and shall reflect all Partnership transactions and shall be appropriate and adequate for all Partnership business. The Partnership books shall also be kept on a fiscal year ending December 31. The Partnership's records shall be maintained at (Your Address).

9.2. Financial Statements.   Within a reasonable period after the close of each fiscal year, the General Partner, at the Partnership's expense, will give a written report to each other Partner indicating such Partner's share of the Partnership income, which requirement may be satisfied by giving each Partner a copy of any K-1 from the tax form that includes such information.

Section 9 deals with the books and the records of the partnership. It details where the records shall be kept and stipulates that each partner will receive a report each year showing the income and expenses for that period.

SECTION 10
Banking

All Partnership funds will be deposited in the Partnership's name in such accounts as the General Partner designates. The General Partner can authorize other persons to draw checks on Partnership bank accounts, but such authority must be in writing and one (1) or more of the Partners may require that such persons be bonded. Each bank in which a Partnership account is maintained is relieved of any responsibility to inquire into the Partners' authority to deal with such funds and absolved of all liability with respect to withdrawals from such Partnership accounts by any person duly authorized by the General Partner.

Section 10 authorizes the opening of bank accounts for the partnership.

SECTION 11
Tax Elections

No election shall be made to exclude the Partnership from the application of the provisions of Subchapter K of the Internal Revenue Code (the "Code") or from any similar provisions of state tax laws. If a Partnership Interest is transferred, a Partner dies, or Partnership assets are distributed to a Partner, the General Partner may, in his or her discretion, cause the Partnership to elect to cause the basis of the Partnership's assets to be adjusted for federal income tax purposes under Code Sections 734 and 743.

Section 11 provides for the tax elections for the partnership. Note that in no case can the entity change from a partnership form.

SECTION 12
Amendments

This Agreement may be amended only with the unanimous consent of the Partners, if the amendment would change their required contributions, their rights and interests in Partnership profits or losses, their rights on liquidation of the Partnership, payment of cash flow, income tax allocations, or the requisite vote needed to expel a member. Any other provision of this Agreement may be amended by the unilateral act of the General Partner.

Section 12 reiterates that except for liquidation rights and allocation of profits and losses, the general partner has the discretion not only to control the partnership, but to amend the partnership agreement itself.

SECTION 13
Admission and Expulsion of Limited Partners

13.1. *Admission of New Limited Partners.*   *A person may be admitted as a Limited Partner by the decision of the General Partner, provided that he or she consents in writing, in a form satisfactory to the Partners, to be bound by this Agreement.*

13.2. *Expulsion of Limited Partners.*   *Any Limited Partner may be expelled from the Partnership on the decision of the General Partner. Upon the expulsion of any Partner, the Partnership shall be required to pay to such Partner an amount equal to the fair market value of such expelled Partner's Partnership Interest. The fair market value of such expelled Partner's Partnership Interest shall be determined by an independent appraisal performed by the Certified Public Accountant regularly employed to prepare the tax returns of the Partnership or, if either there is no such Certified Public Accountant or such Certified Public Accountant is unacceptable to the expelled Partner (as indicated by such expelled Partner's written protest delivered to the General Partner within five days of such expelled Partner's knowledge of his or her expulsion), by another Certified Public Accountant selected by the General Partner, whose decision in this matter shall be conclusive.*

SECTION 14
Limited Partner's Death, Insanity, or Incompetency

A Limited Partner's death or adjudication of insanity or incompetence will not dissolve the Partnership. Rather, the executors or administrators of the estate of the deceased Limited Partner, or the committee or other legal representatives of the estate of the insane or incompetent Limited Partner, will have the same rights (subject to the same limitations) as the deceased, insane, or incompetent Limited Partner.

Section 13 deals with the admission and expulsion of limited partners, and Section 14 details how a limited partner's death, insanity, or incompetency will affect the partnership.

SECTION 15
Dissolution

15.1. *Causes for Dissolution.*   *The Partnership shall be dissolved upon any of the following events:*

A. *The General Partner's withdrawal or adjudication of bankruptcy, or the occurrence of any other event causing dissolution of a Limited Partnership under state law.*

However, if within six (6) months from the General Partner's withdrawal, dissolution, or adjudication of bankruptcy the other Partners elect to continue the Partnership, then: (a) the Partnership will not be dissolved and it will continue under this Agreement; (b) the remaining Limited Partners will elect a new General Partner (and the Agreement and Certificate will be amended); and (c) the Partnership Interest of the former General Partner will be converted into a Limited Partnership interest, and such former General Partner (or his or her Trustee in bankruptcy, successors, or assigns, or other personal or legal representatives) will be a Limited Partner.

B. *Whenever the General Partner and those of the Limited Partners holding a majority of the Partnership Interests of all Limited Partners agree in writing that it be dissolved.*

15.2. Upon Dissolution. Upon its dissolution, the Partnership will terminate and immediately commence to wind up its affairs. The Partners shall continue to share in profits and losses during liquidation in the same manner and proportions as they did before dissolution. The Partnership's assets may be sold if a price deemed reasonable by the Partners may be obtained. The proceeds from liquidation of Partnership assets shall be applied as follows:

A. *First, all of the Partnership's debts and liabilities to persons other than Partners shall be paid and discharged in the order of priority as provided by law.*

B. *Second, all debts and liabilities to Partners shall be paid and discharged in the order of priority as provided by law.*

C. *Third, all remaining assets shall be distributed proportionately among the Partners in the ratios of their respective Partnership Interests.*

15.3. Gain or Loss. Any gain or loss on the disposition of Partnership properties in the process of liquidation shall be credited or charged to the Partners in proportion to their Partnership Interests, provided, however, that gain or loss with respect to property contributed to the Partnership by a Partner shall be shared among the Partners so as to take account of any variation between the basis of the property so contributed and its fair market value at the time of contribution, in accordance with any applicable Treasury regulations. Any property distributed in kind in the liquidation shall be valued and treated as though it were sold and the cash proceeds distributed. The difference between the value of property distributed in kind and its book value shall be treated as a gain or loss on the sale of property and shall be credited or charged to the Partners accordingly.

15.4. Partnership Assets' Sole Source. The Partners shall look solely to the Partnership's assets for the payment of any debts or liabilities owed by the Partnership to the Partners and for the return of their capital contributions and liquidation amounts. If the Partnership property remaining after the payment or discharge of all of its debts and lia-

bilities to persons other than Partners is insufficient to return the Partners' capital contributions, they shall have no recourse therefor against the Partnership or any other Partners, except to the extent that such other Partners may have outstanding debts or obligations owing to the Partnership.

    15.5. _Winding Up._   The winding up of Partnership affairs and the liquidation and distribution of the Partnership's assets shall be conducted by the Partners, who are hereby authorized to do any and all acts and things authorized by law in order to effect such liquidation and distribution of the Partnership's assets.

Section 15 details the causes for dissolution of the partnership and what will happen upon dissolution.

SECTION 16
Power of Attorney

    16.1. _General._   To facilitate the simple operation of the Partnership's business and to avoid frustration of the purposes of the Partnership by minority Partners refusing to cooperate to enforce this Agreement, each Limited Partner names the General Partner as his attorney-in-fact, and gives the General Partner full power and authority, in the place of the Limited Partner, to file and record (1) any amendment to the certificate of Partnership; (2) any documents of any kind required by any state in which the Partnership is doing business; (3) any other documents deemed advisable by the General Partner; (4) any documents required to continue the Partnership, admit additional or substituted Partners, or dissolve or terminate the Partnership or any interest in it; (5) any documents required to obtain or settle any loan; and (6) any documents that may be required to transfer any Partnership assets.

    16.2. _Power with an Interest._   The Power of Attorney granted under Section 16.1 (1) is a power coupled with an interest; (2) is irrevocable and survives the Partner's incompetency; (3) may be exercised by any General Partner by a facsimile signature or by listing all of the Limited Partners executing the instrument, with a signature of the General Partner as the attorney-in-fact for all of them; and (4) survives the assignment of the Limited Partner's interest and empowers the General Partner to act to the same extent for such successor Limited Partner.

Section 16 is very important. This section grants a specific Power of Attorney to the general partner to control all of the operations of the business. It reinforces the complete and absolute control of the general partner over the partnership's activities.

SECTION 17
Miscellaneous

17.1. <u>*Notices.*</u>   *Notice or payment required or permitted under this Agreement shall be given and served either by personal delivery to the party to whom it is directed or by registered or certified mail, postage and charges prepaid, and if it is sent to a Partner, addressed with his or her address as it appears on the records of the Partnership. Any notice is deemed given on the date on which it is personally delivered, or, if mailed, on the date it is deposited in a regularly maintained receptacle for the deposit of United States mail, addressed and sent as required in this section. Any Partner may change his or her address for all purposes of this Agreement by giving notice in writing, stating his or her new address to the General Partner. Such a change of address will be effective fifteen (15) days after the notice is received by the General Partner.*

17.2. <u>*Non-Waiver.*</u>   *Any party's failure to seek redress for violation of or to insist upon the strict performance of any provision of this Agreement will not prevent a subsequent act, which would have originally constituted a violation, from having the effect of an original violation.*

17.3. <u>*Severability.*</u>   *Every provision of this Agreement is intended to be severable. If any term or provision hereof is invalid for any reason whatsoever, its invalidity will not affect the validity of the remainder of the Agreement.*

17.4. <u>*Good Faith.*</u>   *The doing of any act or the failure to do any act by a Partner or the Partnership, the effect of which causes any loss or damage to the Partnership, will not subject such Partner or the Partnership to any liability if done pursuant to advice of the Partnership's legal counsel or in good faith to promote the Partnership's best interests.*

17.5. <u>*Governing Law.*</u>   *This Agreement is to be construed according to the laws of the State of (Your State).*

17.6. <u>*Cumulative Rights.*</u>   *The rights and remedies provided in this Agreement are cumulative, and the use of any right or remedy does not limit a party's right to use any or all other remedies. All rights and remedies in this Agreement are in addition to any other legal rights the parties may have.*

17.7. <u>*Other Activities.*</u>   *Every Partner may also engage in whatever activities he or she chooses without having or incurring any obligation to offer any interest in such activities to any party hereof.*

17.8. <u>*Counterparts.*</u>   *This Agreement may be executed in any number of counterparts with the same effect as if all parties hereto had all signed the same document. All counterparts shall be construed together and shall constitute one (1) agreement.*

17.9. <u>*Binding Terms.*</u>   *The terms of this Agreement are binding upon and inure to the benefit of the parties and, to the extent permitted by this Agreement, their heirs, executors, administrators, legal representatives, successors, and assigns.*

17.10. <u>Personal Property.</u>   The interests of each Partner in the Partnership are personal property.

17.11. <u>"Days" Defined.</u>   For purposes of this Agreement, any reference to a "day" or "days" means a calendar day, including any days that fall on legal holidays or weekends.

17.12. <u>Gender and Number.</u>   Unless the context requires otherwise, the use of a masculine pronoun includes the feminine and the neuter, and vice versa, and the use of the singular includes the plural, and vice versa.

> The preceding paragraphs detail the miscellaneous minutiae required in any well-drafted partnership agreement. They state where notices are to be sent to individual partners, determine what law will control the interpretation of the partnership agreement, define days and personal property, and bind the terms of this agreement on heirs, executors, successors, and assigns.

IN WITNESS WHEREOF, the undersigned have executed this Agreement of Partnership, under seal, on the date written above.

_____ *(Seal)*

(YOUR NAME), General/Limited Partner

_____ *(Seal)*

(SPOUSE'S NAME), Successor General Partner

_____ *(Seal)*

(NAME) AS TRUSTEE OF THE (NAME) TRUST,

Limited Partner

STATE OF (YOUR STATE)

} ss.: Be it Remembered

COUNTY OF (YOUR COUNTY)

that on   , 2000, before me, the subscribers, (YOUR NAME), (SPOUSE'S NAME), and (NAME), AS TRUSTEE OF THE (NAME) TRUST, personally appeared, who, I am satisfied, are the persons named in and who executed the within Agreement, and thereupon said persons acknowledged that they signed, sealed, and delivered the same as the acts and deeds of said persons, for the uses and purposes therein expressed.

_____

(NOTARY)

SCHEDULE A
Partners and Partnership Interests

General Partner   *Capital Account*

Interest

(YOUR NAME)

1.00%

Limited Partners   *Capital Account*

Interest

(NAME)

TRUSTEE OF THE (NAME) TRUST

99.0%

SCHEDULE B
Partnership Property

The preceding paragraphs include your signature and the signature of the other Partners, the notarization of the signatures, the listing of the partners and partnership interest and the listing of the partnership assets.

Remember that if your limited partners are not yet age 18, you need a trust to hold their limited partnership interest until they reach age 18. The trust as follows will accomplish that objective.

THE (NAME) TRUST

THIS AGREEMENT is entered into by and between (YOUR NAME), as Donor, and (NAME), hereinafter referred to as my "Trustee."

WITNESSETH:
ITEM ONE

I hereby irrevocably transfer, set over, assign, and convey unto my Trustee those assets as per Schedule A attached hereto, the receipt of which by my Trustee is hereby acknowledged. I contemplate that I, or others, including the below said beneficiaries, directly or by his or her representative, will also transfer, set over, convey, or assign additional property to be held in trust in conformity with this instrument; and upon any such transfer, conveyance, or assignment from time to time made, my Trustee shall have all the interests, rights, powers, options, incidents of ownership, advantages, titles, benefits, and privileges which I, or said other transferors, now have or hereafter may have in and to said property.

ITEM TWO

My Trustee may receive any other property (provided said property is acceptable to my Trustee), real or personal, transferred, set over, conveyed, or assigned to said Trustee by me, by others, or by my personal representative to constitute a part of the Trust fund hereby created and to be held, invested, managed, and distributed by my Trustee in accordance with the provisions hereof.

ITEM THREE

This Trust shall be irrevocable, and I shall have no right to alter, amend, revoke, or terminate this Trust or any provision hereof. After the execution of this Trust, I shall have no right, title, or interest in the income or principal of this Trust, and I shall have no *interest, right, power, option, incident of ownership, advantage, title, benefit, or privilege in any property constituting a part of this Trust fund. In no event shall I or my estate have any reversionary or similar type interest in this Trust or in the property contained herein.*

> Items One, Two, and Three are the same as the irrevocable trusts we detailed previously. They identify the parties and provide for assets to be irrevocably transferred into the trust both currently and in the future.

ITEM FOUR

My Trustee shall hold said property and all income therefrom, and shall manage, invest, and reinvest same upon the following uses and Trusts:

A. *My Trustee shall pay out each year all of the Trust net income.*

B. *THE BENEFICIARIES OF THIS TRUST, (NAME), (NAME), and any additional children born to (YOUR NAME) and (SPOUSE'S NAME) prior to the eighteenth birthday of (NAME OF YOUNGEST CHILD) in equal separate Subtrusts, shall, during each calendar year, have the power to withdraw from this Trust, by giving written notice to my Trustee, an amount not to exceed the lesser of (1) his or her pro rata share of the amount which I have contributed to this Trust during such calendar year, or (2) an amount equal to the maximum annual gift tax exclusion allowable under Section 2503(b) of the Internal Revenue Code, or any corresponding provision of any subsequent federal tax laws (if the contributor of the property is married at the time of the gift, a demand beneficiary may request from his or her pro rata share of the transferred property an amount not to exceed twice that annual exclusion if the spouse of the contributor elects to split the gift on a timely filed federal gift tax return. This noncumulative right applies only to inter vivos transfers and not to testamentary dispositions, but otherwise applies notwithstanding any provision of this Agreement to the contrary), or (3) an amount equal to the maximum annual amount allowable under Section 2514(e) of the Internal Revenue Code, or any corresponding provision of any subsequent federal tax laws, as to which the lapse of a Power of Appointment shall not be considered a release of such power. The aforesaid powers of my said beneficiaries shall be exercisable in any calendar year for a period of thirty (30) days after my Trustee gives the notice hereby required of said contribution. Each and all of the aforesaid powers shall be noncumulative and to the extent any such power is unexercised (either in whole or in part) in any calendar year, said power (or unexercised part thereof) shall lapse as to such beneficiary and shall not be added to the sums available for withdrawal by any beneficiary under this paragraph in any other calendar year.*

Each above withdrawal right shall be exercisable only by a written instrument executed by the demand beneficiary (if such beneficiary shall be under any legal disability of any kind, execution may be by his or her legal, natural, or general Guardian, other than the Donor, or if there be none, by (NAME)), followed by delivery to the Trustee. Upon receipt of a written request my Trustee shall make distribution within thirty (30) days.

The Trustee, in his, her, their, or its discretion, may fund such withdrawals by distributing cash or other property, or by borrowing. The Trustee's election as to form and source of payment shall be final and binding on any beneficiary.

If such a demand request is not timely made within the thirty (30)-day period following the receipt of notice of any contribution, it will be fully released by the demand beneficiary to the extent provided in Subparagraph C of this ITEM FOUR.

The withdrawal powers held by a demand beneficiary in any one calendar year will be fully released on a cumulative annual basis only to the extent of the greater of (a) $5,000; or (b) 5% of the aggregate value of the assets out of which the powers to withdraw could have been exercised prior to the lapse of any such powers. The amounts not released under this provision can be appointed by the demand beneficiary solely under provisions of Subparagraph C of this ITEM FOUR below.

C. *A demand beneficiary may appoint the portion of the share created for him or her corresponding to the sum of all withdrawal powers that were not fully released under the provisions of Subparagraph B above of this ITEM FOUR to such of those persons who would be his or her heirs at law as he or she directs by specific reference to this Power of Appointment in his or her valid Last Will, but in no event are those assets to be paid to a demand beneficiary's estate, his or her creditors, or the creditors of his or her estate. My Trustee may rely upon an instrument admitted to probate in any jurisdiction as the Last Will of a deceased beneficiary, but if said Trustee has not received written notice of such an instrument within six (6) months after a demand beneficiary's death, it is to be presumed that the demand beneficiary died intestate and said Trustee will not be liable for acting in accordance with that presumption. If a deceased demand beneficiary does not effectively exercise the foregoing Power of Appointment with respect to any portion of the share created for him or her, said Trustee shall add the proceeds to this Trust to be administered under the terms of this Trust as specified herein.*

D. *In creating this power it is the intent of the Donor to create a noncumulative power of invasion which will qualify any transfer or deemed contribution of property to the Trust as transfer or contribution of a present interest under Section 2503(b) of the Internal Revenue Code. The failure of any beneficiary to exercise such power will not be treated as release of such power as that term is defined in Section 2514(e) of the Internal Revenue Code.*

Item Four identifies all of the beneficiaries and provides the Crummey clauses for the transfers made. Note that separate subtrusts are being created for each child under age 18 and that provisions are being made for additional children born to you and your spouse prior to the eighteenth birthday of your youngest child.

ITEM FIVE

My Trustee is authorized to receive from whatever source additional property (as part of the principal of this Trust) and shall hold, manage, invest, reinvest, and distribute same and any property of the Trust held by my Trustee, for the benefit of my said beneficiaries, as hereinafter set out:

A. *All principal and any accumulated income shall be distributed to my said beneficiaries in fee simple absolute on their 18th birthdays. If any of my said beneficiaries do not live to their 18th birthday, said share shall go equally to my surviving beneficiaries, in fee simple, upon their 18th birthdays.*

B. *If I shall not be survived by any of my said beneficiaries, then the property remaining in the hands of my Trustee shall vest in and be distributed as follows:*

IN TRUST, NEVERTHELESS, for the benefit of the issue of my siblings and the issue of the siblings of my said spouse, to be used exclusively for the payment of 50% of the college and graduate school tuition of said beneficiaries. In no event shall I or my estate have any reversionary or similar type interest in this Trust or in the property contained herein.

Item Five provides for the distribution of the assets of the trust (limited partnership shares) to your children upon their eighteenth birthdays. If you prefer, you can provide for such distribution on an aging basis rather than 100 percent upon the eighteenth birthday of the child. Remember, however, that regardless of who owns the limited partnership shares, as long as you or your spouse are alive, the assets of the Partnership are controlled by you (or your spouse).

Item Five also details the maximum disaster clause if your children should not survive to age 18.

ITEM SIX

Whenever my Trustee is directed or authorized to deliver any notice, money, or property (whether income, principal, or upon Trust termination) to any person who has not attained age 18, or to use the same for the benefit of any such person, my Trustee need not, in his, her, their, or its discretion, require the appointment of a Guardian but shall be authorized to deliver the same to the person having custody of such beneficiary, to deliver the same to such beneficiary without the intervention of a Guardian, to deliver the same to a legal Guardian for such beneficiary if one has already been appointed, or to use the same for the benefit of such beneficiary. My Trustee shall have no duty to see to the proper application of such assets by any such recipient.

Item Six provides for the trustee to have control of the assets and to use the assets for the benefit of your beneficiaries rather than distributing those assets to your beneficiaries prior to age 18.

ITEM SEVEN

My Trustee (and his, her, their, or its successor or successors in office) shall have the following privileges and exemptions and shall, without order of any court, have the power to:

1. *Sell or exchange Trust property, at public or private sale, for cash or upon terms with or without advertisement;*

2. *Improve or repair or lease (as lessor or lessee) any real estate and grant or receive options to purchase property; and a lease or option may be made for a term that may extend beyond the period of the Trust;*

3. *Retain any property conveyed to this Trust, including any stock and securities; invest in stocks, bonds, loans, securities, mutual funds, money market funds, or other property; buy securities from or sell securities to the fiduciary as principal or as agent, and pay reasonable compensation therefor, all without regard to any statute or rule of law now or hereafter in force limiting the class of investments for Trustees, and to register any of same in the name of a nominee without indicating that such are held in a fiduciary capacity, maintaining, however, accurate records showing such as Trust assets; and to do all of same without obligation to diversify investments or liability for failure to diversify investments. The foregoing power shall include the power to purchase or invest in assets of my estate after my death, irrespective of whether my Trustee*

may also be serving as a personal representative of my estate, provided that my estate receives full and adequate consideration in money or money's worth; and provided that any such purchase or investment shall not contravene the provisions of Paragraph 14 of this ITEM SEVEN;

4. *Borrow or lend money for any purpose that the Trustee may deem proper, including the power to borrow from or lend to my fiduciary, upon reasonable terms, and to secure such indebtedness by Trust or loan deed, or otherwise;*

5. *Employ real estate brokers, attorneys, accountants, or other expert assistants, including any who may be affiliates or subsidiaries of the fiduciary, and pay reasonable compensation from Trust funds for their services;*

6. *Compromise or settle any and all claims for or against the Trust; and rescind or modify any contract affecting the Trust, all in such manner and upon such terms as my Trustee deems best;*

7. *Make division or distribution in kind or in money, or partly in kind and partly in money; and any asset distributed in kind need not be distributed pro rata or in fractional shares among beneficiaries;*

8. *Vote any stock by itself or by proxy; enter into any plan or agreement for the sale, merger, consolidation, liquidation, recapitalization, or other disposition of any Trust property or of any corporation issuing securities held as part of the Trust; and accept in such transaction any cash, securities, or property that my Trustee deems proper;*

9. *Determine the allocation of dividends, distributions, profits resulting from the maturity or sale of any asset, and any other receipts, and the allocation of payments and expenses as between income and principal; provide (or not provide) reserves from income otherwise distributable for depreciation, obsolescence, or other prospective loss, reduction in value, or casualty; amortize (or not amortize) premiums, and accumulate (or not accumulate) discounts, at which securities or other assets were acquired; provided that all such determinations, allocations, and other actions are reasonable;*

10. *Exercise any and all options, whether such be options to purchase stock (qualified, nonqualified, restricted, or other), or whether such shall be options to purchase other types or kinds of property; INVEST IN OR HOLD LIMITED PARTNERSHIP INTERESTS;*

11. *Make, fail to make, or terminate any election permitted under the Internal Revenue Code (including any election under Subchapter S of said Code and my Trustee may amend this Trust so that it qualifies under said Subchapter S);*

12. *Do all things which may be necessary or proper to protect and preserve the Trust estate or any part thereof, and my Trustee hereunder shall be liable only for the use of ordinary care in his, her, their, or its execution of this Trust;*

13. *This Trust may consist from time to time in whole or in large part of stock in a single corporation, of stock in only a few corporations, or of a substantial concentration in some other investment. I do not desire that my Trustee sell or otherwise dispose of such stock, stocks, or other investment, if such sale or disposition is made solely for purposes of diversification, or solely because there appears to be a limited market for such stock, stocks, or other investment, or for both of such reasons. Accordingly, I hereby relieve my Trustee from any duty to diversify the investments in this Trust and from any duty to sell or dispose of such stock, stocks, or other investment for any one or more of the foregoing reasons; and my Trustee shall have no liability in respect to any such failure to diversify the investments of this Trust or for failure to sell or dispose of such stock, stocks, or other investment;*

14. *Notwithstanding anything herein contained to the contrary, my Trustee shall not have the power to use any assets of this Trust "for the benefit of my estate" in the manner contemplated by Title 26 of the Code of Federal Regulations Section 20.2042-1(b).*

> Item Seven details the rights and obligations of the Trustee with respect to the assets in the trust. Note that it specifically authorizes the trust to invest in or hold limited partnership interest.

ITEM EIGHT

A. *(NAME), hereinbefore designated as "my Trustee," shall be the sole "Trustee" of this Trust, with the full powers, duties, and responsibilities as set forth in this Trust Agreement. In the event my said Trustee shall die or for any reason cease to act as Trustee hereunder prior to my death, then (NAME) shall be the new Trustee of this Trust, with the full powers, duties, and responsibilities as set forth herein this Trust Agreement.*

B. *Upon my death, (NAME), or said Trustee's successor as per above, shall continue to be Trustee of this Trust, and shall have full powers, duties, and responsibilities as set forth herein.*

> Item Eight describes the current and successor trustees of this trust, both during your lifetime and after your death.

ITEM NINE

I direct that all shares and interests in this Trust, whether principal or income while in the hands of my Trustee, shall not be subject to attachment, execution, or sequestration for any debt, contract, obligation, or liability of any beneficiary and shall not be subject to pledge, assignment, conveyance, or anticipation.

Item Nine provides again the same creditor protection and protection against anticipation as in prior documents.

IN WITNESS WHEREOF, I have hereunto set my hand and affixed my seal, this day of   , 2000.

_____(SEAL)

(YOUR NAME)

In token of the acceptance of this Trust and to acknowledge receipt of the property herein described, (NAME) has set said person's hand and affixed said person's seal this   day of   , 2000.

_____(SEAL)

(NAME)

SCHEDULE A

Schedule of property transferred pursuant to the foregoing Trust Agreement between (YOUR NAME), as Donor, and (NAME), as Trustee.

Asset	Date of Transfer	Basis of Asset	Value of Asset

The rest of the document consists of the signing of the document by the grantor and the trustee and a schedule of the assets transferred into the trust. In this trust, that schedule would normally include only the limited partnership interests in your Family Limited Partnership.

EXAMPLES

THE (LAST NAME) FAMILY
LIMITED PARTNERSHIP AGREEMENT

On   , 2000, (YOUR NAME), (SPOUSE'S NAME), and (NAME), AS TRUSTEE OF THE (LAST NAME) TRUST, all living in or doing business in the State of (Your State), in order to centralize management, reduce costs, and minimize potential liability, entered into the following Limited Partnership Agreement:

RECITALS:

A. The Partners all desire to enter into an agreement (the "Agreement") to establish a Limited Partnership (the "Partnership") under the (Your State) Revised Uniform Limited Partnership Act; and

B. The Partners desire that the Partnership be able to do all things legal in the State of (Your State), including, but not limited to, owning certain policies of insurance on the life or lives of any or all of the Partners (the "Policy") described on Schedule B, and that they all share in the risks, benefits, profits, and losses of this investment.

AGREEMENTS:
SECTION 1
Definitions

1.1. <u>Agreement.</u> The "Agreement" is THE (LAST NAME) FAMILY LIMITED PARTNERSHIP AGREEMENT, as amended from time to time. The Agreement includes Schedule A and Schedule B, as amended from time to time.

1.2. <u>Certificate.</u> The "Certificate" is the certificate of Limited Partnership filed on behalf of THE (LAST NAME) FAMILY LIMITED PARTNERSHIP, as amended from time to time.

1.3. <u>General Partner.</u> The "General Partner" shall refer to (YOUR NAME), or if he can not serve, (SPOUSE'S NAME), or any successor General Partner.

1.4. <u>Limited Partner.</u> A "Limited Partner" and the "Limited Partners" shall refer to one (1) or more of the persons whose names are listed on Schedule A to the Agreement as being Limited Partners.

1.5. <u>Net Cash Flow.</u>   Net cash flow is the Partnership's taxable income, increased by (1) any depreciation or depletion deductions taken into account in computing taxable income, and (2) any nontaxable income or receipts (other than capital contributions and the proceeds of any Partnership); and reduced by (a) any principal payments on any Partnership debts, and (b) expenditures to acquire or improve Partnership assets.

1.6. <u>Partners.</u>   The "Partners" or a "Partner," when used without the words "General" or "Limited," shall refer to both the General and Limited Partners.

1.7. <u>Partnership.</u>   The "Partnership" is THE (LAST NAME) FAMILY LIMITED PARTNERSHIP.

1.8. <u>Partnership Capital.</u>   The "Partnership Capital" is the total of the Partners' capital contributions.

1.9. <u>Partnership Interests.</u>   The "Partnership Interests" are the relative interests of the individual Partners in the Partnership, as indicated on Schedule A.

SECTION 2
Name

The Partnership's name is THE (LAST NAME) FAMILY LIMITED PARTNERSHIP.

SECTION 3
Place of Business and Registered Agent

3.1. <u>Place of Business.</u>   The Partnership's principal place of business is at (Your Address). The General Partner may from time to time change the Partnership's principal place of business to another location and add additional places of business.

3.2. <u>Registered Agent.</u>   (YOUR NAME), the GENERAL PARTNER for the Partnership, residing and doing business in the State of (Your State), shall be the Partnership's registered agent. The registered agent's business address is and shall be within the State of (Your State) and is currently (Your Address).

SECTION 4
Business

The Partnership's purposes are owning the Policy and any other investments and the conduct of any other business that shall be legal for a Limited Partnership to conduct in the State of (Your State).

SECTION 5
Term

5.1. <u>Initial Term.</u>   The Partnership begins on the date of this Agreement and ends on December 31, 2070, unless terminated earlier.

5.2. <u>Extension.</u>   The Partnership may be continued beyond its scheduled termination date by an affirmative vote of the Partners holding a majority of the Partnership Interests. However, at any time after the scheduled termination date, any Partner may withdraw his or her capital account by written request to the General Partner, who shall cause the Partnership to distribute such capital account within thirty (30) calendar days of the receipt of such written request.

SECTION 6
Capital and Partnership Interests

6.1. <u>Each Partner's Share.</u>   Each Partner owns that share of the total Partnership Capital in proportion to his or her Partnership Interest.

6.2. <u>Initial Capital Contribution.</u>   The amount of each Partner's capital contribution is set forth in Schedule A.

6.3. <u>Additions.</u>   No Partner will be required to make any additional capital contributions without his or her consent.

6.4. <u>Adjustments.</u>   Each Partner's capital account shall be adjusted whenever necessary to reflect (1) his or her distributive share of Partnership profits and losses, including capital gains and losses; (2) his or her additional contributions to the Partnership; and (3) distributions made by the Partnership to the Partner. A Partner's loans to the Partnership are not to be added to his or her capital account.

6.5. <u>No Interest Paid.</u>   No Partner shall receive any interest on his or her capital contributions or Partnership Interest.

SECTION 7
Profits, Losses, and Cash Flow

7.1. <u>Profits and Losses.</u>   The Partnership's net profits and losses shall be computed in accordance with generally accepted accounting principles, consistently applied. The Partnership's net profits and losses, and every section of income, deduction, gain, loss, and credit therein, shall be allocated proportionately among the Partners according to their Partnership Interests. No Partner has priority over any other Partner as to Partnership profits. Notwithstanding any other provision of this section, income, gain, loss, and deductions with respect to property contributed to the Partnership by a Partner shall be shared among the Partners so as to take account of any variation between the basis of the property so contributed and its fair market value at the time of contribution, in accordance with any applicable Treasury regulations.

7.2. <u>Assignment or Death.</u>   In the event of an assignment of a Partnership Interest or of a Partner's death, retirement, or expulsion, profits and losses shall be allocated based on the number of days in the particular year during which each Partner owned his or her Partnership Interest, or on any other reasonable basis consistent with applicable United States tax laws and regulations.

7.3. <u>Cash Flow.</u>   The General Partner shall have the discretion to cause the Partnership to distribute any or all of its net cash flow to the Partners at least annually. All distributions of Partnership net cash flow shall be distributed to the Partners in proportion to their Partnership Interests.

SECTION 8
Management and Operations

8.1. <u>Limited Partners.</u>   The Limited Partners (not including a Limited Partner who is also the General Partner) shall take no part in and have no vote respecting the Partnership's management and operations.

8.2. <u>General Partner.</u>   The General Partner has the full and exclusive power on the Partnership's behalf, in its name, to manage, control, administer, and operate its business and affairs and to do or cause to be done anything he or she deems necessary or appropriate for the Partnership's business.

8.3. <u>Compensation.</u>   The General Partner shall be entitled to compensation for managing the Partnership's business.

8.4. <u>Expenses.</u>   All reasonable expenses incurred by the General Partner in managing and conducting the Partnership's business, including (but not limited to) overhead, rent, administrative and travel expenses, and professional, technical, administrative, and other services, will be reimbursed by the Partnership.

8.5. <u>Tax Matters Partner.</u>   The General Partner shall also be the Tax Matters Partner and, as such, shall be solely responsible for representing the Partnership in all dealings with the Internal Revenue Service and any state, local, and foreign tax authorities, but the General Partner shall keep the other Partners reasonably informed of any Partnership dealings with any tax agency.

SECTION 9
Books and Records

9.1. <u>General.</u>   The Partnership's books and records will be kept on the cash method of accounting and in accordance with other comprehensive basis of accounting, tax basis, consistently applied, and shall reflect all Partnership transactions and shall be appropriate and adequate for all Partnership business. The Partnership books shall also be kept on a fiscal year ending December 31. The Partnership's records shall be maintained at (Your Address).

9.2. <u>Financial Statements.</u>   Within a reasonable period after the close of each fiscal year, the General Partner, at the Partnership's expense, will give a written report to each other Partner indicating such Partner's share of the Partnership income, which requirement may be satisfied by giving each Partner a copy of any K-1 from the tax form that includes such information.

SECTION 10
Banking

All Partnership funds will be deposited in the Partnership's name in such accounts as the General Partner designates. The General Partner can authorize other persons to draw checks on Partnership bank accounts, but such authority must be in writing and one (1) or more of the Partners may require that such persons be bonded. Each bank in which a Partnership account is maintained is relieved of any responsibility to inquire into the Partners' authority to deal with such funds and absolved of all liability with respect to withdrawals from such Partnership accounts by any person duly authorized by the General Partner.

SECTION 11
Tax Elections

No election shall be made to exclude the Partnership from the application of the provisions of Subchapter K of the Internal Revenue Code (the "Code") or from any similar provisions of state tax laws. If a Partnership Interest is transferred, a Partner dies, or Partnership assets are distributed to a Partner, the General Partner may, in his or her discretion, cause the Partnership to elect to cause the basis of the Partnership's assets to be adjusted for federal income tax purposes under Code Sections 734 and 743.

SECTION 12
Amendments

This Agreement may be amended only with the unanimous consent of the Partners, if the amendment would change their required contributions, their rights and interests in Partnership profits or losses, their rights on liquidation of the Partnership, payment of cash flow, income tax allocations, or the requisite vote needed to expel a member. Any other provision of this Agreement may be amended by the unilateral act of the General Partner.

SECTION 13
Admission and Expulsion of Limited Partners

13.1. <u>Admission of New Limited Partners.</u>   A person may be admitted as a Limited Partner by the decision of the General Partner, provided that he or she consents in writing, in a form satisfactory to the Partners, to be bound by this Agreement.

13.2. <u>Expulsion of Limited Partners.</u> Any Limited Partner may be expelled from the Partnership on the decision of the General Partner. Upon the expulsion of any Partner, the Partnership shall be required to pay to such Partner an amount equal to the fair market value of such expelled Partner's Partnership Interest. The fair market value of such expelled Partner's Partnership Interest shall be determined by an independent appraisal performed by the Certified Public Accountant regularly employed to prepare the tax returns of the Partnership or, if either there is no such Certified Public Accountant or such Certified Public Accountant is unacceptable to the expelled Partner (as indicated by such expelled Partner's written protest delivered to the General Partner within five days of such expelled Partner's knowledge of his or her expulsion), by another Certified Public Accountant selected by the General Partner, whose decision in this matter shall be conclusive.

SECTION 14
Limited Partner's Death, Insanity, or Incompetency

A Limited Partner's death or adjudication of insanity or incompetence will not dissolve the Partnership. Rather, the executors or administrators of the estate of the deceased Limited Partner, or the committee or other legal representatives of the estate of the insane or incompetent Limited Partner, will have the same rights (subject to the same limitations) as the deceased, insane, or incompetent Limited Partner.

SECTION 15
Dissolution

15.1. <u>Causes for Dissolution.</u>   The Partnership shall be dissolved upon any of the following events:

A. The General Partner's withdrawal or adjudication of bankruptcy, or the occurrence of any other event causing dissolution of a Limited Partnership under state law. However, if within six (6) months from the General Partner's withdrawal, dissolution, or adjudication of bankruptcy the other Partners elect to continue the Partnership, then: (a) the Partnership will not be dissolved and it will continue under this Agreement; (b) the remaining Limited Partners will elect a new General Partner (and the Agreement and Certificate will be amended); and (c) the Partnership Interest of the former General Partner will be converted into a Limited Partnership interest, and such former General Partner (or his or her Trustee in bankruptcy, successors, or assigns, or other personal or legal representatives) will be a Limited Partner.

B. Whenever the General Partner and those of the Limited Partners holding a majority of the Partnership Interests of all Limited Partners agree in writing that it be dissolved.

15.2. <u>Upon Dissolution.</u>   Upon its dissolution, the Partnership will terminate and immediately commence to wind up its affairs. The Partners shall continue to share in profits and losses during liquidation in the same manner and proportions as they did before dissolution. The Partnership's assets may be sold if a price deemed reasonable by the Partners may be obtained. The proceeds from liquidation of Partnership assets shall be applied as follows:

A. First, all of the Partnership's debts and liabilities to persons other than Partners shall be paid and discharged in the order of priority as provided by law.

B. Second, all debts and liabilities to Partners shall be paid and discharged in the order of priority as provided by law.

C. Third, all remaining assets shall be distributed proportionately among the Partners in the ratios of their respective Partnership Interests.

15.3. <u>Gain or Loss.</u>   Any gain or loss on the disposition of Partnership properties in the process of liquidation shall be credited or charged to the Partners in proportion to their Partnership Interests, provided, however, that gain or loss with respect to property contributed to the Partnership by a Partner shall be shared among the Partners so as to take account of any variation between the basis of the property so contributed and its fair market value at the time of contribution, in accordance with any applicable Treasury regulations. Any property distributed in kind in the liquidation shall be valued and treated as though it were sold and the cash proceeds distributed. The difference between the value of property distributed in kind and its book value shall be treated as a gain or loss on the sale of property and shall be credited or charged to the Partners accordingly.

15.4. <u>Partnership Assets' Sole Source.</u> The Partners shall look solely to the Partnership's assets for the payment of any debts or liabilities owed by the Partnership to the Partners and for the return of their capital contributions and liquidation amounts. If the Partnership property remaining after the payment or discharge of all of its debts and liabilities to persons other than Partners is insufficient to return the Partners' capital contributions, they shall have no recourse therefor against the Partnership or any other Partners, except to the extent that such other Partners may have outstanding debts or obligations owing to the Partnership.

15.5. <u>Winding Up.</u> The winding up of Partnership affairs and the liquidation and distribution of the Partnership's assets shall be conducted by the Partners, who are hereby authorized to do any and all acts and things authorized by law in order to effect such liquidation and distribution of the Partnership's assets.

SECTION 16
Power of Attorney

16.1. <u>General.</u> To facilitate the simple operation of the Partnership's business and to avoid frustration of the purposes of the Partnership by minority Partners refusing to cooperate to enforce this Agreement, each Limited Partner names the General Partner as his attorney-in-fact, and gives the General Partner full power and authority, in the place of the Limited Partner, to file and record (1) any amendment to the certificate of Partnership; (2) any documents of any kind required by any state in which the Partnership is doing business; (3) any other documents deemed advisable by the General Partner; (4) any documents required to continue the Partnership, admit additional or substituted Partners, or dissolve or terminate the Partnership or any interest in it; (5) any documents required to obtain or settle any loan; and (6) any documents that may be required to transfer any Partnership assets.

16.2. <u>Power with an Interest.</u>   The Power of Attorney granted under Section 16.1 (1) is a power coupled with an interest; (2) is irrevocable and survives the Partner's incompetency; (3) may be exercised by any General Partner by a facsimile signature or by listing all of the Limited Partners executing the instrument, with a signature of the General Partner as the attorney-in-fact for all of them; and (4) survives the assignment of the Limited Partner's interest and empowers the General Partner to act to the same extent for such successor Limited Partner.

SECTION 17
Miscellaneous

17.1. <u>Notices.</u>   Notice or payment required or permitted under this Agreement shall be given and served either by personal delivery to the party to whom it is directed or by registered or certified mail, postage and charges prepaid, and if it is sent to a Partner, addressed with his or her address as it appears on the records of the Partnership. Any notice is deemed given on the date on which it is personally delivered, or, if mailed, on the date it is deposited in a regularly maintained receptacle for the deposit of United States mail, addressed and sent as required in this section. Any Partner may change his or her address for all purposes of this Agreement by giving notice in writing, stating his or her new address to the General Partner. Such a change of address will be effective fifteen (15) days after the notice is received by the General Partner.

17.2. <u>Non-Waiver.</u>   Any party's failure to seek redress for violation of or to insist upon the strict performance of any provision of this Agreement will not prevent a subsequent act, which would have originally constituted a violation, from having the effect of an original violation.

17.3. <u>Severability.</u>   Every provision of this Agreement is intended to be severable. If any term or provision hereof is invalid for any reason whatsoever, its invalidity will not affect the validity of the remainder of the Agreement.

17.4. <u>Good Faith.</u>   The doing of any act or the failure to do any act by a Partner or the Partnership, the effect of which causes any loss or damage to the Partnership, will not subject such Partner or the Partnership to any liability if done pursuant to advice of the Partnership's legal counsel or in good faith to promote the Partnership's best interests.

17.5. <u>Governing Law.</u>   This Agreement is to be construed according to the laws of the State of (Your State).

17.6. <u>Cumulative Rights.</u>   The rights and remedies provided in this Agreement are cumulative, and the use of any right or remedy does not limit a party's right to use any or all other remedies. All rights and remedies in this Agreement are in addition to any other legal rights the parties may have.

17.7. <u>Other Activities.</u>   Every Partner may also engage in whatever activities he or she chooses without having or incurring any obligation to offer any interest in such activities to any party hereof.

17.8. <u>Counterparts.</u>   This Agreement may be executed in any number of counterparts with the same effect as if all parties hereto had all signed the same document. All counterparts shall be construed together and shall constitute one (1) agreement.

17.9. <u>Binding Terms.</u>   The terms of this Agreement are binding upon and inure to the benefit of the parties and, to the extent permitted by this Agreement, their heirs, executors, administrators, legal representatives, successors, and assigns.

17.10. <u>Personal Property.</u>   The interests of each Partner in the Partnership are personal property.

17.11. <u>"Days" Defined.</u>   For purposes of this Agreement, any reference to a "day" or "days" means a calendar day, including any days that fall on legal holidays or weekends.

17.12. <u>Gender and Number.</u>   Unless the context requires otherwise, the use of a masculine pronoun includes the feminine and the neuter, and vice versa, and the use of the singular includes the plural, and vice versa.

IN WITNESS WHEREOF, the undersigned have executed this Agreement of Partnership, under seal, on the date written above.

_____ (Seal)

(YOUR NAME), General/Limited Partner

_____ (Seal)

(SPOUSE'S NAME), Successor General Partner

_____ (Seal)

(NAME) AS TRUSTEE OF THE (NAME) TRUST,

Limited Partner

STATE OF (YOUR STATE)

} ss.: Be it Remembered

COUNTY OF (YOUR COUNTY)

that on _____, 2000, before me, the subscribers, (YOUR NAME), (SPOUSE'S NAME), and (NAME), AS TRUSTEE OF THE (NAME) TRUST, personally appeared, who, I am satisfied, are the persons named in and who executed the within Agreement, and thereupon said persons acknowledged that they signed, sealed, and delivered the same as the acts and deeds of said persons, for the uses and purposes therein expressed.

_____

(NOTARY)

SCHEDULE A
PARTNERS AND PARTNERSHIP INTERESTS

General Partner Interest	**Capital Account**
(YOUR NAME) 1.00%	

Limited Partners Interest	**Capital Account**
(NAME) TRUSTEE OF THE (NAME) TRUST 99.0%	

SCHEDULE B
PARTNERSHIP PROPERTY
THE (NAME) TRUST

THIS AGREEMENT is entered into by and between (YOUR NAME), as Donor, and (NAME), hereinafter referred to as my "Trustee."

WITNESSETH:
ITEM ONE

I hereby irrevocably transfer, set over, assign, and convey unto my Trustee those assets as per Schedule A attached hereto, the receipt of which by my Trustee is hereby acknowledged. I contemplate that I, or others, including the below said beneficiaries, directly or by his or her representative, will also transfer, set over, convey, or assign additional property to be held in trust in conformity with this instrument; and upon any such transfer, conveyance, or assignment from time to time made, my Trustee shall have all the interests, rights, powers, options, incidents of ownership, advantages, titles, benefits, and privileges which I, or said other transferors, now have or hereafter may have in and to said property.

ITEM TWO

My Trustee may receive any other property (provided said property is acceptable to my Trustee), real or personal, transferred, set over, conveyed, or assigned to said Trustee by me, by others, or by my personal representative to constitute a part of the Trust fund hereby created and to be held, invested, managed, and distributed by my Trustee in accordance with the provisions hereof.

ITEM THREE

This Trust shall be irrevocable, and I shall have no right to alter, amend, revoke, or terminate this Trust or any provision hereof. After the execution of this Trust, I shall have no right, title, or interest in the income or principal of this Trust, and I shall have no interest, right, power, option, incident of ownership, advantage, title, benefit, or privilege in any property constituting a part of this Trust fund. In no event shall I or my estate have any reversionary or similar type interest in this Trust or in the property contained herein.

ITEM FOUR

My Trustee shall hold said property and all income therefrom, and shall manage, invest, and reinvest same upon the following uses and Trusts:

A. My Trustee shall pay out each year all of the Trust net income.

B. THE BENEFICIARIES OF THIS TRUST, (NAME), (NAME), and any additional children born to (YOUR NAME) and (SPOUSE'S NAME) prior to the eighteenth birthday of (NAME OF YOUNGEST CHILD) in equal separate Subtrusts, shall, during each calendar year, have the power to withdraw from this Trust, by giving written notice to my Trustee, an amount not to exceed the lesser of (1) his or her pro rata share of the amount which I have contributed to this Trust during such calendar year, or (2) an amount equal to the maximum annual gift tax exclusion allowable under Section 2503(b) of the Internal Revenue Code, or any corresponding provision of any subsequent federal tax laws (if the contributor of the property is married at the time of the gift, a demand beneficiary may request from his or her pro rata share of the transferred property an amount not to exceed twice that annual exclusion if the spouse of the contributor elects to split the gift on a timely filed federal gift tax return. This noncumulative right applies only to inter vivos transfers and not to testamentary dispositions, but otherwise applies notwithstanding any provision of this Agreement to the contrary), or (3) an amount equal to the maximum annual amount allowable under Section 2514(e) of the Internal Revenue Code, or any corresponding provision of any subsequent federal tax laws, as to which the lapse of a Power of Appointment shall not be considered a release of such power. The aforesaid powers of my said beneficiaries shall be exercisable in any calendar year for a period of thirty (30) days after my Trustee gives the notice hereby required of said contribution. Each and all of the aforesaid powers shall be noncumulative and to the extent any such power is unexercised (either in whole or in part) in any calendar year, said power (or unexercised part thereof) shall lapse as to such beneficiary and shall not be added to the sums available for withdrawal by any beneficiary under this paragraph in any other calendar year.

Each above withdrawal right shall be exercisable only by a written instrument executed by the demand beneficiary (if such beneficiary shall be under any legal disability of any kind, execution may be by his or her legal, natural, or general Guardian, other than the Donor, or if there be none, by (NAME)), followed by delivery to the Trustee. Upon receipt of a written request my Trustee shall make distribution within thirty (30) days.

The Trustee, in his, her, their, or its discretion, may fund such withdrawals by distributing cash or other property, or by borrowing. The Trustee's election as to form and source of payment shall be final and binding on any beneficiary.

If such a demand request is not timely made within the thirty (30)-day period following the receipt of notice of any contribution, it will be fully released by the demand beneficiary to the extent provided in Subparagraph C of this ITEM FOUR.

The withdrawal powers held by a demand beneficiary in any one calendar year will be fully released on a cumulative annual basis only to the extent of the greater of (a) $5,000; or (b) 5% of the aggregate value of the assets out of which the powers to withdraw could have been exercised prior to the lapse of any such powers. The amounts not released under this provision can be appointed by the demand beneficiary solely under provisions of Subparagraph C of this ITEM FOUR below.

C. A demand beneficiary may appoint the portion of the share created for him or her corresponding to the sum of all withdrawal powers that were not fully released under the provisions of Subparagraph B above of this ITEM FOUR to such of those persons who would be his or her heirs at law as he or she directs by specific reference to this Power of Appointment in his or her valid Last Will, but in no event are those assets to be paid to a demand beneficiary's estate, his or her creditors, or the creditors of his or her estate. My Trustee may rely upon an instrument admitted to probate in any jurisdiction as the Last Will of a deceased beneficiary, but if said Trustee has not received written notice of such an instrument within six (6) months after a demand beneficiary's death, it is to be presumed that the demand beneficiary died intestate and said Trustee will not be liable for acting in accordance with that presumption. If a deceased demand beneficiary does not effectively exercise the foregoing Power of Appointment with respect to any portion of the share created for him or her, said Trustee shall add the proceeds to this Trust to be administered under the terms of this Trust as specified herein.

D. In creating this power it is the intent of the Donor to create a noncumulative power of invasion which will qualify any transfer or deemed contribution of property to the Trust as transfer or contribution of a present interest under Section 2503(b) of the Internal Revenue Code. The failure of any beneficiary to exercise such power will not be treated as release of such power as that term is defined in Section 2514(e) of the Internal Revenue Code.

ITEM FIVE

My Trustee is authorized to receive from whatever source additional property (as part of the principal of this Trust) and shall hold, manage, invest, re-invest, and distribute same and any property of the Trust held by my Trustee, for the benefit of my said beneficiaries, as hereinafter set out:

A.   All principal and any accumulated income shall be distributed to my said beneficiaries in fee simple absolute on their 18th birthdays. If any of my said beneficiaries do not live to their 18th birthday, said share shall go equally to my surviving beneficiaries, in fee simple, upon their 18th birthdays.

B.   If I shall not be survived by any of my said beneficiaries, then the property remaining in the hands of my Trustee shall vest in and be distributed as follows:

IN TRUST, NEVERTHELESS, for the benefit of the issue of my siblings and the issue of the siblings of my said spouse, to be used exclusively for the payment of 50% of the college and graduate school tuition of said beneficiaries. In no event shall I or my estate have any reversionary or similar type interest in this Trust or in the property contained herein.

ITEM SIX

Whenever my Trustee is directed or authorized to deliver any notice, money, or property (whether income, principal, or upon Trust termination) to any person who has not attained age 18, or to use the same for the benefit of any such person, my Trustee need not, in his, her, their, or its discretion, require the appointment of a Guardian but shall be authorized to deliver the same to the person having custody of such beneficiary, to deliver the same to such beneficiary without the intervention of a Guardian, to deliver the same to a legal Guardian for such beneficiary if one has already been appointed, or to use the same for the benefit of such beneficiary. My Trustee shall have no duty to see to the proper application of such assets by any such recipient.

ITEM SEVEN

My Trustee (and his, her, their, or its successor or successors in office) shall have the following privileges and exemptions and shall, without order of any court, have the power to:

1. Sell or exchange Trust property, at public or private sale, for cash or upon terms with or without advertisement;

2. Improve or repair or lease (as lessor or lessee) any real estate and grant or receive options to purchase property; and a lease or option may be made for a term that may extend beyond the period of the Trust;

3. Retain any property conveyed to this Trust, including any stock and securities; invest in stocks, bonds, loans, securities, mutual funds, money market funds, or other property; buy securities from or sell securities to the fiduciary as principal or as agent, and pay reasonable compensation therefor, all without regard to any statute or rule of law now or hereafter in force limiting the class of investments for Trustees, and to register any of same in the name of a nominee without indicating that such are held in a fiduciary capacity, maintaining, however, accurate records showing such as Trust assets; and to do all of same without obligation to diversify investments or liability for failure to diversify investments. The foregoing power shall include the power to purchase or invest in assets of my estate after my death, irrespective of whether my Trustee may also be serving as a personal representative of my estate, provided that my estate receives full and adequate consideration in money or money's worth; and provided that any such purchase or investment shall not contravene the provisions of Paragraph 14 of this ITEM SEVEN;

4. Borrow or lend money for any purpose that the Trustee may deem proper, including the power to borrow from or lend to my fiduciary, upon reasonable terms, and to secure such indebtedness by Trust or loan deed, or otherwise;

5. Employ real estate brokers, attorneys, accountants, or other expert assistants, including any who may be affiliates or subsidiaries of the fiduciary, and pay reasonable compensation from Trust funds for their services;

6. Compromise or settle any and all claims for or against the Trust; and rescind or modify any contract affecting the Trust, all in such manner and upon such terms as my Trustee deems best;

7. Make division or distribution in kind or in money, or partly in kind and partly in money; and any asset distributed in kind need not be distributed pro rata or in fractional shares among beneficiaries;

8. Vote any stock by itself or by proxy; enter into any plan or agreement for the sale, merger, consolidation, liquidation, recapitalization, or other disposition of any Trust property or of any corporation issuing securities held

as part of the Trust; and accept in such transaction any cash, securities, or property that my Trustee deems proper;

9. Determine the allocation of dividends, distributions, profits resulting from the maturity or sale of any asset, and any other receipts, and the allocation of payments and expenses as between income and principal; provide (or not provide) reserves from income otherwise distributable for depreciation, obsolescence, or other prospective loss, reduction in value, or casualty; amortize (or not amortize) premiums, and accumulate (or not accumulate) discounts, at which securities or other assets were acquired; provided that all such determinations, allocations, and other actions are reasonable;

10. Exercise any and all options, whether such be options to purchase stock (qualified, nonqualified, restricted, or other), or whether such shall be options to purchase other types or kinds of property; INVEST IN OR HOLD LIMITED PARTNERSHIP INTERESTS;

11. Make, fail to make, or terminate any election permitted under the Internal Revenue Code (including any election under Subchapter S of said Code and my Trustee may amend this Trust so that it qualifies under said Subchapter S);

12. Do all things which may be necessary or proper to protect and preserve the Trust estate or any part thereof, and my Trustee hereunder shall be liable only for the use of ordinary care in his, her, their, or its execution of this Trust;

13. This Trust may consist from time to time in whole or in large part of stock in a single corporation, of stock in only a few corporations, or of a substantial concentration in some other investment. I do not desire that my Trustee sell or otherwise dispose of such stock, stocks, or other investment, if such sale or disposition is made solely for purposes of diversification, or solely because there appears to be a limited market for such stock, stocks, or other investment, or for both of such reasons. Accordingly, I hereby relieve my Trustee from any duty to diversify the investments in this Trust and from any duty to sell or dispose of such stock, stocks, or other investment for any one or more of the foregoing reasons; and my Trustee shall have no liability in respect to any such failure to diversify the investments of this Trust or for failure to sell or dispose of such stock, stocks, or other investment;

14. Notwithstanding anything herein contained to the contrary, my Trustee shall not have the power to use any assets of this Trust "for the benefit of my estate" in the manner contemplated by Title 26 of the Code of Federal Regulations Section 20.2042-1(b).

ITEM EIGHT

A. (NAME), hereinbefore designated as "my Trustee," shall be the sole "Trustee" of this Trust, with the full powers, duties, and responsibilities as set forth in this Trust Agreement. In the event my said Trustee shall die or for any reason cease to act as Trustee hereunder prior to my death, then (NAME) shall be the new Trustee of this Trust, with the full powers, duties, and responsibilities as set forth herein this Trust Agreement.

B. Upon my death, (NAME), or said Trustee's successor as per above, shall continue to be Trustee of this Trust, and shall have full powers, duties, and responsibilities as set forth herein.

ITEM NINE

I direct that all shares and interests in this Trust, whether principal or income while in the hands of my Trustee, shall not be subject to attachment, execution, or sequestration for any debt, contract, obligation, or liability of any beneficiary and shall not be subject to pledge, assignment, conveyance, or anticipation.

IN WITNESS WHEREOF, I have hereunto set my hand and affixed my seal, this   day of   , 2000.

_____ (SEAL)

(YOUR NAME)

In token of the acceptance of this Trust and to acknowledge receipt of the property herein described, (NAME) has set said person's hand and affixed said person's seal this   day of   , 2000.

_____ (SEAL)

(NAME)

SCHEDULE A

Schedule of property transferred pursuant to the foregoing Trust Agreement between (YOUR NAME), as Donor, and (NAME), as Trustee.

Asset	Date of Transfer	Basis of Asset	Value of Asset

CHAPTER 8

Charitable Remainder Trusts

A Charitable Remainder Trust (CRT) is possibly the best way for you to have your cake and eat it too. Here's the situation. You have substantially appreciated property with a low cash flow. For example, you may have highly appreciated stocks that are distributing only small amounts of dividends. Alternatively, you may have a substantially appreciated piece of real estate and you no longer want to be bothered with the rental business. In either case, you want to convert an asset into cash flow.

Let's take an example. Assume you have stock that you purchased for $100,000 that now has a fair market value of $1.1 million. If you sold the stock, you would have a gain of $1 million, taxed at 20 percent, leaving you with only $900,000 left after paying the tax (fair market value less tax = $900,000). If that $900,000 were invested at 8 percent, you would have an annual cash flow of $72,000.

Alternatively, you can set up a Charitable Remainder Trust and transfer the assets to that trust. The Charitable Remainder Trust can sell those assets and, because of its charitable nature, pay zero tax. You now have $1.1 million invested at 8 percent, yielding you an annual cash flow of $88,000—$16,000 more than you would have earned had you sold the assets directly.

You now have an added cash flow of $16,000 per year—but it comes with a cost. You will get this cash flow each and every year for the rest of your life, but at your death, whatever is left over goes to the charity. So far, it doesn't sound like such a great idea. You've given up $1.1 million in assets to get an added cash flow of only $16,000 per year. But we're not done yet.

The transfer of those assets to a Charitable Remainder Trust also creates a charitable tax deduction. The tax deduction is based upon the discounted present value of the remainder interest going to charity at your death. The older you are at the time of the transfer—the closer you are to death—the higher the value of your charitable contribution. For example, the present value of the remainder interest of a gift of $1.1 million at your age may be $600,000. In the 30 percent tax bracket, that $600,000 in deductions will save you $180,000 in tax.

In the typical situation, you use the $180,000 of tax savings to purchase an insurance policy that will replace the $1.1 million in assets that you have contributed to the charity.

In fact, if you place the insurance policy in an Irrevocable Life Insurance Trust, the $1.1 million proceeds can be excluded from your estate. In the 50 percent estate tax bracket, had you owned the $1.1 million in stock at your death (rather than insurance), you would have paid $550,000 in tax and would have only had $550,000 (rather than $1.1 million) for your beneficiaries.

A. Assets:

Cost = $100,000	Tax = 20% × $1,000,000 = $200,000
FMV = $1,100,000	Assets remaining 900,000
Gain = $1,000,000	$\underline{\times \qquad 8\%}$
	$ 72,000

versus

$1,100,000

$\underline{\times \qquad 8\%}$

$ 88,000

Extra income = $16,000 per year

B. Tax Deduction on Discounted Present Value of Remainder Interest Going to Charity at Your Death:

Gift:	$1,100,000
Value:	$600,000
Tax savings (30%):	$180,000

There are two types of Charitable Remainder Trusts. The first one is an *annuity trust*. Under an annuity trust, the CRT will pay you a specified sum every year. Alternatively, the trustee could be directed to determine the fair market value of the trust every year and pay you a specific percentage of that value. Trusts set up this way are called Charitable Remainder *Unitrusts*. When you draft the trust, you irrevocably determine which form of payment you desire, and that form is absolute and can never be changed. If you expect the assets to appreciate, you would probably elect a unitrust to maximize your payout.

In terms of beneficiaries, you can elect yourself as the sole beneficiary, or you can name any one or more persons of your own choosing to receive the distributions each year for as long as they might live. Be careful, however, because if you give the income to anyone other than yourself or a spouse, that might result in a gift tax liability.

You can appoint a trustee to administer the trust, or you can serve as trustee yourself. The trustee is required to account for the inflows and outflows of the trust and to file annual tax reports. However, if you serve as trustee you will have almost as much discretion in investing the assets of the trust as you now have in investing your own personal assets. While in most cases the assets of a Charitable Remainder Trust are invested in stocks, bonds, and mutual fund shares, as trustee you will be free to invest in real property, tax-free bonds, annuities, and most forms of property. In fact, if you wish, you can reserve the right not only to change trustees, but to change the designated charitable beneficiaries either during your life or through your Will.

With a Charitable Remainder Trust, you can get an income tax deduction for a gain that has never been taxed to you. And because the trust will be tax exempt, it can sell the appreciated property without incurring a capital gains tax and invest the proceeds in a different way. A Charitable Remainder Trust can be an effective way to convert a risky appreciated growth asset to a conservative income-oriented asset without incurring a capital gains tax.

Your charitable deduction is a function of both your age and the discount rate that is being used. Clearly, the older you are, the higher the deduction. The discount rate that must be used is known as the *applicable federal rate* and is determined and published by the IRS on a monthly basis.

There are a number of excellent tax and financial planning programs that will compute for you the amount of your charitable deduction based upon your age and the then current applicable federal rate. Alternatively, many tax-exempt organizations will be pleased to provide the exact amount of the charitable deduction allowable for any Charitable Remainder Trust you may want to consider. For example, you can call the American Institute for Cancer Research at 1-800-843-8114, and the organization will do the computations for you.

Once you have your computations, you will know exactly how much the Charitable Remainder Trust will increase your cash flow and the amount of wealth (when combined with life insurance in an Irrevocable Life Insurance Trust) that your heirs will inherit. All you need to do then is draft and fund the trust itself. Let's look at the alternative documents for either a Charitable Remainder Annuity Trust or a Charitable Remainder Unitrust.

THE (YOUR NAME) CHARITABLE REMAINDER ANNUITY TRUST

On _____, 2000, (YOUR NAME), of (Your Address), ("the Donor") desiring to establish a Charitable Remainder Annuity Trust, within the meaning of Internal Revenue Service Revenue Procedure 89-21 and Internal Revenue Code Section 664(d)(1), as amended, or the corresponding provision of any successor law ("the Code"), hereby creates The (Your Name) Charitable Remainder Annuity Trust ("the Trust") and designates The (Name) Foundation, a nonprofit organization established and doing business in the State of (State) as the initial Trustee ("the Trustee").

> The preceding paragraph establishes the trust as an annuity trust, identifies the donor, and identifies the initial trustee of the trust.

ARTICLE I
Funding of Trust

The Donor transfers to the Trustee the property described in Schedule A, and the Trustee accepts such property and agrees to hold, manage, and distribute it under the terms of this instrument.

ARTICLE II
Irrevocability and Amendments

This Trust is irrevocable. However, the Trustee shall have the power, acting alone, to amend the Trust in any manner (except to reduce the required payments to the Recipient) required for the sole purpose of ensuring that the Trust qualifies and continues to qualify as a Charitable Remainder Annuity within the meaning of Section 664(d)(2) of the Code.

> These articles detail the property to be included in the trust and the irrevocability of the trust.

ARTICLE III
Payment of Annuity Amount

A. *The Trustee shall pay to (YOUR NAME) ("the Recipient") in each taxable year of the Trust during the Recipient's life an annuity amount equal to eight and 51/100 percent (8.51%) of the net fair market value of the assets of the Trust valued as of this date.*

B. *The annuity amount shall be paid in equal monthly amounts of $,
starting (Date) from income and, to the extent that income is not sufficient, from
principal. Any income of the Trust for a taxable year in excess of the annuity amount
shall be added to principal. Should any annuity payments be received more than ten
(10) days late for any reason other than those out of the control of the Trustee, the
Donor shall have the right to substitute another qualified charitable institution as
remainder beneficiary.*

C. *If the net fair market value of the Trust assets is incorrectly determined, then within
a reasonable period after the value is finally determined for federal tax purposes, but
only after a final judgment of the Tax Court, the Trustee shall pay to the Recipient,
in the case of an undervaluation, or the Recipient shall pay to the Trustee, in the case
of an overvaluation, an amount equal to the difference between the annuity amount
properly payable and the annuity amount actually paid.*

D. *In determining the annuity amount, the Trustee shall prorate the annuity amount on
a daily basis for a short taxable year and for the taxable year of the Recipient's death.*

The preceding article details the payment of the annuity amount. You
should maximize the amount of the annuity that comes to you; however,
under the law, at least 10 percent of the value of the contribution should
actually be available to the charity at the termination of the annuity.

The document details how much should be paid out in the annuity (in
this case, 8.51 percent of the initial value of the assets of the date of the
transfer) and how the annuity should be paid out.

ARTICLE IV
Distribution to Charity

*When the Recipient dies, the Trustee shall distribute all of the then principal and
income of the Trust, other than the amounts due to the Recipient or his estate under Article
III, to THE (NAME) FOUNDATION, a nonprofit corporation established and doing business in the State of (State), (the "Remainder Beneficiary") to be used for its general purposes.
If THE (NAME) FOUNDATION is not an organization described in Sections 170(c),
2055(a), and 2522(a) of the Code at the time when any principal or income of the Trust is
to be distributed to it, then the Trustee shall distribute such principal and income to one or
more organizations that, at that time, are described in Sections 170(c), 170(b)(1)(A),
2055(a), and 2522(a) of the Code, as the Trustee shall select in its sole discretion.*

The preceding article determines who shall get the remainder principal at
your death when the annuity terminates.

ARTICLE V
Additional Contributions

No additional contributions shall be made to the Trust after the initial contribution.

ARTICLE VI
Prohibited Transactions

The income of the Trust for each taxable year shall be distributed at such time and in such manner as not to subject the Trust to tax under Section 4942 of the Code. Except for the payment of the annuity amount to the Recipient, the Trustee shall not engage in any act of self-dealing, as defined in Section 4941(d) of the Code, and shall not make any taxable expenditures, as defined in Section 4945(d) of the Code. The Trustee shall not make any investments that jeopardize the charitable purpose of the Trust, within the meaning of the Section 4944 of the Code, or retain any excess business holdings, within the meaning of Section 4943 of the Code.

> The preceding articles describe those transactions that are prohibited and indicate that no additional contributions can be made to the trust after the initial contribution.

ARTICLE VII
Trustee and Successor Trustee

A. *THE (NAME) FOUNDATION will be the Initial Trustee.*

B. *The Donor retains the right to dismiss the Trustee and to appoint a successor Trustee.*

C. *The Trustee may designate any individual or institution as a Co-Trustee by a written instrument. Any Co-Trustee or successor Trustee may, without liability, accept without examination or review the accounts rendered and the property delivered by any predecessor Trustee, without any liability. Each successor Trustee has the same title, powers, and duties as the Trustee succeeded, without any additional conveyance. Any reference to a "Trustee" refers equally to any successor Trustee.*

D. *No Trustee named in Paragraph A shall be required to provide surety or other security on a bond.*

E. *Any Trustee may resign by giving written notice specifying the resignation's effective date to the designated successor Trustee, if there is one, or to the Donor. If no successor Trustee is named in Paragraph A, the successor Trustee shall be named by the Donor, or, if he or she is not able, by the remainder beneficiary.*

F. *No Trustee shall be required (1) to obtain the order of any court to exercise any power or discretion under this Trust, or (2) to file any accounting with any public official, although the Trustee must maintain accurate records concerning the Trust and shall send to the Donor, the Recipient, and the remainder beneficiary an annual accounting of the Trust's condition, including receipts and disbursements, which may be satisfied by a copy of the Trust's federal income tax return, if one is required.*

G. *The Trustee accepts this Trust with compensation not to exceed 1% of the value of said Trust each year on the anniversary date of this Trust for services in administering this Trust. SAID COMPENSATION SHALL NOT REDUCE THE AMOUNT DUE TO THE RECIPIENT.*

> Article VII defines the trustee, the successor trustee, and the compensation of the trustee.

ARTICLE VIII
Taxable Year

The taxable year of the Trust shall be the calendar year.

ARTICLE IX
Governing Law

The operation of the Trust shall be governed by the laws of the State of (State). However, the Trustee is prohibited from exercising any power or discretion granted under said laws that would be inconsistent with the qualification of the Trust under Section 664(d)(1) of the Code and the corresponding regulations.

> The preceding articles determine both the calendar year of the trust and the state whose laws will govern the operation of the trust.

ARTICLE X
Trust Investments

Nothing in this Trust instrument shall be construed to restrict the Trustee from investing the Trust assets in a manner that could result in the annual realization of a reasonable amount of income or gain from the sale or disposition of Trust assets. Consistent with this limitation and with the qualification of the Trust as a Charitable Remainder Annuity Trust under Section 664(d)(1) of the Code, the Trustee is authorized to:

A. *Hold assets given to the Trust or invest and reinvest them (or leave them temporarily uninvested) in any type of property and every kind of investment, including (but not limited to) corporate obligations of every kind, preferred or common stocks, securities of any regulated investment trust, and partnership interests. Notwithstanding the previous statements, during any period in which the Donor is also a Trustee, the Trustee may not invest any of the Trust funds in hard-to-value assets, such as real estate or closely held stocks.*

B. *Keep all or part of the Trust property at any place within the United States or abroad.*

C. *Deposit Trust funds in any commercial savings or savings and loan accounts.*

D. *Sell or otherwise dispose of Trust assets, including (but not limited to) Trust real property, for cash or credit, at public or private sale, and with such warranties or indemnifications as the Trustee deems advisable.*

E. *Hold property in the name of any Trustee or any custodian or nominee, without disclosing this Trust, but the Trustee is responsible for the acts of any custodian or nominee the Trustee so uses.*

F. *Pay and advance money for the Trust's protection and for all expenses, losses, and liabilities sustained in its administration, at the expense of the Trustee.*

G. *Prosecute or defend any action for the protection of the Trust, the Trustee in the performance of the Trustee's duties, or both, and pay, contest, or settle any claim by or against the Trust or the Trustee in the performance of the Trustee's duties, at the expense of the Trustee.*

H. *Employ persons, even if they are associated with the Trustee, to advise or assist the Trustee in the performance of the Trustee's duties, at the expense of said Trustee.*

I. *Distribute Trust assets in kind or in cash, without the consent of any beneficiary.*

J. *Execute and deliver any instruments necessary or useful in the exercise of any of these powers.*

Article X discusses what the trust can invest in and the limitations of a trust investment.

ARTICLE XI
Death Taxes

No estate, inheritance, or other death taxes with respect to the Trust shall be allocated to or recoverable from the Trust, notwithstanding any inconsistent statements in the Donor's Last Will or in any other instrument.

ARTICLE XII
Facility of Payment

The Trustee may, in its discretion, do one or more of the following with respect to any payment which would be made to the Recipient at a time when he or she is legally disabled: (1) take any action necessary to have a legal guardian appointed for the Recipient, if none has already been appointed, and make the payment to such legal guardian, without having to see to the proper application of such payment; or (2) expend such payment for the Recipient's benefit.

ARTICLE XIII
Miscellaneous

A. *The headings in this Trust are inserted for convenience only and are not a part of this Trust.*

B. *Whenever the context of this Trust requires, the masculine gender includes the feminine or neuter, and vice versa, and the singular number includes the plural, and vice versa.*

> The preceding articles deal with how the annuities can be paid, limitations in terms of payment, and miscellaneous trust provisions.

IN WITNESS WHEREOF, (YOUR NAME), the Donor, and The (Name) Foundation, of (Address), the Trustee, by its duly authorized officer have signed this agreement the day and year first above written.

_____

(Your Name), Donor

_____

(Name) Foundation, Trustee

By:

_____

(NAME), EXECUTIVE DIRECTOR

STATE OF (YOUR STATE) _____

COUNTY OF (YOUR COUNTY) _____

 BE IT REMEMBERED, that on _____ *, 2000, before me, the undersigned authority, personally appeared (YOUR NAME) and (NAME) AS EXECUTIVE DIREC-TOR OF THE (NAME) FOUNDATION, who, I am satisfied, are the persons named in and who executed the above document, and I having first made known to such persons the contents thereof, such persons acknowledged that they are of sound mind, free of duress or undue influence, and that such persons signed, sealed, and delivered the same as their voluntary act and deed. All of which is hereby certified.*

_____

(NOTARY)

SCHEDULE A

The trust is then signed by the donor and the trustee, both signatures are notarized, and the property is transferred into the trust is then scheduled.

 The preceding trust is a Charitable Remainder "Annuity" Trust. The trust that follows is a Charitable Remainder Unitrust. With the unitrust, rather than having the charity act as trustee, the trust provides for a financial institution—in this case the Merrill Lynch Trust Company of America—to act as trustee.

THE (NAME) CHARITABLE REMAINDER UNITRUST

On (Date), (Name) and (Name), of (Address), ("the Donor") desiring to establish a Charitable Remainder Unitrust, within the meaning of Internal Revenue Service Revenue Procedure 90-32 and Code Section 664(d)(1), as amended, or the corresponding provision of any successor law ("the Code"), hereby create The (Name) Charitable Remainder Unitrust ("the Trust") and designate (Name), a (State) corporation, as the initial Trustee ("the Trustee").

ARTICLE I
Funding of Trust

The Donor transfers to the Trustee the property described in Schedule A, and the Trustee accepts such property and agrees to hold, manage, and distribute it under the terms of this instrument.

ARTICLE II
Irrevocability and Amendments

This Trust is irrevocable. However, the Trustee shall have the power, acting alone, to amend the Trust in any manner required for the sole purpose of ensuring that the Trust qualifies and continues to qualify as a Charitable Remainder Unitrust within the meaning of Section 664(d)(2) of the Code.

These trust provisions are very similar to the annuity trust provisions. The big difference is found in Article III.

ARTICLE III
Payment of Annuity Amount

A. *In each taxable year of the Trust, the Trustee shall pay to (NAME) and (NAME) (hereinafter referred to as "the Recipients"), in equal shares during their lifetimes, a unitrust amount equal to ten percent (10%) of the net fair market value of the assets of the Trust valued as of the first day of each taxable year of the Trust (the "Valuation Date"). At the death of the first Recipient (as defined below), the surviving Recipient shall receive the entire unitrust annuity amount.*

B. *The unitrust amount shall be paid in equal quarterly amounts (starting September 1, 2000) from income and, to the extent that income is not sufficient, from principal. Any income of the Trust for a taxable year in excess of the unitrust amount shall be added to principal.*

C.   *If the net fair market value of the Trust assets is incorrectly determined, then within a reasonable period after the value is finally determined for federal tax purposes, the Trustee shall pay to the Recipient, in the case of an undervaluation, or the Recipient shall pay to the Trustee, in the case of an overvaluation, an amount equal to the difference between the unitrust amount properly payable and the unitrust amount actually paid.*

D.   *In determining the unitrust amount, the Trustee shall prorate the unitrust amount on a daily basis for a short taxable year and for the taxable year of death of the later to die of the Recipients.*

Note that in this article, the trustee is required to value the assets of the trust each year and the amount of distribution is a percentage (in this case 10 percent) of the net fair market value of those assets annually.

ARTICLE IV
Distribution to Charity

Immediately following the death of the later of the Recipients to die, the Trustee shall distribute all of the then principal and income of the Trust, other than any amounts due to the Recipient or his or her estate under Article III, to (NAME), to be used for its general educational purposes. If (NAME) is not an organization described in Code Sections 170(c), 170(b)(1)(A), 2055(a), and 2522(a) at the time when any principal or income of the Trust is to be distributed to it, then the Trustee shall distribute such principal and income to one or more organizations that, at that time, are described in Code Sections 170(c), 170(b)(1)(A), 2055(a), and 2522(a), as the Trustee shall select in its sole discretion. The Donor has the discretion, during his or her lifetime, to change the beneficiary so long as said change is to a qualifying charitable organization as per above. Said change shall be made by certified letter to the Trustee.

Article IV details who will be the charitable recipient of the assets upon your death.

ARTICLE V
Additional Contributions

If additional contributions are made to the Trust after the initial contribution, the unitrust amount for the year in which the additional contribution is made shall be ten percent (10%) of the sum of (a) the net fair market value of the Trust assets as of the first day of the taxable year (excluding the assets added and any income from or appreciation on such assets) and (b) that proportion of the value of the assets so added that was excluded under (a) that the number of days in the period which begins with the date of the contribution and ends with the earlier of the last day of the taxable year or the date of death of the later to die of the Recipients bears to the number of days in the period that begins on the first day of such taxable year and ends with the earlier of the last day in such taxable year or the date of death of the later to die of the Recipients. In the case where there is no valuation after the time of contribution, the assets so added shall be valued at the time of contribution. Any additional contributions must be acceptable to the Trustee.

> Because this is a unitrust, additional contributions can always be made. Note that with a unitrust, the distributions are based upon an annual valuation of the trust assets. With an annuity trust, any percentage distribution is limited exclusively to the initial value of the assets when they are put into the trust.

ARTICLE VI
Prohibited Transactions

The income of the Trust for each taxable year shall be distributed at such time and in such manner as not to subject the Trust to tax under Section 4942 of the Code. Except for the payment of the annuity amount to the Recipients, the Trustee shall not engage in any act of self-dealing, as defined in Section 4941(d) of the Code, and shall not make any taxable expenditures, as defined in Section 4945(d) of the Code. The Trustee shall not make any investments that jeopardize the charitable purpose of the Trust, within the meaning of Section 4944 of the Code, or retain any excess business holdings, within the meaning of Section 4943 of the Code.

ARTICLE VII
Trustee and Successor Trustee

A. *(Name), a (State) corporation, will be the Initial Trustee.*

B. *The Donor retains the right to dismiss the Trustee and to appoint a successor Trustee.*

C. *The Trustee may designate any individual or institution as a Co-Trustee, by a written instrument. Any Co-Trustee or successor Trustee may, without liability, accept without examination or review the accounts rendered and the property delivered by any predecessor Trustee, without any liability. Each successor Trustee has the same title, powers, and duties as the Trustee succeeded, without any additional conveyance. Any reference to a "Trustee" refers equally to any successor Trustee.*

D. No Trustee named in Paragraph A shall be required to provide surety or other security on a bond.

E. Any Trustee may resign by giving written notice specifying the resignation's effective date as per ARTICLE XIII, Paragraph F below.

F. No Trustee shall be required (1) to obtain the order of any court to exercise of any power or discretion under this Trust or (2) to file any accounting with any public official, although the Trustee must maintain accurate records concerning the Trust and shall send to the Donor, each Recipient, and the remainderman an annual accounting of the Trust's condition, including receipts and disbursements, which may be satisfied by a copy of the Trust's federal income tax return, if one is required, or, at the option of the Trustee, by providing monthly statements.

G. Each Trustee is entitled to compensation based on its published fee schedule in effect at the time services are rendered.

ARTICLE VIII
Taxable Year

The taxable year of the Trust shall be the calendar year.

ARTICLE IX
Governing Law

The operation of the Trust shall be governed by the laws of the State of (State). However, the Trustee is prohibited from exercising any power or discretion granted under said laws that would be inconsistent with the qualification of the Trust under Section 664(d)(1) of the Code and the corresponding regulations.

ARTICLE X
Trust Investments

Nothing in this Trust instrument shall be construed to restrict the Trustee from investing the Trust assets in a manner that could result in the annual realization of a reasonable amount of income or gain from the sale or disposition of Trust assets. Consistent with this limitation and with the qualification of the Trust as a Charitable Remainder Unitrust under Section 664(d)(1) of the Code, the Trustee is authorized to:

A. Hold assets given to the Trust or invest and reinvest them (or leave them temporarily uninvested) in any type of property and every kind of investment, including (but not limited to) corporate obligations of every kind, preferred or common stocks, securities of any regulated investment Trust, and partnership interests. Notwithstanding the previous statements, during any period in which the Donor is also a Trustee, the

Trustee may not invest any of the Trust funds in hard-to-value assets, such as real estate or closely held stocks.

B. Keep all or part of the Trust property at any place within the United States or abroad.

C. Deposit Trust funds in any commercial savings or savings and loan accounts.

D. Sell or otherwise dispose of Trust assets, including (but not limited to) Trust real property, for cash or credit, at public or private sale, and with such warranties or indemnifications as the Trustee deems advisable.

E. Hold property in the name of any Trustee or any custodian or nominee, without disclosing this Trust, but the Trustee is responsible for the acts of any custodian or nominee the Trustee so uses.

F. Pay and advance money for the Trust's protection and for all expenses, losses, and liabilities sustained in its administration.

G. Prosecute or defend any action for the protection of the Trust, the Trustee in the performance of the Trustee's duties, or both, and to pay, contest, or settle any claim by or against the Trust or the Trustee in the performance of the Trustee's duties.

H. Employ persons, even if they are associated with the Trustee, to advise or assist the Trustee in the performance of the Trustee's duties.

I. Distribute Trust assets in kind or in cash, without the consent of any beneficiary.

J. Execute and deliver any instruments necessary or useful in the exercise of any of these powers.

ARTICLE XI
Death Taxes

No estate, inheritance, or other death taxes with respect to the Trust shall be allocated to or recoverable from the Trust, notwithstanding any inconsistent statements in the Donor's Last Will or in any other instrument. This Trust shall terminate unless the surviving beneficiary pays for any state death taxes or federal estate taxes due, if any, from the Trust on the death of the first beneficiary to die.

ARTICLE XII
Facility of Payment

The Trustee may, in its discretion, do one or more of the following with respect to any payment which would be made to the Recipient at a time when he is legally disabled: (1) take any action necessary to have a legal guardian appointed for the Recipient, if none has already been appointed, and make the payment to such legal guardian, without having to see to the proper application of such payment, or (2) expend such payment for the Recipient's benefit.

ARTICLE XIII
Miscellaneous

A. This Trust will be construed according to the laws of (State).

B. Whenever the context of this Trust requires, the masculine gender includes the feminine or neuter, and vice versa, and the singular number includes the plural, and vice versa.

C. The Trustee shall have the following specific powers as to Trust property and may exercise the same in its sole and absolute discretion without Court order or approval:

(a) To engage any corporation, partnership, or other entity affiliated with the Trustee (an "Affiliated Entity") to render services to any Trust hereunder, including, without limitation:

(i) To manage or advise on the investments of such Trust on a discretionary or nondiscretionary basis.

(ii) To act as a broker or dealer to execute transactions, including the purchase of any securities currently distributed, underwritten, or issued by an Affiliated Entity, at standard commission rates, markups, or concessions, and to provide other management or investment services with respect to such Trust, including the custody of assets; provided, however, that an Affiliated Entity that is a "disqualified person" for purposes of Section 4941 of the Internal Revenue Code of 1986, as amended, shall only act as agent and not as Principal (except with regard to the purchase of money market mutual funds), and to pay for any such services from Trust property, without reduction for any compensation paid to the Trustee for its services as Trustee.

(b) To invest in mutual funds offered by an Affiliated Entity or to which an Affiliated Entity may render services and from which an affiliate Entity receives compensation.

(c) To cause or permit all or any part of any Trust hereunder to be held, maintained, or managed in any jurisdiction and to hold any Trust property in the name of its nominee or a nominee of any Affiliated Entity.

D. This Trust shall be effective upon the later of the execution of the Trust instrument by the Trustee or the transfer of the assets or property to the Trustee. For purposes of this Trust, the term "transfer" shall mean the moment in time when the Trustee actually receives the assets or title to the property in the name of the Trustee or by confirming evidence of ownership of it in a Trust account held in the name of this Trust.

E. The Trustee, and any successor corporate Trustee, shall receive payment for its services in accordance with its schedule of rates in effect at the time such compensation becomes payable, without reduction for any other fees or other compensation paid to said Trustee or an *Affiliated Entity*, including (but not limited to) such fees or other compensation paid by any mutual fund, unit investment trust, or other investment vehicle, or an agent. Such compensation may be paid without Court approval.

F.   The Trustee may resign as Trustee of any Trust hereunder at any time by written notice delivered to any Co-Trustee(s) and to all beneficiaries to whom current Trust payments may or must then be distributed, or to the natural or legal guardians of such beneficiaries. Such resignation shall be effective upon the written appointment of a successor Trustee. A majority of such beneficiaries or such natural or legal guardians, as the case may be, shall have the power to appoint a successor Trustee, or in default of such appointment, the Trustee shall have the same power. All of the Trustee's fees and expenses (including reasonable attorney's fees) attributable to the appointment of a successor Trustee shall be paid by such Trust. No bond or other security shall be required of the Trustee or any successor Trustee in any jurisdiction. Any successor Trustee shall have the same powers, authorities, and discretions as though originally named as the Trustee.

G.   The Trustee shall have the power to employ, and to delegate any of its discretionary powers to agents, including (but not limited to) attorneys, investment advisors, appraisers, or accountants as it deems necessary and proper and to pay for such services from the Trust property.

IN WITNESS WHEREOF, (NAME) and (NAME), the Donor, and (NAME), a (State) Corporation, the Trustee, by its duly authorized officer have signed this agreement the day and year first above written.

_____

(NAME), DONOR

_____

(NAME), DONOR

_____

(NAME), a (State) Corporation (TRUSTEE)

By:

_____

(NAME) Executive Director

STATE OF (YOUR STATE) _____

COUNTY OF (YOUR COUNTY) _____

BE IT REMEMBERED, that on   , before me, the undersigned author-ity, personally appeared, (NAME) and (NAME), who, I am satisfied, are the persons named in and who executed the above document, and I having first made known to such persons the contents thereof, such persons acknowledged that they are of sound mind, free of duress or undue influence, and that such persons signed, sealed, and delivered the same as their voluntary act and deed. All of which is hereby certified.

_____

(NOTARY)

SCHEDULE A

The remainder of the document is basically the same as with the annuity trust. Note the modifications that were made because we had a third-party independent trustee. Otherwise, the structure of the Charitable Remainder Unitrust document is essentially identical to that of the Charitable Remainder Annuity Trust document.

EXAMPLES

THE (YOUR NAME) CHARITABLE REMAINDER ANNUITY TRUST

On _____, 2000, (YOUR NAME), of (Your Address), ("the Donor") desiring to establish a Charitable Remainder Annuity Trust, within the meaning of Internal Revenue Service Revenue Procedure 89-21 and Internal Revenue Code Section 664(d)(1), as amended, or the corresponding provision of any successor law ("the Code"), hereby creates The (Your Name) Charitable Remainder Annuity Trust ("the Trust") and designates The (Name) Foundation, a nonprofit organization established and doing business in the State of (State) as the initial Trustee ("the Trustee").

ARTICLE I
Funding of Trust

The Donor transfers to the Trustee the property described in Schedule A, and the Trustee accepts such property and agrees to hold, manage, and distribute it under the terms of this instrument.

ARTICLE II
Irrevocability and Amendments

This Trust is irrevocable. However, the Trustee shall have the power, acting alone, to amend the Trust in any manner (except to reduce the required payments to the Recipient) required for the sole purpose of ensuring that the Trust qualifies and continues to qualify as a Charitable Remainder Annuity within the meaning of Section 664(d)(2) of the Code.

ARTICLE III
Payment of Annuity Amount

A. The Trustee shall pay to (YOUR NAME) ("the Recipient") in each taxable year of the Trust during the Recipient's life an annuity amount equal to eight and 51/100 percent (8.51%) of the net fair market value of the assets of the Trust valued as of this date.

B. The annuity amount shall be paid in equal monthly amounts of $, starting (Date) from income and, to the extent that income is not sufficient, from principal. Any income of the Trust for a taxable year in excess of the annuity amount shall be added to principal. Should any annuity payments be received more than ten (10) days late for any reason other than those out of the control of the Trustee, the Donor shall have the right to substitute another qualified charitable institution as remainder beneficiary.

C. If the net fair market value of the Trust assets is incorrectly determined, then within a reasonable period after the value is finally determined for federal tax purposes, but only after a final judgment of the Tax Court, the Trustee shall pay to the Recipient, in the case of an undervaluation, or the Recipient shall pay to the Trustee, in the case of an overvaluation, an amount equal to the difference between the annuity amount properly payable and the annuity amount actually paid.

D. In determining the annuity amount, the Trustee shall prorate the annuity amount on a daily basis for a short taxable year and for the taxable year of the Recipient's death.

ARTICLE IV
Distribution to Charity

When the Recipient dies, the Trustee shall distribute all of the then principal and income of the Trust, other than the amounts due to the Recipient or his estate under Article III, to THE (NAME) FOUNDATION, a nonprofit corporation established and doing business in the State of (State), (the "Remainder Beneficiary") to be used for its general purposes. If THE (NAME) FOUNDATION is not an organization described in Sections 170(c), 2055(a), and 2522(a) of the Code at the time when any principal or income of the Trust is to be distributed to it, then the Trustee shall distribute such principal and income to one or more organizations that, at that time, are described in Sections 170(c), 170(b)(1)(A), 2055(a), and 2522(a) of the Code, as the Trustee shall select in its sole discretion.

ARTICLE V
Additional Contributions

No additional contributions shall be made to the Trust after the initial contribution.

ARTICLE VI
Prohibited Transactions

The income of the Trust for each taxable year shall be distributed at such time and in such manner as not to subject the Trust to tax under Section 4942 of the Code. Except for the payment of the annuity amount to the Recipient, the Trustee shall not engage in any act of self-dealing, as defined in Section 4941(d) of the Code, and shall not make any taxable expenditures, as defined in Section 4945(d) of the Code. The Trustee shall not make any investments that jeopardize the charitable purpose of the Trust, within the meaning of Section 4944 of the Code, or retain any excess business holdings, within the meaning of Section 4943 of the Code.

ARTICLE VII
Trustee and Successor Trustee

A. THE (NAME) FOUNDATION will be the Initial Trustee.

B. The Donor retains the right to dismiss the Trustee and to appoint a successor Trustee.

C. The Trustee may designate any individual or institution as a Co-Trustee by a written instrument. Any Co-Trustee or successor Trustee may, without liability, accept without examination or review the accounts rendered and the property delivered by any predecessor Trustee, without any liability. Each successor Trustee has the same title, powers, and duties as the Trustee succeeded, without any additional conveyance. Any reference to a "Trustee" refers equally to any successor Trustee.

D. No Trustee named in Paragraph A shall be required to provide surety or other security on a bond.

E. Any Trustee may resign by giving written notice specifying the resignation's effective date to the designated successor Trustee, if there is one, or to the Donor. If no successor Trustee is named in Paragraph A, the successor Trustee shall be named by the Donor, or, if she is not able, by the remainder beneficiary.

F. No Trustee shall be required (1) to obtain the order of any court to exercise any power or discretion under this Trust, or (2) to file any accounting with any public official, although the Trustee must maintain accurate records concerning the Trust and shall send to the Donor, the Recipient, and the remainder beneficiary an annual accounting of the Trust's condition, including receipts and disbursements, which may be satisfied by a copy of the Trust's federal income tax return, if one is required.

G. The Trustee accepts this Trust with compensation not to exceed 1% of the value of said Trust each year on the anniversary date of this Trust for services in administering this Trust. SAID COMPENSATION SHALL NOT REDUCE THE AMOUNT DUE TO THE RECIPIENT.

ARTICLE VIII
Taxable Year

The taxable year of the Trust shall be the calendar year.

ARTICLE IX
Governing Law

The operation of the Trust shall be governed by the laws of the State of (State). However, the Trustee is prohibited from exercising any power or discretion granted under said laws that would be inconsistent with the qualification of the Trust under Section 664(d)(1) of the Code and the corresponding regulations.

ARTICLE X
Trust Investments

Nothing in this Trust instrument shall be construed to restrict the Trustee from investing the Trust assets in a manner that could result in the annual realization of a reasonable amount of income or gain from the sale or disposition of Trust assets. Consistent with this limitation and with the qualification of the Trust as a Charitable Remainder Annuity Trust under Section 664(d)(1) of the Code, the Trustee is authorized to:

A. Hold assets given to the Trust or invest and reinvest them (or leave them temporarily uninvested) in any type of property and every kind of investment, including (but not limited to) corporate obligations of every kind, preferred or common stocks, securities of any regulated investment trust, and partnership interests. Notwithstanding the previous statements, during any period in which the Donor is also a Trustee, the Trustee may not invest any of the Trust funds in hard-to-value assets, such as real estate or closely held stocks.

B. Keep all or part of the Trust property at any place within the United States or abroad.

C. Deposit Trust funds in any commercial savings or savings and loan accounts.

D. Sell or otherwise dispose of Trust assets, including (but not limited to) Trust real property, for cash or credit, at public or private sale, and with such warranties or indemnifications as the Trustee deems advisable.

E. Hold property in the name of any Trustee or any custodian or nominee, without disclosing this Trust, but the Trustee is responsible for the acts of any custodian or nominee the Trustee so uses.

F. Pay and advance money for the Trust's protection and for all expenses, losses, and liabilities sustained in its administration, at the expense of the Trustee.

G. Prosecute or defend any action for the protection of the Trust, the Trustee in the performance of the Trustee's duties, or both, and pay, contest, or settle any claim by or against the Trust or the Trustee in the performance of the Trustee's duties, at the expense of the Trustee.

H. Employ persons, even if they are associated with the Trustee, to advise or assist the Trustee in the performance of the Trustee's duties, at the expense of said Trustee.

I. Distribute Trust assets in kind or in cash, without the consent of any beneficiary.

J. Execute and deliver any instruments necessary or useful in the exercise of any of these powers.

ARTICLE XI
Death Taxes

No estate, inheritance, or other death taxes with respect to the Trust shall be allocated to or recoverable from the Trust, notwithstanding any inconsistent statements in the Donor's Last Will or in any other instrument.

ARTICLE XII
Facility of Payment

The Trustee may, in its discretion, do one or more of the following with respect to any payment which would be made to the Recipient at a time when he or she is legally disabled: (1) take any action necessary to have a legal guardian appointed for the Recipient, if none has already been appointed, and make the payment to such legal guardian, without having to see to the proper application of such payment; or (2) expend such payment for the Recipient's benefit.

ARTICLE XIII
Miscellaneous

A. The headings in this Trust are inserted for convenience only and are not a part of this Trust.

B. Whenever the context of this Trust requires, the masculine gender includes the feminine or neuter, and vice versa, and the singular number includes the plural, and vice versa.

IN WITNESS WHEREOF, (YOUR NAME), the Donor, and The (Name) Foundation, of (Address), the Trustee, by its duly authorized officer have signed this agreement the day and year first above written.

_____

(Your Name), Donor

_____

(Name) Foundation, Trustee

By:

_____

(NAME), EXECUTIVE DIRECTOR

STATE OF (YOUR STATE)_____

COUNTY OF (YOUR COUNTY)_____

BE IT REMEMBERED, that on   , 2000, before me, the under-signed authority, personally appeared (YOUR NAME) and (NAME) AS EXEC-UTIVE DIRECTOR OF THE (NAME) FOUNDATION, who, I am satisfied, are the persons named in and who executed the above document, and I having first made known to such persons the contents thereof, such persons acknowledged that they are of sound mind, free of duress or undue influence, and that such persons signed, sealed, and delivered the same as their voluntary act and deed. All of which is hereby certified.

_____

(NOTARY)

SCHEDULE A

THE (NAME) CHARITABLE REMAINDER UNITRUST

On (Date), (Name) and (Name), of (Address), ("the Donor") desiring to establish a Charitable Remainder Unitrust, within the meaning of Internal Revenue Service Revenue Procedure 90-32 and Code Section 664(d)(1), as amended, or the corresponding provision of any successor law ("the Code"), hereby create The (Name) Charitable Remainder Unitrust ("the Trust") and designate (Name), a (State) corporation, as the initial Trustee ("the Trustee").

ARTICLE I
Funding of Trust

The Donor transfers to the Trustee the property described in Schedule A, and the Trustee accepts such property and agrees to hold, manage, and distribute it under the terms of this instrument.

ARTICLE II
Irrevocability and Amendments

This Trust is irrevocable. However, the Trustee shall have the power, acting alone, to amend the Trust in any manner required for the sole purpose of ensuring that the Trust qualifies and continues to qualify as a Charitable Remainder Unitrust within the meaning of Section 664(d)(2) of the Code.

ARTICLE III
Payment of Annuity Amount

A. In each taxable year of the Trust, the Trustee shall pay to (NAME) and (NAME) (hereinafter referred to as "the Recipients"), in equal shares during their lifetimes, a unitrust amount equal to ten percent (10%) of the net fair market value of the assets of the Trust valued as of the first day of each taxable year of the Trust (the "Valuation Date"). At the death of the first Recipient (as defined below), the surviving Recipient shall receive the entire unitrust annuity amount.

B. The unitrust amount shall be paid in equal quarterly amounts (starting September 1, 2000) from income and, to the extent that income is not sufficient, from principal. Any income of the Trust for a taxable year in excess of the unitrust amount shall be added to principal.

C. If the net fair market value of the Trust assets is incorrectly determined, then within a reasonable period after the value is finally determined for federal tax purposes, the Trustee shall pay to the Recipient, in the case of an undervaluation, or the Recipient shall pay to the Trustee, in the case of an overvaluation, an amount equal to the difference between the unitrust amount properly payable and the unitrust amount actually paid.

D. In determining the unitrust amount, the Trustee shall prorate the unitrust amount on a daily basis for a short taxable year and for the taxable year of death of the later to die of the Recipients.

ARTICLE IV
Distribution to Charity

Immediately following the death of the later of the Recipients to die, the Trustee shall distribute all of the then principal and income of the Trust, other than any amounts due to the Recipient or his or her estate under Article III, to (NAME), to be used for its general educational purposes. If (NAME) is not an organization described in Code Sections 170(c), 170(b)(1)(A), 2055(a), and 2522(a) at the time when any principal or income of the Trust is to be distributed to it, then the Trustee shall distribute such principal and income to one or more organizations that, at that time, are described in Code Sections 170(c), 170(b)(1)(A), 2055(a), and 2522(a), as the Trustee shall select in its sole discretion. The Donor has the discretion, during his or her lifetime, to change the beneficiary so long as said change is to a qualifying charitable organization as per above. Said change shall be made by certified letter to the Trustee.

ARTICLE V
Additional Contributions

If additional contributions are made to the Trust after the initial contribution, the unitrust amount for the year in which the additional contribution is made shall be ten percent (10%) of the sum of (a) the net fair market value of the Trust assets as of the first day of the taxable year (excluding the assets added and any income from or appreciation on such assets) and (b) that proportion of the value of the assets so added that was excluded under (a) that the number of days in the period which begins with the date of the contribution and ends with the earlier of the last day of the taxable year or the date of death of the later to die of the Recipients bears to the number of days in the period that begins on the first day of such taxable year and ends with the earlier of the last day in such taxable year or the date of death of the later to die of the Recipients. In the case where there is no valuation after the time of contribution, the assets so added shall be valued at the time of contribution. Any additional contributions must be acceptable to the Trustee.

ARTICLE VI
Prohibited Transactions

The income of the Trust for each taxable year shall be distributed at such time and in such manner as not to subject the Trust to tax under Section 4942 of the Code. Except for the payment of the annuity amount to the Recipients, the Trustee shall not engage in any act of self-dealing, as defined in Section 4941(d) of the Code, and shall not make any taxable expenditures, as defined in Section 4945(d) of the Code. The Trustee shall not make any investments that jeopardize the charitable purpose of the Trust, within the meaning of Section 4944 of the Code, or retain any excess business holdings, within the meaning of Section 4943 of the Code.

ARTICLE VII
Trustee and Successor Trustee

A. (Name), a (State) corporation, will be the Initial Trustee.
B. The Donor retains the right to dismiss the Trustee and to appoint a successor Trustee.
C. The Trustee may designate any individual or institution as a Co-Trustee, by a written instrument. Any Co-Trustee or successor Trustee may, without liability, accept without examination or review the accounts rendered and the property delivered by any predecessor Trustee, without any liability. Each successor Trustee has the same title, powers, and duties as the Trustee succeeded, without any additional conveyance. Any reference to a "Trustee" refers equally to any successor Trustee.

D. No Trustee named in Paragraph A shall be required to provide surety or other security on a bond.

E. Any Trustee may resign by giving written notice specifying the resignation's effective date as per ARTICLE XIII, Paragraph F below.

F. No Trustee shall be required (1) to obtain the order of any court to exercise of any power or discretion under this Trust or (2) to file any accounting with any public official, although the Trustee must maintain accurate records concerning the Trust and shall send to the Donor, each Recipient, and the remainderman an annual accounting of the Trust's condition, including receipts and disbursements, which may be satisfied by a copy of the Trust's federal income tax return, if one is required, or, at the option of the Trustee, by providing monthly statements.

G. Each Trustee is entitled to compensation based on its published fee schedule in effect at the time services are rendered.

ARTICLE VIII
Taxable Year

The taxable year of the Trust shall be the calendar year.

ARTICLE IX
Governing Law

The operation of the Trust shall be governed by the laws of the State of (State). However, the Trustee is prohibited from exercising any power or discretion granted under said laws that would be inconsistent with the qualification of the Trust under Section 664(d)(1) of the Code and the corresponding regulations.

ARTICLE X
Trust Investments

Nothing in this Trust instrument shall be construed to restrict the Trustee from investing the Trust assets in a manner that could result in the annual realization of a reasonable amount of income or gain from the sale or disposition of Trust assets. Consistent with this limitation and with the qualification of the Trust as a Charitable Remainder Unitrust under Section 664(d)(1) of the Code, the Trustee is authorized to:

A. Hold assets given to the Trust or invest and reinvest them (or leave them temporarily uninvested) in any type of property and every kind of investment, including (but not limited to) corporate obligations of every kind, preferred or common stocks, securities of any regulated investment Trust and, partnership interests. Notwithstanding the previous statements, during any period in which the Donor is also a Trustee, the Trustee may not invest any of the Trust funds in hard-to-value assets, such as real estate or closely held stocks.

B. Keep all or part of the Trust property at any place within the United States or abroad.

C. Deposit Trust funds in any commercial savings or savings and loan accounts.

D. Sell or otherwise dispose of Trust assets, including (but not limited to) Trust real property, for cash or credit, at public or private sale, and with such warranties or indemnifications as the Trustee deems advisable.

E. Hold property in the name of any Trustee or any custodian or nominee, without disclosing this Trust, but the Trustee is responsible for the acts of any custodian or nominee the Trustee so uses.

F. Pay and advance money for the Trust's protection and for all expenses, losses, and liabilities sustained in its administration.

G. Prosecute or defend any action for the protection of the Trust, the Trustee in the performance of the Trustee's duties, or both, and to pay, contest, or settle any claim by or against the Trust or the Trustee in the performance of the Trustee's duties.

H. Employ persons, even if they are associated with the Trustee, to advise or assist the Trustee in the performance of the Trustee's duties.

I. Distribute Trust assets in kind or in cash, without the consent of any beneficiary.

J. Execute and deliver any instruments necessary or useful in the exercise of any of these powers.

ARTICLE XI
Death Taxes

No estate, inheritance, or other death taxes with respect to the Trust shall be allocated to or recoverable from the Trust, notwithstanding any inconsistent statements in the Donor's Last Will or in any other instrument. This Trust shall terminate unless the surviving beneficiary pays for any state death taxes or federal estate taxes due, if any, from the Trust on the death of the first beneficiary to die.

ARTICLE XII
Facility of Payment

The Trustee may, in its discretion, do one or more of the following with respect to any payment which would be made to the Recipient at a time when he is legally disabled: (1) take any action necessary to have a legal guardian appointed for the Recipient, if none has already been appointed, and make the payment to such legal guardian, without having to see to the proper application of such payment, or (2) expend such payment for the Recipient's benefit.

ARTICLE XIII
Miscellaneous

A. This Trust will be construed according to the laws of (State).

B. Whenever the context of this Trust requires, the masculine gender includes the feminine or neuter, and vice versa, and the singular number includes the plural, and vice versa.

C. The Trustee shall have the following specific powers as to Trust property and may exercise the same in its sole and absolute discretion without Court order or approval:

(a) To engage any corporation, partnership, or other entity affiliated with the Trustee (an "Affiliated Entity") to render services to any Trust hereunder, including, without limitation:

(i) To manage or advise on the investments of such Trust on a discretionary or nondiscretionary basis.

(ii) To act as a broker or dealer to execute transactions, including the purchase of any securities currently distributed, underwritten, or issued by an Affiliated Entity, at standard commission rates, markups, or concessions, and to provide other management or investment services with respect to such Trust, including the custody of assets; provided, however, that an Affiliated Entity that is a "disqualified person" for purposes of Section 4941 of the Internal Revenue Code of 1986, as amended, shall only act as agent and not as Principal (except with regard to the purchase of money market mutual funds), and to pay for any such services from Trust property, without reduction for any compensation paid to the Trustee for its services as Trustee.

(b) To invest in mutual funds offered by an Affiliated Entity or to which an Affiliated Entity may render services and from which an affiliate Entity receives compensation.

(c) To cause or permit all or any part of any Trust hereunder to be held, maintained, or managed in any jurisdiction and to hold any Trust property in the name of its nominee or a nominee of any Affiliated Entity.

D. This Trust shall be effective upon the later of the execution of the Trust instrument by the Trustee or the transfer of the assets or property to the Trustee. For purposes of this Trust, the term "transfer" shall mean the moment in time when the Trustee actually receives the assets or title to the property in the name of the Trustee or by confirming evidence of ownership of it in a Trust account held in the name of this Trust.

E. The Trustee, and any successor corporate Trustee, shall receive payment for its services in accordance with its schedule of rates in effect at the time such compensation becomes payable, without reduction for any other fees or other compensation paid to said Trustee or an Affiliated Entity, including (but not limited to) such fees or other compensation paid by any mutual fund, unit investment trust, or other investment vehicle, or an agent. Such compensation may be paid without Court approval.

F. The Trustee may resign as Trustee of any Trust hereunder at any time by written notice delivered to any Co-Trustee(s) and to all beneficiaries to whom current Trust payments may or must then be distributed, or to the natural or legal guardians of such beneficiaries. Such resignation shall be effective upon the written appointment of a successor Trustee. A majority of such beneficiaries or such natural or legal guardians, as the case may be, shall have the power to appoint a successor Trustee, or in default of such appointment, the Trustee shall have the same power. All of the Trustee's fees and expenses (including reasonable attorney's fees) attributable to the appointment of a successor Trustee shall be paid by such Trust. No bond or other security shall be required of the Trustee or any successor Trustee in any jurisdiction. Any successor Trustee shall have the same powers, authorities, and discretions as though originally named as the Trustee.

G. The Trustee shall have the power to employ, and to delegate any of its discretionary powers to agents, including (but not limited to) attorneys, investment advisors, appraisers, or accountants as it deems necessary and proper and to pay for such services from the Trust property.

IN WITNESS WHEREOF, (NAME) and (NAME), the Donor, and (NAME), a (State) Corporation, the Trustee, by its duly authorized officer have signed this agreement the day and year first above written.

_____

(NAME), DONOR

_____

(NAME), DONOR

_____

(NAME), a (State) Corporation (TRUSTEE)

By:

_____

(NAME) Executive Director

STATE OF (YOUR STATE)_____

COUNTY OF (YOUR COUNTY)_____

BE IT REMEMBERED, that on   , before me, the undersigned authority, personally appeared, (NAME) and (NAME), who, I am satisfied, are the persons named in and who executed the above document, and I having first made known to such persons the contents thereof, such persons acknowledged that they are of sound mind, free of duress or undue influence, and that such persons signed, sealed, and delivered the same as their voluntary act and deed. All of which is hereby certified.

_____

(NOTARY)

SCHEDULE A

CHAPTER 9

Private Annuities

The preceding chapters and documents should be sufficient to eliminate any federal estate tax on estates of as much as $3 million plus held by husband and wife. The following documents are for those whose estates exceed that value. They represent more sophisticated techniques that can be used to further reduce your federal estate tax to zero.

An annuity is a contractual agreement whereby, in exchange for a single payment or a series of payments, an individual or an institution will give you a series of payments over a period of time. With the traditional annuity, you make a lump sum payment to an insurance company and that company will give you a series of payments of dollars either for your lifetime or over a specified term of years. A private annuity is exactly the same thing except that it is contracted between private individuals rather than with a financial institution.

Assume you have property that you expect to appreciate and you want to get that property out of your estate. Also assume that you are not in good health and, while you clearly expect to live for the next 12 months, you don't expect to reach your statistical life expectancy. Here's where a private annuity agreement might help. You transfer the property to your beneficiaries (your children) in exchange for their promise to pay you an annuity for the rest of your life. The amount that they will have to pay you will be a function of your life expectancy as per IRS tables rather than your true, shorter life expectancy. The IRS tables must be used unless "death is imminent." *Imminent* has been defined to mean that you are expected to die within the next 12 months.

Because your statistical life expectancy is greater than your actual life expectancy, the payments will be smaller and will be projected over a longer time than they actually should be. At your death, the payments will terminate. Because the actual payments will be less than they should have been using your true life expectancy, there is, in effect, a *nontaxable* gift to your children for the difference.

Normally, if you have an annuity with an insurance company and outlive your life expectancy, you're the winner. In this case, where the transfer is made to your children, everyone wins (at least from a financial point of view) if you die prior to your statistically computed life expectancy. (You may be dead, but at least you're dead as a winner with the IRS!)

While you are alive and are receiving the annuity payments, those payments will consist of part interest, part capital gain, and part nontaxable return of capital. In the appropriate situation, however, the private annuity is an excellent vehicle for transferring assets to your beneficiaries for less than full and adequate consideration, but without the imposition of a gift or estate tax.

Let's take a look at the document itself:

PRIVATE ANNUITY AGREEMENT

*AN ANNUITY AGREEMENT made this, the   day of   ,
2000, by and between the State (Your State), hereinafter called Transferor, and (NAME),
hereinafter called Transferee.*

RECITALS

*Transferor is the owner of certain property listed on Schedule A attached hereto and
made an integral part of this Agreement.*

*Transferor is age (age), and will be (age) in (Month), 2000, an age where he or she
wishes to be free of the responsibilities of the management of said property and wishes to be
assured of a fixed annual income for the remainder of his or her life, regardless of whether
such property produces income.*

The value of said property is (Dollar Amount).

*Transferee wishes to acquire said property and is willing to make fixed annual pay-
ments of (Dollar Amount), in monthly installments of (Dollar Amount), for the remainder
of Transferor's life in exchange for said property.*

> The preceding paragraphs detail who is making the transfer, who is to pay
> the annuity, the age of the transferor, and the value of the property. Based
> on IRS life expectancy and annuity tables, the amount of the annuity per
> year and in monthly installments is set.

COVENANTS AND AGREEMENTS

*NOW THEREFORE, for and in consideration of the mutual promises made by each
party to the other and of the mutual Agreements contained herein, the parties hereto agree
with each other as follows:*

*(1)   Transferor shall this day execute and deliver to the Transferee all of his or her right,
title, and interest in and to the above described property.*

*(2)   Transferee, for his heirs and legal representatives, does hereby agree to pay to Trans-
feror the sum of (Dollar Amount) each month for his or her lifetime payable the
day of   , 2000, and the same day of each month thereafter.*

*(3)   The aforesaid payments to Transferor are to be made without reference to the trans-
ferred property and irrespective of any income earned by the property. These payments
are obligations of the transferee and are not limited in any way to the value of the
property.*

(4) Transferee is given the right to sell, transfer, assign, or pledge the property free and clear of any claims whatsoever by Transferor and it is understood that the payments to be made to Transferor are not secured by the property.

This Agreement shall inure to the benefit of and shall be binding upon Transferee's heirs and legal representatives.

> These paragraphs detail the rights and obligations of the parties and the binding nature of the agreement. Note that the payments of income to you are not at all tied to the income earned by the property or to any changes in value of the property.

IN WITNESS WHEREOF this Annuity Agreement is signed, sealed, and delivered in duplicate on the day and year first herein written, it being agreed that each copy of this Agreement shall constitute an original.

_____ *(L.S.)*

(NAME), Transferor

Signed, sealed, and delivered
in the presence of: (As to Transferor)

_____

_____

Notary Public, _____ *County,* _____

_____ *(L.S.)*

(NAME), Transferee

Signed, sealed, and delivered
in the presence of: (As to Transferee)

_____

_____

Notary Public, _____ *County,* _____

SCHEDULE A

> The annuity agreement is signed by both parties and notarized, and the annuity assets are listed in Schedule A.
>
> The private annuity agreement is a simple document, but one that, in the appropriate situation, can be extremely useful in transferring assets at a discounted value.

EXAMPLE

PRIVATE ANNUITY AGREEMENT

AN ANNUITY AGREEMENT made this, the   day of   , 2000, by and between the State of (Your State), hereinafter called Transferor, and (NAME), hereinafter called Transferee.

RECITALS

Transferor is the owner of certain property listed on Schedule A attached hereto and made an integral part of this Agreement.

Transferor is age (age), and will be (age) in (Month), 2000, an age where he or she wishes to be free of the responsibilities of the management of said property and wishes to be assured of a fixed annual income for the remainder of his or her life, regardless of whether such property produces income.

The value of said property is (Dollar Amount).

Transferee wishes to acquire said property and is willing to make fixed annual payments of (Dollar Amount), in monthly installments of (Dollar Amount), for the remainder of Transferor's life in exchange for said property.

COVENANTS AND AGREEMENTS

NOW THEREFORE, for and in consideration of the mutual promises made by each party to the other and of the mutual Agreements contained herein, the parties hereto agree with each other as follows:

(1) Transferor shall this day execute and deliver to the Transferee all of his or her right, title, and interest in and to the above described property.

(2) Transferee, for his heirs, and legal representatives, does hereby agree to pay to Transferor the sum of (Dollar Amount) each month for his or her lifetime payable the _____ day of _____, 2000, and the same day of each month thereafter.

(3) The aforesaid payments to Transferor are to be made without reference to the transferred property and irrespective of any income earned by the property. These payments are obligations of the transferee and are not limited in any way to the value of the property.

(4) Transferee is given the right to sell, transfer, assign, or pledge the property free and clear of any claims whatsoever by Transferor and it is understood that the payments to be made to Transferor are not secured by the property.

This Agreement shall inure to the benefit of and shall be binding upon Transferee's heirs and legal representatives.

IN WITNESS WHEREOF this Annuity Agreement is signed, sealed, and delivered in duplicate on the day and year first herein written, it being agreed that each copy of this Agreement shall constitute an original.

_____ (L.S.)

(NAME), Transferor

Signed, sealed, and delivered
in the presence of: (As to Transferor)

_____

_____

Notary Public, _____ County, _____

_____ (L.S.)

(NAME), Transferee

Signed, sealed, and delivered
in the presence of: (As to Transferee)

_____

_____

Notary Public, _____ County, _____

SCHEDULE A

CHAPTER 10

Self-Canceling Installment Notes (SCINs)

The Self-Canceling Installment Note serves basically the same purpose as the private annuity. In both cases you are trying to get assets to your beneficiaries at less than their full and adequate consideration. With a Self-Canceling Installment Note, you are selling property to your beneficiaries (children) and taking back a note. In effect, you are actually acting as the bank and financing the transaction.

Because this note will be canceled at your death, you should use a higher interest rate than you would if the note were not self-destructing. As with a private annuity, this technique is most effective when your actual life expectancy is less than your statistical life expectancy. If you die before the note is paid in full, any balance escapes both gift and estate taxation. Also, similar to the case with a private annuity, during your lifetime each payment received will include not only interest and capital gains, but a nontaxable return of your capital. Let's look at the note itself:

PROMISSORY NOTE

(YOUR NAME), of (Your Address) ("Borrower"), promises to pay (NAME), of (Address) ("Lender"), six hundred thousand dollars ($600,000), together with simple interest on the unpaid principal balance at the rate of thirteen percent (13%) per annum.

SECTION 1
Payments

1.1. <u>Maturity.</u>   This note matures on the sixth (6th) anniversary of the date the note was made.

1.2. <u>Amortization Schedule.</u>   Borrower will pay Lender one hundred thousand dollars ($100,000) on or before each anniversary date of this note:

Date	Principal	Interest
First anniversary	$100,000	$ 78,000
Second anniversary	100,000	65,000
Third anniversary	100,000	52,000
Fourth anniversary	100,000	39,000
Fifth anniversary	100,000	26,000
Sixth anniversary	100,000	13,000
Total	$700,000	$273,000

Borrower and Lender agree that this amortization schedule is accurate and will control, absent any prepayment. Both parties also agree to report their interest and principal payments and balances for tax and financial purposes according to this schedule.

> The preceding paragraphs detail the debtor and creditor of the note, the maturity of the note, and the amortization schedule for the note.

1.3. <u>Cancellation at Lender's Death.</u>   Notwithstanding this amortization schedule, this note and the underlying obligation to pay shall be canceled and terminated as if paid in full upon Lender's death, if he or she dies prior to the note's stated maturity date. This cancellation shall not apply with respect to any overdue or late payments of principal or interest outstanding at the time of Lender's death.

> This paragraph is the self-destructing element of the installment note. It provides that no further payments will be due upon your death. Any principal then outstanding escapes both gift and estate taxation.

1.4. Holidays.   If the anniversary date of this note falls on a Saturday, a Sunday, or a day that is a legal holiday under the laws of the United States, the payment for that year shall be due on the next succeeding business day.

1.5. "Timely Payment" Defined.   Payment is timely made if it is actually received by Lender or his or her legal representatives on or before the date on which it is due, or if it is mailed by the United States Postal Service and is postmarked on or before the date on which it is due.

1.6. Medium of Payment.   Payment may be made by cash, personal check, certified check, cashier's check, money order, or any other additional means acceptable to Lender.

1.7. Where Payment Made.   Payment may be made to Lender at (Address), or at such other place as he or she may designate in writing from time to time.

1.8. Prepayment.   Borrower may prepay all or any portion of the principal balance of this note at any time, without penalty or premium.

The preceding paragraphs define when payment is timely, how payment should be made, and where payment can be made.

SECTION 2
Security

This note is secured specifically by a deed of trust on the real property owned by Borrower and described in Schedule A, but it also is secured by the full assets of Borrower, including all assets hereafter acquired, other than the specific property purchased by Borrower from Lender for which this note is full payment, described in Schedule B.

This section describes the security that is being given to secure the note.

SECTION 3
Default

3.1. "Default" Defined.   Borrower will be in default if he fails to pay any installment of principal or interest when due and does not cure his deficiency within thirty (30) calendar days of the date the payment was due.

3.2. Acceleration.   Whenever Borrower is in default, Lender may declare the entire principal balance in default, and immediately due and payable.

3.3. Lender's Remedies.   Upon any default, Lender may foreclose upon the specific security, or take such other legal actions as he deems necessary or appropriate to collect the amounts in default.

3.4. <u>Confession of Judgment.</u>   Upon any default, except where prohibited by law, Borrower empowers any attorney of any Court of record within the state of (State) to appear for him and, after one or more declarations or complaints have been filed, to confess judgment against him for any sums due under this instrument, including attorney's fees of fifteen percent (15%) of the outstanding principal balance of the debt evidenced by this instrument. All exemptions from levy, garnishment, attachment, or seizure of assets are hereby waived by Borrower with respect to amounts due under this instrument.

These provisions are standard note provisions defining default, acceleration, and the remedies of the creditor upon default.

SECTION 4
Cancellation

Upon payment of all principal and interest required to be paid under this note, Lender will return to Borrower all copies of this note, marked "CANCELED/PAID IN FULL," and all of Borrower's obligations under this note will be terminated.

SECTION 5
Miscellaneous

5.1. <u>Headings.</u>   The headings in this instrument are inserted for convenience and shall not be considered a part of this instrument or used in its interpretation.

5.2. <u>State Law.</u>   This note, and the parties, rights, and liabilities thereunder, shall be construed under the law of the state of (State).

_____

Date: (Date)

_____

(NAME), Borrower

<u>*STATE OF (YOUR STATE)*</u>

<u>*COUNTY OF (YOUR COUNTY)*</u>

BE IT REMEMBERED, that on   , 2000, before me, the undersigned authority, personally appeared (YOUR NAME) and (NAME) AS EXECUTIVE DIRECTOR OF THE (NAME) FOUNDATION, who I am satisfied are the persons named in and who executed the above document, and I having first made known to such persons the contents thereof, such persons acknowledged that they are of sound mind, free of duress or undue influence, and that such persons signed, sealed, and delivered the same as their voluntary act and deed. All of which is hereby certified.

(NOTARY)

The remainder of the note is standard form. Although multiple additional provisions can be added, since this is normally an intra-family transaction, I prefer to keep the document as clean and as simple as possible.

Similar to the private annuity, the Self-Canceling Installment Note allows you to transfer assets to "the object of your bounty" without the imposition of any gift or estate taxes. In the appropriate circumstances, it is another arrow in your quiver of estate reduction techniques and can be an important element in achieving your aim of paying zero estate taxes.

EXAMPLE

PROMISSORY NOTE

(YOUR NAME), of (Your Address) ("Borrower"), promises to pay (NAME), of (Address) ("Lender"), six hundred thousand dollars ($600,000), together with simple interest on the unpaid principal balance at the rate of thirteen percent (13%) per annum.

SECTION 1
Payments

1.1. <u>Maturity.</u>   This note matures on the sixth (6th) anniversary of the date the note was made.

1.2. <u>Amortization Schedule.</u> Borrower will pay Lender one hundred thousand dollars ($100,000) on or before each anniversary date of this note:

Date	Principal	Interest
First anniversary	$100,000	$ 78,000
Second anniversary	100,000	65,000
Third anniversary	100,000	52,000
Fourth anniversary	100,000	39,000
Fifth anniversary	100,000	26,000
Sixth anniversary	100,000	13,000
Total	$700,000	$273,000

Borrower and Lender agree that this amortization schedule is accurate and will control, absent any prepayment. Both parties also agree to report their interest and principal payments and balances for tax and financial purposes according to this schedule.

1.3. <u>Cancellation at Lender's Death.</u>   Notwithstanding this amortization schedule, this note and the underlying obligation to pay shall be canceled and terminated as if paid in full upon Lender's death, if he or she dies prior to the note's stated maturity date. This cancellation shall not apply with respect to any overdue or late payments of principal or interest outstanding at the time of Lender's death.

1.4. <u>Holidays.</u> If the anniversary date of this note falls on a Saturday, a Sunday, or a day that is a legal holiday under the laws of the United States, the payment for that year shall be due on the next succeeding business day.

1.5. <u>"Timely Payment" Defined.</u> Payment is timely made if it is actually received by Lender or his or her legal representatives on or before the date on which it is due, or if it is mailed by the United States Postal Service and is postmarked on or before the date on which it is due.

1.6. <u>Medium of Payment.</u> Payment may be made by cash, personal check, certified check, cashier's check, money order, or any other additional means acceptable to Lender.

1.7. <u>Where Payment Made.</u> Payment may be made to Lender at (Address), or at such other place as he or she may designate in writing from time to time.

1.8. <u>Prepayment.</u> Borrower may prepay all or any portion of the principal balance of this note at any time, without penalty or premium.

SECTION 2
Security

This note is secured specifically by a deed of trust on the real property owned by Borrower and described in Schedule A, but it also is secured by the full assets of Borrower, including all assets hereafter acquired, other than the specific property purchased by Borrower from Lender for which this note is full payment, described in Schedule B.

SECTION 3
Default

3.1. "Default" Defined.   Borrower will be in default if he fails to pay any installment of principal or interest when due and does not cure his deficiency within thirty (30) calendar days of the date the payment was due.

3.2. Acceleration.   Whenever Borrower is in default, Lender may declare the entire principal balance in default, and immediately due and payable.

3.3. Lender's Remedies.   Upon any default, Lender may foreclose upon the specific security, or take such other legal actions as he deems necessary or appropriate to collect the amounts in default.

3.4. Confession of Judgment.   Upon any default, except where prohibited by law, Borrower empowers any attorney of any Court of record within the state of (State) to appear for him and, after one or more declarations or complaints have been filed, to confess judgment against him for any sums due under this instrument, including attorney's fees of fifteen percent (15%) of the outstanding principal balance of the debt evidenced by this instrument. All exemptions from levy, garnishment, attachment, or seizure of assets are hereby waived by Borrower with respect to amounts due under this instrument.

SECTION 4
Cancellation

Upon payment of all principal and interest required to be paid under this note, Lender will return to Borrower all copies of this note, marked "CANCELED/PAID IN FULL," and all of Borrower's obligations under this note will be terminated.

SECTION 5
Miscellaneous

5.1. <u>Headings.</u>   The headings in this instrument are inserted for convenience and shall not be considered a part of this instrument or used in its interpretation.

5.2. <u>State Law.</u>   This note, and the parties, rights, and liabilities thereunder, shall be construed under the law of the state of (State).

_____

Date: (Date)

_____

(NAME), Borrower

STATE OF (YOUR STATE) _____

COUNTY OF (YOUR COUNTY) _____

BE IT REMEMBERED, that on   , 2000, before me, the undersigned authority, personally appeared (YOUR NAME) and (NAME) AS EXECUTIVE DIRECTOR OF THE (NAME) FOUNDATION, who I am satisfied are the persons named in and who executed the above document, and I having first made known to such persons the contents thereof, such persons acknowledged that they are of sound mind, free of duress or undue influence, and that such persons signed, sealed, and delivered the same as their voluntary act and deed. All of which is hereby certified.

_____

(NOTARY)

CHAPTER 11

Qualified Personal Residence Trusts (QPRTs)

A Qualified Personal Residence Trust (QPRT) is a trust established to hold title to your personal residence. Under the trust, your retain the right to use that residence for a fixed term of years. A Qualified Personal Residence Trust can be established for two residences and can be used with a cooperative apartment or a condominium. During the trust's term, you continue to benefit from the mortgage interest and real estate tax deductions.

When the selected term expires, the property passes either outright to, or in trust for the benefit of, your selected beneficiaries. Those beneficiaries can be your spouse, children, or grandchildren or others.

However, to achieve the desired estate tax benefits, you must survive the term of the trust. If you die earlier, the residence will be included in your estate, just as if you had never done the transaction, and the anticipated estate tax benefits will be lost. Your loss will be the cost of setting up the Qualified Personal Residence Trust. However, anytime you have a "heads I win, tails I break even" proposition, that's a technique you should look at.

When you transfer a residence to a Qualified Personal Residence Trust, you have made a taxable gift. The value of the gift for tax purposes is equal to the present value of the beneficiary's contingent right to receive the residence at the end of the trust's term. You have *not* made a gift of that portion of the value of the residence represented by your right to continue to live in that residence during the trust's term. The value of that right is increased (and the taxable gift reduced) because of the contingency that the residence will be returned to your estate if you die before the term expires.

If you survive the term, you will have removed the full value of the residence (including all appreciation after the date of the transfer) at a gift tax cost based upon only a fraction of the total value of the residence. Because this is a gift of a "future interest," the $10,000/$20,000 exclusion does not apply.

The value of your gift is a function of the term of the trust and the assumed interest rate. The IRS publishes, on a monthly basis, the interest rate to be used. For example, if you are 50 years old and give a $1 million residence to a 15-year Qualified Personal Residence Trust, depending upon the interest rate for that month, you may be treated as making a gift of only 28 percent or $280,000. If, in 15 years, the residence has appreciated at only 4.8 percent per year, it is now worth $2 million. You will have given your beneficiaries $2 million, but at the same tax cost as if you had given them only $280,000. Had you made it a 20-year Qualified Personal Residence Trust, the $280,000 gift could have been reduced to only $170,000. By using $170,000 out of your $675,000–$1 million exclusion amount, you have eliminated the estate tax on an asset now worth $2 million.

Let's take a look at the Qualified Personal Residence Trust drafted to hold your vacation house for 10 years and then distribute the assets to your son.

THE (YOUR NAME) QUALIFIED PERSONAL RESIDENCE TRUST

On   , 2000, this Trust was created by (YOUR NAME) (sometimes the "Grantor" and sometimes the "Trustee"), who declared that she held certain property as Trustee, on the following terms and conditions:

ARTICLE I
Trust Created; Purposes

A. *The Grantor holds as Trustee the real property listed on Schedule A, to be administered according to the terms of this instrument. The Grantor and anyone else may transfer additional property to the Trustee, to be held and administered according to the Trust's terms. The Grantor retains no right, title, or interest in any Trust property, except as specifically provided in Article III.*

B. *This paragraph contains a statement of the Grantor's reasons for establishing this Trust. Every provision of this instrument shall be construed consistent with these expressed intentions and purposes.*

1. *The Grantor intends by this Trust to make a completed gift to her son, (NAME), of a vested remainder in the Trust property, subject only to the Grantor's retention of a right to the use of and the income from the Trust for ten (10) years. The Grantor intends that, except as may be provided expressly herein, her interest in this Trust shall give her only those rights which are ordinarily associated with an income interest in trust for a term-for-years and that it endow her with no rights inconsistent therewith.*

2. *The Grantor intends that this Trust constitute a Qualified Personal Residence Trust pursuant to the applicable regulations of the U.S. Department of the Treasury promulgated with respect to Section 2702(b) of the Internal Revenue Code of 1986, as amended ("Code"), and all terms used herein shall have the same meaning in this instrument as they do in the Code and the said regulations.*

The preceding paragraphs establish the grantor and the trustee of the trust. In this case, you are serving both as grantor and trustee; you have set up a 10-year trust; and at the end of the 10 years the property in the trust will go to your son.

ARTICLE II
Irrevocability

This Trust and all interests in it are irrevocable, and the Grantor has no power to alter, amend, revoke, or terminate any Trust provision or interest, whether under this instrument or any statute or rule of law.

Article II establishes the irrevocability of the trust.

ARTICLE III
During Trust's Term

A. *During the Trust's term, the Trustee shall hold the Trust property for the Grantor's exclusive personal use and benefit. The Trustee shall permit the Grantor to use such property as her personal residence without rent or other charge, and the Trustee shall maintain such property from the Trust funds, including any rental income received by the Trustee. To the extent that the Trustee incurs expenses for the maintenance of the Trust property in excess of the Trust's cash assets, the Trustee shall notify the Grantor, who may pay such expenses directly, without any right to reimbursement from the Trust.*

1. *Rental of Property.   The Trustee may, with the Grantor's written consent, rent the property on such terms and conditions as the Trustee shall deem appropriate.*

2. *No Distributions to Others.   The Trustee may distribute neither income nor corpus to anyone other than the Grantor before the termination of the Trust.*

3. *Trust Assets.   Except as provided in this ITEM 3, the Trustee may hold as part of this Trust nothing other than real property constituting the Grantor's personal residence. The Trustee shall accept no gifts or other transfers to the Trust of any property not permitted under this ITEM 3.*

    3.1. *Cash.   The Trustee may hold cash as an asset of the Trust, but not in excess of the amounts required for payment of Trust expenses (including mortgage payments) already incurred or reasonably expected to be incurred within the next three (3) months following the date on which such cash is first held, and for improvements to the residence held by the Trust to be paid within the next three (3) months following the date on which such cash is first held.*

    3.2. *Proceeds of Sale.   The Trustee may hold any proceeds from the sale of the Trust's real estate (including any income thereon) for a period not to exceed* two (2) years from the date of sale, if the Trustee intends to use the proceeds within that period to buy another residence to be used as a personal residence of the Grantor.

    3.3. <u>Insurance Proceeds.</u> The Trustee may hold the proceeds of any insurance paid to the Trust as a result of the damage to or destruction of the Trust's real property for a period not to exceed two (2) years if the Trustee intends to use the proceeds for repair, improvement, or replacement of the Trust real property.

    3.4. <u>Prompt Distribution of Cash.</u> The Trustee shall distribute all cash in excess of the amounts permitted under this ITEM 3 to the Grantor not less often than quarterly.

B. If the Grantor dies before the tenth (10th) anniversary of the date of this instrument, the Trustee shall distribute the Trust funds to the Grantor's estate, and this Trust shall terminate. If the Grantor is alive on the tenth (10th) anniversary of the date of this instrument, the Trustee shall distribute the Trust real property to (NAME) (or, if he is not then living, to his estate), and distribute to the Grantor any cash held by the Trust for the payment of expenses or for any other purpose, and this Trust shall terminate.

C. Notwithstanding the provisions of Paragraph B, the date on which the real property held by the Trust ceases to be a personal residence of the Grantor because of a change in its use, or if earlier, the date on which sales proceeds are received on account of the sale of such personal residence, shall be known as the "Cessation Date." On the Cessation Date, the Trust shall immediately convert to an annuity trust, and shall be held and administered as follows:

1. From the Cessation Date until the termination of this Trust, the Trust shall function exclusively as a qualified annuity trust. During such term, the Trustee shall pay to the Grantor an "annuity amount" determined by dividing the value for federal gift tax purposes of all interests retained by the Grantor in the property transferred to this Trust (as of the date of such transfer) by the annuity factor for the initial term of the Trust determined under Section 7520 of the Code (as of the date of such transfer).

2. The annuity amount shall be paid in equal quarterly installments from income and, to the extent income is insufficient, from principal.

3. In determining the annuity amount, the Trustee shall prorate the annuity amount on a daily basis for short taxable years.

4. Any Trust income not distributed to the Grantor as part of the annuity amount shall be added to principal.

5. *If the initial net fair market value of the Trust assets is incorrectly determined by the Trustee, then within a reasonable period after the final determination of the correct value, the Trustee shall pay the Grantor, in case of an undervaluation, or the Grantor shall pay the Trustee, in the case of an overvaluation, an amount equal to the difference between the annuity amount properly payable and the annuity amount actually paid, plus interest on such amounts computed at the rate required by the applicable Treasury Department regulations or, if there are no such regulations, the rate used for valuing annuity interests under Code Section 664, compounded annually.*

6. *It is the Grantor's intent that the provisions under this paragraph create a Trust which would be a qualified annuity trust from the Cessation Date, and all provisions of this instrument shall be construed consistent with this intent.*

D. *The Grantor's interest in this Trust may not be commuted.*

Article III details the duties of the trustee during the trust's term. The trustee can rent or sell the property, but the trust may hold nothing other than real property constituting a personal residence of the grantor (you). If you die before the trust is terminated, the proceeds then go to your beneficiary or to his or her estate. If the property is sold, the document provides that the trust will immediately convert into an annuity trust wherein the trustee (you) pays to the grantor (you) an annuity amount.

ARTICLE IV
Definitions

A. *The Grantor is unmarried at the time this Trust is executed, and she has only one (1) child, (NAME).*

B. *A Trustee is "disabled" or under a "disability" whenever any Trustee other than a disabled Trustee or, if there is no such Trustee, any person who would become successor Trustee on such determination of disability, receives written certification from two (2) physicians regularly attending the Trustee, at least one (1) of whom is board certified in the specialty most closely associated with the alleged disability, that such Trustee has become physically or mentally incapacitated, regardless of cause and regardless of whether or not there has been any adjudication of incompetence, mental illness, or need for a committee, conservator, Guardian, or other personal representative. A Trustee is recovered from his or her disability whenever the then serving Trustee receives written certification from two (2) physicians regularly attending such disabled Trustee, at least one (1) of whom is board certified in the specialty most closely associated with the alleged disability, that he or she is no longer incapacitated and is again able to manage his or her own personal and financial affairs. No Trustee is liable to anyone for removing anyone from the Trusteeship, if the Trustee relied in good faith on the aforementioned physicians' certifications. No one else is liable to anyone for dealing with a Trustee other than the one removed for disability, if such removal was made upon good faith reliance on the aforementioned physicians' certifications.*

C.   *All tax-related terms mean the same things in this Trust instrument as they mean in the Internal Revenue Code of 1986, as amended.*

This article defines when the trustee becomes disabled and can no longer serve as trustee.

ARTICLE V
Trustee's Powers

The Trustee is exclusively empowered to do the following:

A.   *To hold and retain any real property received that constitutes a personal residence of the Grantor, regardless of the source of such property and without regard to diversification.*

B.   *To deposit Trust funds temporarily in any commercial interest-bearing savings or savings and loan accounts, and to invest the Trust funds (after the Cessation Date) in any type of investment asset, including stocks, bonds, and partnership interests, to the extent suitable for investment by Trusts generally.*

C.   *To borrow money for any reasonable Trust purpose and upon such terms, including (but not limited to) interest rates, security, and loan duration, as the Trustee deems advisable.*

D.   *To sell or otherwise dispose of Trust assets, including (but not limited to) Trust real property, for cash or credit, at public or private sale, and with such warranties or indemnifications as the Trustee deems advisable.*

E.   *To improve, develop, manage, lease, or abandon any Trust assets, as the Trustee deems advisable, consistent with the purposes of this Trust.*

F.   *To pay and advance money for the Trust's protection and for all expenses, losses, and liabilities sustained in its administration.*

G.   *To prosecute or defend any action for the protection of the Trust, the Trustee in the performance of the Trustee's duties, or both, and to pay, contest, or settle any claim by or against the Trust for the Trustee in the performance of the Trustee's duties.*

H. *To employ persons, even if they are associated with the Trustee, to advise or assist the Trustee in the performance of the Trustee's duties.*

I. *To distribute Trust assets in kind or in cash.*

J. *To allocate receipts and disbursements to principal or income, in accordance with applicable local law and practice, except that in the absence of any specific local law, the Trustee shall follow the rules and principles of the Revised Uniform Principal and Income Act, as adopted and most recently revised (at the time of such allocation) by the National Conference of Commissioners on Uniform State Laws.*

K. *To execute and deliver any instruments necessary or useful in the exercise of any of these powers.*

Article V details the powers of the trustee. Remember, since you are going to be trustee here, if you so choose, you want these powers to be as expansive as possible.

ARTICLE VI
The Trustee

A. *The Grantor is the initial Trustee of this Trust. If the Grantor is ever unwilling or unable to continue serving, her sibling, (NAME), will become the Trustee.*

B. *A Trustee may designate any individual or institution as a Co-Trustee by a written instrument. Any Co-Trustee or successor Trustee may, without liability, accept without examination or review the accounts rendered and the property delivered by any predecessor Trustee. Each successor Trustee has the same title, powers, and duties as the Trustee succeeded, without any additional conveyance. A Co-Trustee so named shall serve only as long as the Trustee who appointed such Co-Trustee (or, if such Co-Trustee was named by more than one (1) Trustee acting together, by the last to serve of such Trustees), and such Co-Trustee shall not become a successor Trustee upon the death, resignation, or disability of the Trustee who appointed such Co-Trustee, unless such Co-Trustee is elected as successor Trustee pursuant to Paragraph E of this article. Any reference to a "Trustee" refers equally to any successor Trustee.*

C. *Any Trustee may, from time to time, delegate to any other Trustee by written instrument any or all of such Trustee's powers (except those, if any, not exercisable by such other Trustee). Such delegation may be temporary or permanent, and, if temporary, may be for any duration of time or until any event specified by the delegating Trustee. Any person dealing in good faith with any Trustee may rely without inquiry upon the Trustee's certificate with respect to any delegation.*

D. *No Trustee shall be required to provide surety or other security on a bond.*

E. *Any Trustee may resign by giving written notice specifying the resignation's effective date to the Grantor or her legal Guardian. Whenever there shall be a vacancy in the office of Trustee, a successor Trustee shall be named by the Grantor, her legal Guardian, or her personal representative, as the case may be.*

F. *No Trustee shall be required to obtain the order of any Court to exercise any power or discretion under this Trust.*

G. *No Trustee shall be required to file any accounting with any public official. The Trustee must, however, maintain accurate records concerning the Trust. Each year, furthermore, the Trustee shall furnish an annual accounting of the Trust's condition, including receipts and disbursements, to the Grantor or her legal Guardian. This required accounting may be satisfied by a copy of the Trust's federal income tax return, if one is required.*

H. *Each Trustee (other than the Grantor) is entitled to reasonable compensation for services in administering this Trust and to reimbursement for expenses. If the Grantor is the Trustee of this Trust, she will be entitled to no compensation but she will be entitled to reimbursement for expenses.*

Article VI details who the successor trustee shall be and specifically does not require the trustee to provide surety or other security on a bond or to obtain the order of any court to exercise any power or discretion under this trust. The trustee is entitled to compensation, but is not required to file any accounting with any public official.

ARTICLE VII
Miscellaneous

A. *This Trust shall be governed by and construed according to the law of (State).*

B. *Whenever the context of this Trust requires, the masculine gender includes the feminine or neuter, and vice versa, and the singular number includes the plural, and vice versa.*

IN WITNESS WHEREOF, (NAME), the Grantor and Trustee, has hereunto set her hand and seal, all as of the day and year first above written.

_____
Grantor

_____

Trustee

STATE OF (YOUR STATE)

COUNTY OF (YOUR COUNTY)

    BE IT REMEMBERED, that on   , 2000, before me, the undersigned authority, personally appeared (YOUR NAME) and (NAME) AS EXECUTIVE DIRECTOR OF THE (NAME) FOUNDATION, who I am satisfied are the persons named in and who executed the above document, and I having first made known to such persons the contents thereof, such persons acknowledged that they are of sound mind, free of duress or undue influence, and that such persons signed, sealed, and delivered the same as their voluntary act and deed. All of which is hereby certified.

_____

(NOTARY)

SCHEDULE A

> The preceding paragraphs complete the Qualified Personal Residence Trust document. The Qualified Personal Residence Trust is another tactic for estate and gift reduction techniques, and, where appropriate, should be considered in your efforts to reduce your estate tax down to zero.

EXAMPLE

THE (YOUR NAME) QUALIFIED PERSONAL RESIDENCE TRUST

On   , 2000, this Trust was created by (YOUR NAME) (sometimes the "Grantor" and sometimes the "Trustee"), who declared that she held certain property as Trustee, on the following terms and conditions:

ARTICLE I
Trust Created; Purposes

A. The Grantor holds as Trustee the real property listed on Schedule A, to be administered according to the terms of this instrument. The Grantor and anyone else may transfer additional property to the Trustee, to be held and administered according to the Trust's terms. The Grantor retains no right, title, or interest in any Trust property, except as specifically provided in Article III.

B. This paragraph contains a statement of the Grantor's reasons for establishing this Trust. Every provision of this instrument shall be construed consistent with these expressed intentions and purposes.

  1. The Grantor intends by this Trust to make a completed gift to her son, (NAME), of a vested remainder in the Trust property, subject only to the Grantor's retention of a right to the use of and the income from the Trust for ten (10) years. The Grantor intends that, except as may be provided expressly herein, her interest in this Trust shall give her only those rights which are ordinarily associated with an income interest in trust for a term-for-years and that it endow her with no rights inconsistent therewith.

  2. The Grantor intends that this Trust constitute a Qualified Personal Residence Trust pursuant to the applicable regulations of the U.S. Department of the Treasury promulgated with respect to Section 2702(b) of the Internal Revenue Code of 1986, as amended ("Code"), and all terms used herein shall have the same meaning in this instrument as they do in the Code and the said regulations.

ARTICLE II
Irrevocability

This Trust and all interests in it are irrevocable, and the Grantor has no power to alter, amend, revoke, or terminate any Trust provision or interest, whether under this instrument or any statute or rule of law.

ARTICLE III
During Trust's Term

A. During the Trust's term, the Trustee shall hold the Trust property for the Grantor's exclusive personal use and benefit. The Trustee shall permit the Grantor to use such property as her personal residence without rent or other charge, and the Trustee shall maintain such property from the Trust funds, including any rental income received by the Trustee. To the extent that the Trustee incurs expenses for the maintenance of the Trust property in excess of the Trust's cash assets, the Trustee shall notify the Grantor, who may pay such expenses directly, without any right to reimbursement from the Trust.

   1. <u>Rental of Property.</u>   The Trustee may, with the Grantor's written consent, rent the property on such terms and conditions as the Trustee shall deem appropriate.

   2. <u>No Distributions to Others.</u>   The Trustee may distribute neither income nor corpus to anyone other than the Grantor before the termination of the Trust.

   3. <u>Trust Assets.</u>   Except as provided in this ITEM 3, the Trustee may hold as part of this Trust nothing other than real property constituting the Grantor's personal residence. The Trustee shall accept no gifts or other transfers to the Trust of any property not permitted under this ITEM 3.

      3.1. <u>Cash.</u>   The Trustee may hold cash as an asset of the Trust, but not in excess of the amounts required for payment of Trust expenses (including mortgage payments) already incurred or reasonably expected to be incurred within the next three (3) months following the date on which such cash is first held, and for improvements to the residence held by the Trust to be paid within the next three (3) months following the date on which such cash is first held.

3.2. <u>Proceeds of Sale.</u> The Trustee may hold any proceeds from the sale of the Trust's real estate (including any income thereon) for a period not to exceed two (2) years from the date of sale, if the Trustee intends to use the proceeds within that period to buy another residence to be used as a personal residence of the Grantor.

3.3. <u>Insurance Proceeds.</u> The Trustee may hold the proceeds of any insurance paid to the Trust as a result of the damage to or destruction of the Trust's real property for a period not to exceed two (2) years if the Trustee intends to use the proceeds for repair, improvement, or replacement of the Trust real property.

3.4. <u>Prompt Distribution of Cash.</u> The Trustee shall distribute all cash in excess of the amounts permitted under this ITEM 3 to the Grantor not less often than quarterly.

B. If the Grantor dies before the tenth (10th) anniversary of the date of this instrument, the Trustee shall distribute the Trust funds to the Grantor's estate, and this Trust shall terminate. If the Grantor is alive on the tenth (10th) anniversary of the date of this instrument, the Trustee shall distribute the Trust real property to (NAME) (or, if he is not then living, to his estate), and distribute to the Grantor any cash held by the Trust for the payment of expenses or for any other purpose, and this Trust shall terminate.

C. Notwithstanding the provisions of Paragraph B, the date on which the real property held by the Trust ceases to be a personal residence of the Grantor because of a change in its use, or if earlier, the date on which sales proceeds are received on account of the sale of such personal residence, shall be known as the "Cessation Date." On the Cessation Date, the Trust shall immediately convert to an annuity trust, and shall be held and administered as follows:

1. From the Cessation Date until the termination of this Trust, the Trust shall function exclusively as a qualified annuity trust. During such term, the Trustee shall pay to the Grantor an "annuity amount" determined by dividing the value for federal gift tax purposes of all interests retained by the Grantor in the property transferred to this Trust (as of the date of such transfer) by the annuity factor for the initial term of the Trust determined under Section 7520 of the Code (as of the date of such transfer).

2. The annuity amount shall be paid in equal quarterly installments from income and, to the extent income is insufficient, from principal.

3. In determining the annuity amount, the Trustee shall prorate the annuity amount on a daily basis for short taxable years.

4. Any Trust income not distributed to the Grantor as part of the annuity amount shall be added to principal.

5. If the initial net fair market value of the Trust assets is incorrectly determined by the Trustee, then within a reasonable period after the final determination of the correct value, the Trustee shall pay the Grantor, in case of an undervaluation, or the Grantor shall pay the Trustee, in the case of an overvaluation, an amount equal to the difference between the annuity amount properly payable and the annuity amount actually paid, plus interest on such amounts computed at the rate required by the applicable Treasury Department regulations or, if there are no such regulations, the rate used for valuing annuity interests under Code Section 664, compounded annually.

6. It is the Grantor's intent that the provisions under this paragraph create a Trust which would be a qualified annuity trust from the Cessation Date, and all provisions of this instrument shall be construed consistent with this intent.

D. The Grantor's interest in this Trust may not be commuted.

ARTICLE IV
Definitions

A. The Grantor is unmarried at the time this Trust is executed, and she has only one (1) child, (NAME).

B. A Trustee is "disabled" or under a "disability" whenever any Trustee other than a disabled Trustee or, if there is no such Trustee, any person who would become successor Trustee on such determination of disability, receives written certification from two (2) physicians regularly attending the Trustee, at least one (1) of whom is board certified in the specialty most closely associated with the alleged disability, that such Trustee has become physically or mentally incapacitated, regardless of cause and regardless of whether or not there has been any adjudication of incompetence, mental illness, or need for a committee, conservator, Guardian, or other personal representative. A Trustee is recovered from his or her disability whenever the then serving Trustee receives written certification from two (2) physicians regularly attending such disabled Trustee, at least one (1) of whom is board certified in the specialty most closely associated with the alleged disability, that he or she is no longer incapacitated and is again able to manage his or her own personal and financial affairs. No Trustee is liable to anyone for removing anyone from the Trusteeship, if the Trustee relied in good faith on the aforementioned physicians' certifications. No one else is liable to anyone for dealing with a Trustee other than the one removed for disability, if such removal was made upon good faith reliance on the aforementioned physicians' certifications.

C. All tax-related terms mean the same things in this Trust instrument as they mean in the Internal Revenue Code of 1986, as amended.

ARTICLE V
Trustee's Powers

The Trustee is exclusively empowered to do the following:

A. To hold and retain any real property received that constitutes a personal residence of the Grantor, regardless of the source of such property and without regard to diversification.

B. To deposit Trust funds temporarily in any commercial interest-bearing savings or savings and loan accounts, and to invest the Trust funds (after the Cessation Date) in any type of investment asset, including stocks, bonds, and partnership interests, to the extent suitable for investment by Trusts generally.

C. To borrow money for any reasonable Trust purpose and upon such terms, including (but not limited to) interest rates, security, and loan duration, as the Trustee deems advisable.

D. To sell or otherwise dispose of Trust assets, including (but not limited to) Trust real property, for cash or credit, at public or private sale, and with such warranties or indemnifications as the Trustee deems advisable.

E. To improve, develop, manage, lease, or abandon any Trust assets, as the Trustee deems advisable, consistent with the purposes of this Trust.

F. To pay and advance money for the Trust's protection and for all expenses, losses, and liabilities sustained in its administration.

G. To prosecute or defend any action for the protection of the Trust, the Trustee in the performance of the Trustee's duties, or both, and to pay, contest, or settle any claim by or against the Trust for the Trustee in the performance of the Trustee's duties.

H. To employ persons, even if they are associated with the Trustee, to advise or assist the Trustee in the performance of the Trustee's duties.

I. To distribute Trust assets in kind or in cash.

J. To allocate receipts and disbursements to principal or income, in accordance with applicable local law and practice, except that in the absence of any specific local law, the Trustee shall follow the rules and principles of the Revised Uniform Principal and Income Act, as adopted and most recently revised (at the time of such allocation) by the National Conference of Commissioners on Uniform State Laws.

K. To execute and deliver any instruments necessary or useful in the exercise of any of these powers.

ARTICLE VI
The Trustee

A. The Grantor is the initial Trustee of this Trust. If the Grantor is ever unwilling or unable to continue serving, her sibling, (NAME), will become the Trustee.

B. A Trustee may designate any individual or institution as a Co-Trustee by a written instrument. Any Co-Trustee or successor Trustee may, without liability, accept without examination or review the accounts rendered and the property delivered by any predecessor Trustee. Each successor Trustee has the same title, powers, and duties as the Trustee succeeded, without any additional conveyance. A Co-Trustee so named shall serve only as long as the Trustee who appointed such Co-Trustee (or, if such Co-Trustee was named by more than one (1) Trustee acting together, by the last to serve of such Trustees), and such Co-Trustee shall not become a successor Trustee upon the death, resignation, or disability of the Trustee who appointed such Co-Trustee, unless such Co-Trustee is elected as successor Trustee pursuant to Paragraph E of this article. Any reference to a "Trustee" refers equally to any successor Trustee.

C. Any Trustee may, from time to time, delegate to any other Trustee by written instrument any or all of such Trustee's powers (except those, if any, not exercisable by such other Trustee). Such delegation may be temporary or permanent, and, if temporary, may be for any duration of time or until any event specified by the delegating Trustee. Any person dealing in good faith with any Trustee may rely without inquiry upon the Trustee's certificate with respect to any delegation.

D. No Trustee shall be required to provide surety or other security on a bond.

E. Any Trustee may resign by giving written notice specifying the resignation's effective date to the Grantor or her legal Guardian. Whenever there shall be a vacancy in the office of Trustee, a successor Trustee shall be named by the Grantor, her legal Guardian, or her personal representative, as the case may be.

F. No Trustee shall be required to obtain the order of any court to exercise any power or discretion under this Trust.

G. No Trustee shall be required to file any accounting with any public official. The Trustee must, however, maintain accurate records concerning the Trust. Each year, furthermore, the Trustee shall furnish an annual accounting of the Trust's condition, including receipts and disbursements, to the Grantor or her legal Guardian. This required accounting may be satisfied by a copy of the Trust's federal income tax return, if one is required.

H. Each Trustee (other than the Grantor) is entitled to reasonable compensation for services in administering this Trust and to reimbursement for expenses. If the Grantor is the Trustee of this Trust, she will be entitled to no compensation but she will be entitled to reimbursement for expenses.

ARTICLE VII
Miscellaneous

A. This Trust shall be governed by and construed according to the law of (State).

B. Whenever the context of this Trust requires, the masculine gender includes the feminine or neuter, and vice versa, and the singular number includes the plural, and vice versa.

IN WITNESS WHEREOF, (NAME), the Grantor and Trustee, has hereunto set her hand and seal, all as of the day and year first above written.

_____
Grantor

_____
Trustee

STATE OF (YOUR STATE)

COUNTY OF (YOUR COUNTY)

BE IT REMEMBERED, that on   , 2000, before me, the under-signed authority, personally appeared (YOUR NAME) and (NAME) AS EXEC-UTIVE DIRECTOR OF THE (NAME) FOUNDATION, who I am satisfied are the persons named in and who executed the above document, and I having first made known to such persons the contents thereof, such persons acknowledged that they are of sound mind, free of duress or undue influence, and that such persons signed, sealed, and delivered the same as their voluntary act and deed. All of which is hereby certified.

_____

(NOTARY)

SCHEDULE A

CHAPTER 12

Grantor Retained Annuity Trusts (GRATs) and Grantor Retained Unitrusts (GRUTs)

If your estate exceeds $3 million in value, you may very well need to consider estate reduction techniques in addition to those already discussed. The basic concept of a Grantor Retained Annuity Trust (GRAT) is simple. You create a trust that, at the end of its life, will transfer the assets remaining in the trust to someone else—for example, your children. While the trust is in existence, it pays you a fixed amount each year—an annuity.

The GRAT is a sophisticated way to remove assets from your estate with minimal gift tax consequences. It also allows you to enjoy the income from the assets transferred to the GRAT for a predetermined period of time. At the end of that term, family member GRAT beneficiaries will ultimately receive the gift.

Let's see how this works. The first question is, how much of the money in the trust isn't subject to gift tax? This depends partly on the amount of money the trust will pay you each year, the number of years the trust will run, your life expectancy, and the return the IRS expects the assets in the trust to earn each year.

The rate of return used in this calculation is set monthly by the IRS, according to a formula that is pegged to intermediate-term Treasury rates. If the interest rates are low, the amount of money that is needed to fund those annual payments—and the amount of money in the trust that passes on tax free to the beneficiaries—is higher.

Additional discounting can be achieved if the assets transferred to the GRAT constitute minority or nonmarketable business interest property. Properties such as nonvoting S corporation stock or Family Limited Partnership interests can enhance the already substantial gift discounting available with GRATs.

The real tax savings is a function of how much the value of the trust assets actually increases during the term of the trust. In effect, the GRAT freezes the value of the assets, for tax purposes, at what they are worth at the time the trust is established. If the trust earns more than the IRS expects, that excess appreciation passes on tax free to your beneficiaries.

Because the IRS rate is locked in at the time you establish the GRAT, this strategy is especially effective when interest rates are low. For example, assume you fund a GRAT with stock currently valued at $1 million. Assume that the stock returns 10 percent per year during the trust's 12-year life. If the IRS applicable federal rate is 9 percent (the IRS expects the trust to earn 9 percent annually), creating a GRAT will result in a tax-free gift of $858,300 when the trust expires. But, if the IRS mandated rate is just 5.4 percent, the tax-free gift will be $993,800—nearly 16 percent more.

Remember, the tax savings increase over time. The longer the property stays in the trust, beating the IRS mandated interest rate, the more growth moves on to your beneficiaries tax free. Beating the IRS rate is crucial. If the trust earns less than the IRS mandated rate, setting up the GRAT will be a mistake. The gift tax bill will be higher than either the gift or estate tax levy on the remaining assets would have been had those assets been passed on without a GRAT.

Here, similar to the situation with Qualified Personal Residence Trusts, you want to outlive the trust term. If the person establishing the trust dies before the trust expires, most or all of the remaining assets will be subject to estate tax.

With a GRAT, each year you receive a fixed amount in either dollars or a percentage of the initial valuation of the trust. With a Grantor Retained Unitrust (GRUT), you receive a fixed percentage of the fair market value of the assets in the trust, valued each year. The analogy is similar again to charitable remainder annuity trusts and charitable remainder unitrusts.

According to *The Wall Street Journal,* tax experts say, "The cost of setting up a GRAT can be $2,500 to $25,000 or more, depending upon its complexity." Let's save you some money—see the following example of a GRAT document.

This is a Grantor Retained Annuity Trust with a 10 percent annuity to you for 10 years, ending with a distribution to your child.

THE (NAME) RETAINED ANNUITY TRUST

On   , 2000, this Trust was created by (YOUR NAME) (the "Grantor"), who agreed with her sibling, (NAME) (the "Trustee"), that the Trustee shall hold and administer the Trust fund as follows:

> This paragraph identifies you as the grantor and designates your sibling as the trustee of this GRAT.

ARTICLE I
Trust Created and Purposes

A. The Grantor transfers to the Trustee the assets listed on Schedule A, to be held and administered according to the terms of this instrument. No one may transfer any additional assets to the Trust. The Grantor retains no right, title, or interest in any Trust property, except as specifically provided in ARTICLE III.

B. This paragraph contains a statement of the Grantor's reasons for establishing this Trust. Every provision of this instrument shall be construed consistent with these expressed intentions and purposes.

    1. The Grantor intends by this Trust to make a completed gift to her son, (NAME), of a vested remainder in the Trust property, subject only to the Grantor's retention of a right to the annuity described in ARTICLE III for ten (10) years. The Grantor intends that, except as may be provided expressly herein, her interest in this Trust shall give her only those rights which are ordinarily associated with an annuity interest in Trust for a term-for-years and that it shall endow her with no rights inconsistent therewith.

    2. The Grantor intends that this Trust constitute a qualified Grantor Retained Annuity Trust pursuant to the applicable regulations of the U.S. Department of Treasury promulgated with respect to Section 2702 of the Internal Revenue Code of 1986, as amended ("Code"), and all terms used herein shall have the same meaning in this instrument as they do in the Code and the said regulations.

> The preceding article details your intent to gift a remainder interest in the trust property to your son while retaining an income interest for 10 years.

ARTICLE II
Irrevocability

This Trust and all interests in it are irrevocable, and the Grantor has no power to alter, amend, revoke, or terminate any Trust provision or interest, whether under this instrument or any statute or rule of law.

Article II makes the trust irrevocable—you have no power to alter, amend, revoke, or terminate any trust provision.

ARTICLE III
During Trust's Term

A. *From the date of this instrument until the tenth (10th) anniversary thereof, the Trustee shall pay to the Grantor (or, if she is not then living, to her estate) an "annuity amount" equal to ten percent (10%) of the initial value of the Trust fund. The annuity amount shall be paid in equal quarterly installments from income and, to the extent income is insufficient, from principal.*

   1. *Computation of Annuity Amount in Certain Circumstances.   In determining the annuity amount, the Trustee shall prorate the annuity amount on a daily basis for short taxable years.*

   2. *Excess Income.   Any Trust income not distributed to the Grantor as part of the annuity amount shall be added to principal.*

   3. *No Distributions to Others.   The Trustee may distribute neither income nor corpus to anyone other than the Grantor before the termination of the Trust.*

   4. *Quarterly Payments.   The annuity amount shall be paid in equal quarterly installments from income and, to the extent income is insufficient, from principal.*

   5. *Incorrect Valuation of Trust Property.   If the initial net fair market value of the Trust assets is incorrectly determined by the Trustee, then within a reasonable period after the final determination of the correct value, the Trustee shall pay the Grantor, in case of an undervaluation, or the Grantor shall pay to the Trustee, in the case of an overvaluation, an amount equal to the difference between the annuity amount properly payable and the annuity amount actually paid, plus interest on such amounts computed at the rate required by the applicable Treasury Department regulations or, if there are no such regulations, the rate used for valuing annuity interests under Code Section 664, compounded annually.*

B. *On the tenth (10th) anniversary of the date of this instrument, the Trustee shall distribute the Trust real property to (NAME) (or, if he is not then living, to his estate), and this Trust shall terminate.*

C. *The Grantor's interest in this Trust may not be commuted.*

Article III details the amount of the annuity that you are going to receive (10 percent of the initial value of the trust fund). It also discusses how you are to be paid (in equal quarterly installments) and what will happen when the trust terminates.

ARTICLE IV
Definitions

A. *The Grantor is unmarried at the time this Trust is executed.*

B. *At the time this Trust is executed, the Grantor has one child, (NAME).*

C. *A Trustee is "disabled" or under a "disability" whenever any Trustee other than a disabled Trustee or, if there is no such Trustee, any person who would become successor Trustee on such determination of disability, receives written certification of two (2) physicians regularly attending the Trustee, at least one (1) of whom is board certified in the specialty most closely associated with the alleged disability that such Trustee has become physically or mentally incapacitated, regardless of cause and regardless of whether or not there has been any adjudication of incompetence, mental illness, or need for a committee, conservator, Guardian, or other personal representative. A Trustee is recovered from his or her disability whenever the then serving Trustee receives written certification from two (2) physicians regularly attending such disabled Trustee, at least one (1) of whom is board certified in the specialty most closely associated with the alleged disability, that he or she is no longer incapacitated and is again able to manage his or her own personal and financial affairs. No Trustee is liable to anyone for removing anyone from the Trusteeship, if the Trustee relied in good faith on the aforementioned physicians' certifications. No one else is liable to anyone for dealing with a Trustee other than the one removed for disability, if such removal was made upon good faith reliance on the aforementioned physicians' certifications.*

D. *All tax-related terms mean the same things in this Trust instrument as they mean in the Internal Revenue Code of 1986, as amended.*

Article IV provides the definitions and details what will happen should your trustee become disabled.

ARTICLE V
Trustee's Powers

The Trustee is exclusively empowered to do the following:

A. *To hold and retain all or any property received from any source, without regard to diversification.*

B. *To invest and reinvest the Trust funds in any type of property and every kind of investment, including (but not limited to) corporate obligations of every kind, preferred or common stocks, securities of any regulated investment Trust, state and local bonds, and partnership interests.*

C. *To participate passively in the operation of any productive business or other enterprise, and to incorporate, dissolve, or otherwise change the form of such business, but the Trustee shall do nothing which would constitute the conduct of an active trade or business by the Trust.*

D. *To deposit Trust funds in any commercial interest-bearing savings or savings and loan accounts.*

E. *To borrow money for any reasonable Trust purpose and upon such terms, including (but not limited to) interest rates, security, and loan duration, as the Trustee deems advisable.*

F. *To lend Trust funds to such persons and on such terms including (but not limited to) interest rates, security, and loan duration, as the Trustee deems advisable, but the Trustee may not lend Trust funds without an adequate rate of interest.*

G. *To sell or otherwise dispose of Trust assets, including (but not limited to) Trust real property, for cash or credit, at public or private sale, and with such warranties or indemnifications as the Trustee deems advisable.*

H. *To buy assets of any type from any person on such terms, including (but not limited to) cash or credit, interest rates, and security, as the Trustee deems advisable.*

I. *To improve, develop, manage, lease, or abandon any Trust assets, as the Trustee deems advisable.*

J. *To hold property in the name of any Trustee or any custodian or nominee, without disclosing this Trust, but the Trustee is responsible for the acts of any custodian or nominee the Trustee so uses.*

K. *To pay and advance money for the Trust's protection and for all expenses, losses, and liabilities sustained in its administration.*

L. *To prosecute or defend any action for the protection of the Trust, the Trustee in the performance of the Trustee's duties, or both, and to pay, contest, or settle any claim by or against the Trust or the Trustee in the performance of the Trustee's duties.*

M. *To employ persons, even if they are associated with the Trustee, to advise or assist the Trustee in the performance of the Trustee's duties.*

N. *To distribute Trust assets in kind or in cash.*

O. *To allocate receipts and disbursements to principal or income, in accordance with applicable local law and practice, except that in the absence of any specific local law, the Trustee shall follow the rules and principles of the Revised Uniform Principal and Income Act, as adopted and most recently revised (at the time of such allocation) by the National Conference of Commissioners on Uniform State Laws.*

P. *To execute and deliver any instruments necessary or useful in the exercise of any of these powers.*

Article V details the powers of the trustee. Remember, you want to give maximum flexibility to the trustee.

ARTICLE VI
The Trustee

A. *(NAME) will be the Trustee, until his resignation, death, or disability, at which time the Grantor's sister, (NAME), will become successor Trustee.*

B. *A Trustee may designate any individual or institution as a Co-Trustee by a written instrument. Any Co-Trustee or successor Trustee may, without liability, accept without examination or review the accounts rendered and the property delivered by any predecessor Trustee. Each successor Trustee has the same title, powers, and duties as the Trustee succeeded, without any additional conveyance. A Co-Trustee so named shall serve only as long as the Trustee who appointed such Co-Trustee (or, if such Co-Trustee was named by more than one (1) Trustee acting together, by the last to serve of such Trustees), and such Co-Trustee shall not become a successor Trustee upon the death, resignation, or disability of the Trustee who appointed such Co-Trustee, unless such Co-Trustee is elected as successor Trustee pursuant to Paragraph E of this article. Any reference to a "Trustee" refers equally to any successor Trustee.*

C. *Any Trustee may, from time to time, delegate to any other Trustee by written instrument any or all of such Trustee's powers (except those, if any, not exercisable by such other Trustee). Such delegation may be temporary or permanent, and if temporary, may be for any duration of time or until any event specified by the delegating Trustee. Any person dealing in good faith with any Trustee may rely without inquiry upon the Trustee's certificate with respect to any delegation.*

D.   *No Trustee shall be required to provide surety or other security on a bond.*

E.   *Any Trustee may resign by giving written notice specifying the resignation's effective date to each adult beneficiary of the current Trust income, to a custodial parent or legal Guardian of each minor beneficiary of current Trust income, or, if there is no custodial parent or legal Guardian, to an appropriate person selected by the Trustee to represent such minor beneficiary. Whenever there shall be a vacancy in the office of Trustee, a successor Trustee shall be named by a majority vote of the income beneficiaries, with the votes being cast by those persons to whom notice was given under this paragraph. The successor Trustee named by vote of the income beneficiaries must be a corporation authorized under the laws of (State) to render Trust services. Under no circumstance may the Grantor become a Trustee of this Trust.*

F.   *No Trustee shall be required to obtain the order of any Court to exercise any power or discretion under this Trust.*

G.   *No Trustee shall be required to file any accounting with any public official. The Trustee must, however, maintain accurate records concerning the Trust. Each year, furthermore, the Trustee shall furnish an annual accounting of the Trust's condition, including receipts and disbursements, to each adult beneficiary of the current Trust income, to a custodial parent of each minor beneficiary of current Trust income, and to the legal Guardian of any beneficiary of current Trust income having a legal Guardian, each determined at the time such notice is given. This required accounting may be satisfied by a copy of the Trust's federal income tax return, if one is required.*

H.   *Each Trustee is entitled to reasonable compensation for services in administering this Trust and to reimbursement for expenses.*

Article VI identifies both the current trustee and the successor trustee. It specifically waives any surety or bond for the trustee. It also specifically waives the requirement to file any accounting with any public official and the need to obtain the order of any court to exercise any power or discretion under the trust.

ARTICLE VII
Miscellaneous

A. This Trust shall be governed by and construed according to the law of (Your State).

B. Whenever the context of this Trust requires, the masculine gender includes the feminine or neuter, and vice versa, and the singular number includes the plural, and vice versa.

IN WITNESS WHEREOF, (YOUR NAME), the Grantor, and (NAME), the Trustee, have hereunto set their hands and seals, all as of the day and year first above written.

_____ (Seal)

Grantor

_____ (Seal)

Trustee

STATE OF (YOUR STATE) _____

COUNTY OF (YOUR COUNTY) _____

BE IT REMEMBERED, that on   , 2000, before me, the undersigned authority, personally appeared (YOUR NAME) and (NAME) AS EXECUTIVE DIRECTOR OF THE (NAME) FOUNDATION, who I am satisfied are the persons named in and who executed the above document, and I having first made known to such persons the contents thereof, such persons acknowledged that they are of sound mind, free of duress or undue influence, and that such persons signed, sealed, and delivered the same as their voluntary act and deed. All of which is hereby certified.

_____

(NOTARY)

SCHEDULE A

The preceding paragraphs complete the document by identifying the choice of law and providing the signatures (notarized) of both the grantor and the trustee.

The following document is an example of a Grantor Retained Unitrust. The only difference is Article III, which stipulates that rather than getting a fixed annuity, you (the grantor) will receive a variable annuity equal to 10 percent of the net fair market value of the trust assets valued as of the first day of each trust taxable year.

THE (YOUR NAME) GRANTOR RETAINED UNITRUST

On _____, 2000, this Trust was created by (YOUR NAME) (the "Grantor"), who agreed with her sibling, (NAME) (the "Trustee") that the Trustee shall hold and administer the Trust fund as follows:

ARTICLE I
Trust Created, Additions, and Purpose

A. The Grantor transfers to the Trustee the property listed on Schedule A, as amended from time to time, to be held and administered according to the terms of this Trust instrument. The Grantor and anyone else may transfer additional property to the Trustee, to be held and administered according to the Trust's terms. The Grantor retains no right, title, or interest in any Trust property, except as specifically provided in Article III.

B. Any additions to this Trust after the original contribution shall be held together with the existing Trust funds.

C. The Grantor intends by this Trust to make a completed gift to her son, (NAME), on the date of any gift to the Trust, of a vested remainder in the Trust assets, subject only to the Grantor's retention of a unitrust interest for a specified term-of-years. The Grantor intends that her interest in this Trust shall give her only those rights which are ordinarily associated with a unitrust interest in trust for a term-for-years, and that it shall endow her with no rights inconsistent therewith. The Grantor also intends that her interest in this Trust shall constitute a "qualified interest" as defined in Section 2702 of the Internal Revenue Code of 1986. Every provision of this instrument shall be construed consistent with these expressed intentions and purposes.

ARTICLE II
Irrevocability

This Trust and all interests in it are irrevocable, and the Grantor has no power to alter, amend, revoke, or terminate any Trust provision or interest, whether under this instrument or any statute or rule of law.

ARTICLE III
During Trust's Term

A. *From the date of this instrument until the tenth (10th) anniversary thereof, the Trustee shall pay to the Grantor (or, if she is not then living, to her estate) a "unitrust amount" equal to ten percent (10%) of the net fair market value of the Trust assets valued as of the first day of each Trust taxable year. The unitrust amount shall be paid in equal quarterly installments from income and, to the extent income is insufficient, from principal. In determining the unitrust amount, the Trustee shall prorate the annuity amount on a daily basis for short taxable years. Any Trust income not distributed to the Grantor as part of the annuity amount shall be added to principal.*

1. *If the net fair market value of the Trust assets is incorrectly determined by the Trustee for any taxable year, then within a reasonable period after the final determination of the correct value, the Trustee shall pay the Grantor, in case of an undervaluation, or the Grantor shall pay to the Trustee, in the case of an overvaluation, an amount equal to the difference between the unitrust amount properly payable and the unitrust amount actually paid, plus interest on such amounts computed at the rate required by the applicable Treasury Department regulations or, if there are no such regulations, the rate used for valuing unitrust interests under Section 664 of the Internal Revenue Code of 1986, compounded annually.*

2. *If any additional contributions are made to the Trust after the initial contribution, the unitrust amount for the taxable year in which the assets are added shall be ten percent (10%) of the sum of (a) the net fair market value of the Trust assets (excluding the assets added and any income from or appreciation on such assets) and (b) that proportion of the value of the assets so added that was excluded under (a) which the number of days in the period which begins with the date of contribution and ends with the last day of the taxable year bears to the number of days in the period which begins on the first day of such taxable year and ends with the last day of such taxable year. If there is no valuation date after the time of contribution, the assets so added shall be valued at the time of contribution.*

B. *Immediately following the tenth (10th) anniversary of date of this instrument, the Trustee shall distribute the Trust fund to (NAME), or if he is not then living, to his estate.*

C. *In making any payment to a disabled beneficiary under this article, the Trustee may make such payments to such beneficiary, or to his or her Guardian, personal representative, or the person with whom he or she resides, without having to look to the proper application of those payments.*

ARTICLE IV
Definitions

A. The Grantor is unmarried at the time this Trust is executed.

B. At the time this Trust is executed, the Grantor has one (1) child, (NAME).

C. A Trustee is "disabled" or under a "disability" whenever any Trustee other than a disabled Trustee or, if there is no such Trustee, any person who would become successor Trustee on such determination of disability, receives written certification from two (2) physicians regularly attending the Trustee, at least one (1) of whom is board certified in the specialty most closely associated with the alleged disability, that such Trustee has become physically or mentally incapacitated, regardless of cause and regardless of whether or not there has been any adjudication of incompetence, mental illness, or need for a committee, conservator, Guardian, or other personal representative. A Trustee is recovered from his or her disability whenever the then serving Trustee receives written certification from two (2) physicians regularly attending such disabled Trustee, at least one (1) of whom is board certified in the specialty most closely associated with the alleged disability, that he or she is no longer incapacitated and is again able to manage his or her own personal and financial affairs. No Trustee is liable to anyone for removing anyone from the Trusteeship, if the Trustee relied in good faith on the aforementioned physicians' certifications. No one else is liable to anyone for dealing with a Trustee other than the one removed for disability, if such removal was made upon good faith reliance on the aforementioned physicians' certifications.

D. All tax-related terms mean the same things in this Trust instrument as they mean in the Internal Revenue Code of 1986, as amended.

ARTICLE V
Trustee's Powers

The Trustee is exclusively empowered to do the following:

A. To hold and retain all or any property received from any source, without regard to diversification.

B. To invest and reinvest the Trust funds in any type of property and every kind of investment, including (but not limited to) corporate obligations of every kind, preferred or common stocks, securities of any regulated investment Trust, state and local bonds, and partnership interests.

C. To participate passively in the operation of any productive business or other enterprise, and to incorporate, dissolve, or otherwise change the form of such business, but the Trustee shall do nothing which would constitute the conduct of an active trade or business by the Trust.

D. To deposit Trust funds in any commercial interest-bearing savings or savings and loan accounts.

E. To borrow money for any reasonable Trust purpose and upon such terms, including (but not limited to) interest rates, security, and loan duration, as the Trustee deems advisable.

F. To lend Trust funds to such persons and on such terms including (but not limited to) interest rates, security, and loan duration, as the Trustee deems advisable, but the Trustee may not lend Trust funds without an adequate rate of interest.

G. To sell or otherwise dispose of Trust assets, including (but not limited to) Trust real property, for cash or credit, at public or private sale, and with such warranties or indemnifications as the Trustee deems advisable.

H. To buy assets of any type from any person on such terms, including (but not limited to) cash or credit, interest rates, and security, as the Trustee deems advisable.

I. To improve, develop, manage, lease, or abandon any Trust assets, as the Trustee deems advisable.

J. To hold property in the name of any Trustee or any custodian or nominee, without disclosing this Trust, but the Trustee is responsible for the acts of any custodian or nominee the Trustee so uses.

K. To pay and advance money for the Trust's protection and for all expenses, losses, and liabilities sustained in its administration.

L. To prosecute or defend any action for the protection of the Trust, the Trustee in the performance of the Trustee's duties, or both, and to pay, contest, or settle any claim by or against the Trust or the Trustee in the performance of the Trustee's duties.

M. To employ persons, even if they are associated with the Trustee, to advise or assist the Trustee in the performance of the Trustee's duties.

N. To distribute Trust assets in kind or in cash.

O. To allocate receipts and disbursements to principal or income, in accordance with applicable local law and practice, except that in the absence of any specific local law, the Trustee shall follow the rules and principles of the Revised Uniform Principal and Income Act, as adopted and most recently revised (at the time of such allocation) by the National Conference of Commissioners on Uniform State Laws.

P. To execute and deliver any instruments necessary or useful in the exercise of any of these powers.

ARTICLE VI
The Trustee

A. (NAME) will be the Trustee, until his resignation, death, or disability, at which time the Grantor's sister, (NAME), will become successor Trustee.

B. A Trustee may designate any individual or institution as a Co-Trustee by a written instrument. Any Co-Trustee or successor Trustee may, without liability, accept without examination or review the accounts rendered and the property delivered by any predecessor Trustee. Each successor Trustee has the same title, powers, and duties as the Trustee succeeded, without any additional conveyance. A Co-Trustee so named shall serve only as long as the Trustee who appointed such Co-Trustee (or, if such Co-Trustee was named by more than one (1) Trustee acting together, by the last to serve of such Trustees), and such Co-Trustee shall not become a successor Trustee upon the death, resignation, or disability of the Trustee who appointed such Co-Trustee, unless such Co-Trustee is elected as successor Trustee pursuant to Paragraph E of this article. Any reference to a "Trustee" refers equally to any successor Trustee.

C. Any Trustee may, from time to time, delegate to any other Trustee by written instrument any or all of such Trustee's powers (except those, if any, not exercisable by such other Trustee). Such delegation may be temporary or permanent, and if temporary, may be for any duration of time or until any event specified by the delegating Trustee. Any person dealing in good faith with any Trustee may rely without inquiry upon the Trustee's certificate with respect to any delegation.

D. No Trustee shall be required to provide surety or other security on a bond.

E. Any Trustee may resign by giving written notice specifying the resignation's effective date to the beneficiary to whom distributions may be made at that time.

F. Whenever there shall be a vacancy in the office of Trustee, a successor Trustee shall be named by the person to whom notice of resignation would be given.

G. No Trustee shall be required to obtain the order of any Court to exercise any power or discretion under this Trust.

H. No Trustee shall be required to file any accounting with any public official. The Trustee must, however, maintain accurate records concerning the Trust. Each year, furthermore, the Trustee shall furnish an annual accounting of the Trust's condition, including receipts and disbursements, to each beneficiary to whom distributions have been made during the year.

I. Each Trustee is entitled to reasonable compensation for services in administering this Trust and to reimbursement for expenses.

ARTICLE VII
Miscellaneous

A. This Trust shall be governed by and construed according to the law of (State).

B. Whenever the context of this Trust requires, the masculine gender includes the feminine or neuter, and vice versa, and the singular number includes the plural, and vice versa.

IN WITNESS WHEREOF, (YOUR NAME), the Grantor, and (NAME), the Trustee, have hereunto set their hands and seals, all as of the day and year first above written.

_____ (Seal)

Grantor

_____ (Seal)

Trustee

STATE OF (YOUR STATE) _____

COUNTY OF (YOUR COUNTY) _____

BE IT REMEMBERED, that on   , 2000, before me, the undersigned authority, personally appeared (YOUR NAME) and (NAME) AS EXECUTIVE DIRECTOR OF THE (NAME) FOUNDATION, who I am satisfied are the persons named in and who executed the above document, and I having first made known to such persons the contents thereof, such persons acknowledged that they are of sound mind, free of duress or undue influence, and that such persons signed, sealed, and delivered the same as their voluntary act and deed. All of which is hereby certified.

_____

(NOTARY)

SCHEDULE A

Grantor retained trusts are additional ways to eliminate estate tax. While they don't give you the charitable deduction that is found in Charitable Remainder Trusts, they do enable you to transfer assets to your beneficiaries at a substantially discounted value.

EXAMPLES

THE (NAME) RETAINED ANNUITY TRUST

On   , 2000, this Trust was created by (YOUR NAME) (the "Grantor"), who agreed with her sibling, (NAME) (the "Trustee"), that the Trustee shall hold and administer the Trust fund as follows:

ARTICLE I
Trust Created and Purposes

A. The Grantor transfers to the Trustee the assets listed on Schedule A, to be held and administered according to the terms of this instrument. No one may transfer any additional assets to the Trust. The Grantor retains no right, title, or interest in any Trust property, except as specifically provided in ARTICLE III.

B. This paragraph contains a statement of the Grantor's reasons for establishing this Trust. Every provision of this instrument shall be construed consistent with these expressed intentions and purposes.

  1. The Grantor intends by this Trust to make a completed gift to her son, (NAME), of a vested remainder in the Trust property, subject only to the Grantor's retention of a right to the annuity described in ARTICLE III for ten (10) years. The Grantor intends that, except as may be provided expressly herein, her interest in this Trust shall give her only those rights which are ordinarily associated with an annuity interest in Trust for a term-for-years and that it shall endow her with no rights inconsistent therewith.

  2. The Grantor intends that this Trust constitute a qualified Grantor Retained Annuity Trust pursuant to the applicable regulations of the U.S. Department of Treasury promulgated with respect to Section 2702 of the Internal Revenue Code of 1986, as amended ("Code"), and all terms used herein shall have the same meaning in this instrument as they do in the Code and the said regulations.

ARTICLE II
Irrevocability

This Trust and all interests in it are irrevocable, and the Grantor has no power to alter, amend, revoke, or terminate any Trust provision or interest, whether under this instrument or any statute or rule of law.

ARTICLE III
During Trust's Term

A. From the date of this instrument until the tenth (10th) anniversary thereof, the Trustee shall pay to the Grantor (or, if she is not then living, to her estate) an "annuity amount" equal to ten percent (10%) of the initial value of the Trust fund. The annuity amount shall be paid in equal quarterly installments from income and, to the extent income is insufficient, from principal.

   1. <u>Computation of Annuity Amount in Certain Circumstances.</u>   In determining the annuity amount, the Trustee shall prorate the annuity amount on a daily basis for short taxable years.

   2. <u>Excess Income.</u>   Any Trust income not distributed to the Grantor as part of the annuity amount shall be added to principal.

   3. <u>No Distributions to Others.</u>   The Trustee may distribute neither income nor corpus to anyone other than the Grantor before the termination of the Trust.

   4. <u>Quarterly Payments.</u>   The annuity amount shall be paid in equal quarterly installments from income and, to the extent income is insufficient, from principal.

   5. <u>Incorrect Valuation of Trust Property.</u>   If the initial net fair market value of the Trust assets is incorrectly determined by the Trustee, then within a reasonable period after the final determination of the correct value, the Trustee shall pay the Grantor, in case of an undervaluation, or the Grantor shall pay to the Trustee, in the case of an overvaluation, an amount equal to the difference between the annuity amount properly payable and the annuity amount actually paid, plus interest on such amounts computed at the rate required by the applicable Treasury Department regulations or, if there are no such regulations, the rate used for valuing annuity interests under Code Section 664, compounded annually.

B. On the tenth (10th) anniversary of the date of this instrument, the Trustee shall distribute the Trust real property to (NAME) (or, if he is not then living, to his estate), and this Trust shall terminate.

C. The Grantor's interest in this Trust may not be commuted.

ARTICLE IV
Definitions

A. The Grantor is unmarried at the time this Trust is executed.

B. At the time this Trust is executed, the Grantor has one child, (NAME).

C. A Trustee is "disabled" or under a "disability" whenever any Trustee other than a disabled Trustee or, if there is no such Trustee, any person who would become successor Trustee on such determination of disability, receives written certification of two (2) physicians regularly attending the Trustee, at least one (1) of whom is board certified in the specialty most closely associated with the alleged disability that such Trustee has become physically or mentally incapacitated, regardless of cause and regardless of whether or not there has been any adjudication of incompetence, mental illness, or need for a committee, conservator, Guardian, or other personal representative. A Trustee is recovered from his or her disability whenever the then serving Trustee receives written certification from two (2) physicians regularly attending such disabled Trustee, at least one (1) of whom is board certified in the specialty most closely associated with the alleged disability, that he or she is no longer incapacitated and is again able to manage his or her own personal and financial affairs. No Trustee is liable to anyone for removing anyone from the Trusteeship, if the Trustee relied in good faith on the aforementioned physicians' certifications. No one else is liable to anyone for dealing with a Trustee other than the one removed for disability, if such removal was made upon good faith reliance on the aforementioned physicians' certifications.

D. All tax-related terms mean the same things in this Trust instrument as they mean in the Internal Revenue Code of 1986, as amended.

ARTICLE V
Trustee's Powers

The Trustee is exclusively empowered to do the following:

A. To hold and retain all or any property received from any source, without regard to diversification.

B. To invest and reinvest the Trust funds in any type of property and every kind of investment, including (but not limited to) corporate obligations of every kind, preferred or common stocks, securities of any regulated investment Trust, state and local bonds, and partnership interests.

C. To participate passively in the operation of any productive business or other enterprise, and to incorporate, dissolve, or otherwise change the form of such business, but the Trustee shall do nothing which would constitute the conduct of an active trade or business by the Trust.

D. To deposit Trust funds in any commercial interest-bearing savings or savings and loan accounts.

E. To borrow money for any reasonable Trust purpose and upon such terms, including (but not limited to) interest rates, security, and loan duration, as the Trustee deems advisable.

F. To lend Trust funds to such persons and on such terms including (but not limited to) interest rates, security, and loan duration, as the Trustee deems advisable, but the Trustee may not lend Trust funds without an adequate rate of interest.

G. To sell or otherwise dispose of Trust assets, including (but not limited to) Trust real property, for cash or credit, at public or private sale, and with such warranties or indemnifications as the Trustee deems advisable.

H. To buy assets of any type from any person on such terms, including (but not limited to) cash or credit, interest rates, and security, as the Trustee deems advisable.

I. To improve, develop, manage, lease, or abandon any Trust assets, as the Trustee deems advisable.

J. To hold property in the name of any Trustee or any custodian or nominee, without disclosing this Trust, but the Trustee is responsible for the acts of any custodian or nominee the Trustee so uses.

K. To pay and advance money for the Trust's protection and for all expenses, losses, and liabilities sustained in its administration.

L. To prosecute or defend any action for the protection of the Trust, the Trustee in the performance of the Trustee's duties, or both, and to pay, contest, or settle any claim by or against the Trust or the Trustee in the performance of the Trustee's duties.

M. To employ persons, even if they are associated with the Trustee, to advise or assist the Trustee in the performance of the Trustee's duties.

N. To distribute Trust assets in kind or in cash.

O. To allocate receipts and disbursements to principal or income, in accordance with applicable local law and practice, except that in the absence of any specific local law, the Trustee shall follow the rules and principles of the Revised Uniform Principal and Income Act, as adopted and most recently revised (at the time of such allocation) by the National Conference of Commissioners on Uniform State Laws.

P. To execute and deliver any instruments necessary or useful in the exercise of any of these powers.

ARTICLE VI
The Trustee

A. (NAME) will be the Trustee, until his resignation, death, or disability, at which time the Grantor's sister, (NAME), will become successor Trustee.

B. A Trustee may designate any individual or institution as a Co-Trustee by a written instrument. Any Co-Trustee or successor Trustee may, without liability, accept without examination or review the accounts rendered and the property delivered by any predecessor Trustee. Each successor Trustee has the same title, powers, and duties as the Trustee succeeded, without any additional conveyance. A Co-Trustee so named shall serve only as long as the Trustee who appointed such Co-Trustee (or, if such Co-Trustee was named by more than one (1) Trustee acting together, by the last to serve of such Trustees), and such Co-Trustee shall not become a successor Trustee upon the death, resignation, or disability of the Trustee who appointed such Co-Trustee, unless such Co-Trustee is elected as successor Trustee pursuant to Paragraph E of this article. Any reference to a "Trustee" refers equally to any successor Trustee.

C. Any Trustee may, from time to time, delegate to any other Trustee by written instrument any or all of such Trustee's powers (except those, if any, not exercisable by such other Trustee). Such delegation may be temporary or permanent, and if temporary, may be for any duration of time or until any event specified by the delegating Trustee. Any person dealing in good faith with any Trustee may rely without inquiry upon the Trustee's certificate with respect to any delegation.

D. No Trustee shall be required to provide surety or other security on a bond.

E. Any Trustee may resign by giving written notice specifying the resignation's effective date to each adult beneficiary of the current Trust income, to a custodial parent or legal Guardian of each minor beneficiary of current Trust income, or, if there is no custodial parent or legal Guardian, to an appropriate person selected by the Trustee to represent such minor beneficiary. Whenever there shall be a vacancy in the office of Trustee, a successor Trustee shall be named by a majority vote of the income beneficiaries, with the votes being cast by those persons to whom notice was given under this paragraph. The successor Trustee named by vote of the income beneficiaries must be a corporation authorized under the laws of (State) to render Trust services. Under no circumstance may the Grantor become a Trustee of this Trust.

F. No Trustee shall be required to obtain the order of any Court to exercise any power or discretion under this Trust.

G. No Trustee shall be required to file any accounting with any public official. The Trustee must, however, maintain accurate records concerning the Trust. Each year, furthermore, the Trustee shall furnish an annual accounting of the Trust's condition, including receipts and disbursements, to each adult beneficiary of the current Trust income, to a custodial parent of each minor beneficiary of current Trust income, and to the legal Guardian of any beneficiary of current Trust income having a legal Guardian, each determined at the time such notice is given. This required accounting may be satisfied by a copy of the Trust's federal income tax return, if one is required.

H. Each Trustee is entitled to reasonable compensation for services in administering this Trust and to reimbursement for expenses.

ARTICLE VII
Miscellaneous

A. This Trust shall be governed by and construed according to the law of (Your State).

B. Whenever the context of this Trust requires, the masculine gender includes the feminine or neuter, and vice versa, and the singular number includes the plural, and vice versa.

IN WITNESS WHEREOF, (YOUR NAME), the Grantor, and (NAME), the Trustee, have hereunto set their hands and seals, all as of the day and year first above written.

_____(Seal)

Grantor

_____(Seal)

Trustee

STATE OF (YOUR STATE)_____

COUNTY OF (YOUR COUNTY)

    BE IT REMEMBERED, that on   , 2000, before me, the under-signed authority, personally appeared (YOUR NAME) and (NAME) AS EXEC-UTIVE DIRECTOR OF THE (NAME) FOUNDATION, who I am satisfied are the persons named in and who executed the above document, and I having first made known to such persons the contents thereof, such persons acknowledged that they are of sound mind, free of duress or undue influence, and that such persons signed, sealed, and delivered the same as their voluntary act and deed. All of which is hereby certified.

                                       _____

                                       (NOTARY)

SCHEDULE A

THE (YOUR NAME) GRANTOR RETAINED UNITRUST

On   , 2000, this Trust was created by (YOUR NAME) (the "Grantor"), who agreed with her sibling, (NAME) (the "Trustee") that the Trustee shall hold and administer the Trust fund as follows:

ARTICLE I
Trust Created, Additions, and Purpose

A. The Grantor transfers to the Trustee the property listed on Schedule A, as amended from time to time, to be held and administered according to the terms of this Trust instrument. The Grantor and anyone else may transfer additional property to the Trustee, to be held and administered according to the Trust's terms. The Grantor retains no right, title, or interest in any Trust property, except as specifically provided in Article III.

B. Any additions to this Trust after the original contribution shall be held together with the existing Trust funds.

C. The Grantor intends by this Trust to make a completed gift to her son, (NAME), on the date of any gift to the Trust, of a vested remainder in the Trust assets, subject only to the Grantor's retention of a unitrust interest for a specified term-of-years. The Grantor intends that her interest in this Trust shall give her only those rights which are ordinarily associated with a unitrust interest in trust for a term-for-years, and that it shall endow her with no rights inconsistent therewith. The Grantor also intends that her interest in this Trust shall constitute a "qualified interest" as defined in Section 2702 of the Internal Revenue Code of 1986. Every provision of this instrument shall be construed consistent with these expressed intentions and purposes.

ARTICLE II
Irrevocability

This Trust and all interests in it are irrevocable, and the Grantor has no power to alter, amend, revoke, or terminate any Trust provision or interest, whether under this instrument or any statute or rule of law.

ARTICLE III
During Trust's Term

A. From the date of this instrument until the tenth (10th) anniversary thereof, the Trustee shall pay to the Grantor (or, if she is not then living, to her estate) a "unitrust amount" equal to ten percent (10%) of the net fair market value of the Trust assets valued as of the first day of each Trust taxable year. The unitrust amount shall be paid in equal quarterly installments from income and, to the extent income is insufficient, from principal. In determining the unitrust amount, the Trustee shall prorate the annuity amount on a daily basis for short taxable years. Any Trust income not distributed to the Grantor as part of the annuity amount shall be added to principal.

1. If the net fair market value of the Trust assets is incorrectly determined by the Trustee for any taxable year, then within a reasonable period after the final determination of the correct value, the Trustee shall pay the Grantor, in case of an undervaluation, or the Grantor shall pay to the Trustee, in the case of an overvaluation, an amount equal to the difference between the unitrust amount properly payable and the unitrust amount actually paid, plus interest on such amounts computed at the rate required by the applicable Treasury Department regulations or, if there are no such regulations, the rate used for valuing unitrust interests under Section 664 of the Internal Revenue Code of 1986, compounded annually.

2. If any additional contributions are made to the Trust after the initial contribution, the unitrust amount for the taxable year in which the assets are added shall be ten percent (10%) of the sum of (a) the net fair market value of the Trust assets (excluding the assets added and any income from or appreciation on such assets) and (b) that proportion of the value of the assets so added that was excluded under (a) which the number of days in the period which begins with the date of contribution and ends with the last day of the taxable year bears to the number of days in the period which begins on the first day of such taxable year and ends with the last day of such taxable year. If there is no valuation date after the time of contribution, the assets so added shall be valued at the time of contribution.

B. Immediately following the tenth (10th) anniversary of date of this instrument, the Trustee shall distribute the Trust fund to (NAME), or if he is not then living, to his estate.

C. In making any payment to a disabled beneficiary under this article, the Trustee may make such payments to such beneficiary, or to his or her Guardian, personal representative, or the person with whom he or she resides, without having to look to the proper application of those payments.

ARTICLE IV
Definitions

A. The Grantor is unmarried at the time this Trust is executed.

B. At the time this Trust is executed, the Grantor has one (1) child, (NAME).

C. A Trustee is "disabled" or under a "disability" whenever any Trustee other than a disabled Trustee or, if there is no such Trustee, any person who would become successor Trustee on such determination of disability, receives written certification from two (2) physicians regularly attending the Trustee, at least one (1) of whom is board certified in the specialty most closely associated with the alleged disability, that such Trustee has become physically or mentally incapacitated, regardless of cause and regardless of whether or not there has been any adjudication of incompetence, mental illness, or need for a committee, conservator, Guardian, or other personal representative. A Trustee is recovered from his or her disability whenever the then serving Trustee receives written certification from two (2) physicians regularly attending such disabled Trustee, at least one (1) of whom is board certified in the specialty most closely associated with the alleged disability, that he or she is no longer incapacitated and is again able to manage his or her own personal and financial affairs. No Trustee is liable to anyone for removing anyone from the Trusteeship, if the Trustee relied in good faith on the aforementioned physicians' certifications. No one else is liable to anyone for dealing with a Trustee other than the one removed for disability, if such removal was made upon good faith reliance on the aforementioned physicians' certifications.

D. All tax-related terms mean the same things in this Trust instrument as they mean in the Internal Revenue Code of 1986, as amended.

ARTICLE V
Trustee's Powers

The Trustee is exclusively empowered to do the following:

A. To hold and retain all or any property received from any source, without regard to diversification.

B. To invest and reinvest the Trust funds in any type of property and every kind of investment, including (but not limited to) corporate obligations of every kind, preferred or common stocks, securities of any regulated investment Trust, state and local bonds, and partnership interests.

C. To participate passively in the operation of any productive business or other enterprise, and to incorporate, dissolve, or otherwise change the form of such business, but the Trustee shall do nothing which would constitute the conduct of an active trade or business by the Trust.

D. To deposit Trust funds in any commercial interest-bearing savings or savings and loan accounts.

E. To borrow money for any reasonable Trust purpose and upon such terms, including (but not limited to) interest rates, security, and loan duration, as the Trustee deems advisable.

F. To lend Trust funds to such persons and on such terms including (but not limited to) interest rates, security, and loan duration, as the Trustee deems advisable, but the Trustee may not lend Trust funds without an adequate rate of interest.

G. To sell or otherwise dispose of Trust assets, including (but not limited to) Trust real property, for cash or credit, at public or private sale, and with such warranties or indemnifications as the Trustee deems advisable.

H. To buy assets of any type from any person on such terms, including (but not limited to) cash or credit, interest rates, and security, as the Trustee deems advisable.

I. To improve, develop, manage, lease, or abandon any Trust assets, as the Trustee deems advisable.

J. To hold property in the name of any Trustee or any custodian or nominee, without disclosing this Trust, but the Trustee is responsible for the acts of any custodian or nominee the Trustee so uses.

K. To pay and advance money for the Trust's protection and for all expenses, losses, and liabilities sustained in its administration.

L. To prosecute or defend any action for the protection of the Trust, the Trustee in the performance of the Trustee's duties, or both, and to pay, contest, or settle any claim by or against the Trust or the Trustee in the performance of the Trustee's duties.

M. To employ persons, even if they are associated with the Trustee, to advise or assist the Trustee in the performance of the Trustee's duties.

N. To distribute Trust assets in kind or in cash.

O. To allocate receipts and disbursements to principal or income, in accordance with applicable local law and practice, except that in the absence of any specific local law, the Trustee shall follow the rules and principles of the Revised Uniform Principal and Income Act, as adopted and most recently revised (at the time of such allocation) by the National Conference of Commissioners on Uniform State Laws.

P. To execute and deliver any instruments necessary or useful in the exercise of any of these powers.

ARTICLE VI
The Trustee

A. (NAME) will be the Trustee, until his resignation, death, or disability, at which time the Grantor's sister, (NAME), will become successor Trustee.

B. A Trustee may designate any individual or institution as a Co-Trustee by a written instrument. Any Co-Trustee or successor Trustee may, without liability, accept without examination or review the accounts rendered and the property delivered by any predecessor Trustee. Each successor Trustee has the same title, powers, and duties as the Trustee succeeded, without any additional conveyance. A Co-Trustee so named shall serve only as long as the Trustee who appointed such Co-Trustee (or, if such Co-Trustee was named by more than one (1) Trustee acting together, by the last to serve of such Trustees), and such Co-Trustee shall not become a successor Trustee upon the death, resignation, or disability of the Trustee who appointed such Co-Trustee, unless such Co-Trustee is elected as successor Trustee pursuant to Paragraph E of this article. Any reference to a "Trustee" refers equally to any successor Trustee.

C. Any Trustee may, from time to time, delegate to any other Trustee by written instrument any or all of such Trustee's powers (except those, if any, not exercisable by such other Trustee). Such delegation may be temporary or permanent, and if temporary, may be for any duration of time or until any event specified by the delegating Trustee. Any person dealing in good faith with any Trustee may rely without inquiry upon the Trustee's certificate with respect to any delegation.

D. No Trustee shall be required to provide surety or other security on a bond.

E. Any Trustee may resign by giving written notice specifying the resignation's effective date to the beneficiary to whom distributions may be made at that time.

F. Whenever there shall be a vacancy in the office of Trustee, a successor Trustee shall be named by the person to whom notice of resignation would be given.

G. No Trustee shall be required to obtain the order of any Court to exercise any power or discretion under this Trust.

H. No Trustee shall be required to file any accounting with any public official. The Trustee must, however, maintain accurate records concerning the Trust. Each year, furthermore, the Trustee shall furnish an annual accounting of the Trust's condition, including receipts and disbursements, to each beneficiary to whom distributions have been made during the year.

I. Each Trustee is entitled to reasonable compensation for services in administering this Trust and to reimbursement for expenses.

ARTICLE VII
Miscellaneous

A. This Trust shall be governed by and construed according to the law of (State).

B. Whenever the context of this Trust requires, the masculine gender includes the feminine or neuter, and vice versa, and the singular number includes the plural, and vice versa.

IN WITNESS WHEREOF, (YOUR NAME), the Grantor, and (NAME), the Trustee, have hereunto set their hands and seals, all as of the day and year first above written.

_____ (Seal)

Grantor

_____ (Seal)

Trustee

STATE OF (YOUR STATE) _____

COUNTY OF (YOUR COUNTY) _____

BE IT REMEMBERED, that on   , 2000, before me, the undersigned authority, personally appeared (YOUR NAME) and (NAME) AS EXECUTIVE DIRECTOR OF THE (NAME) FOUNDATION, who I am satisfied are the persons named in and who executed the above document, and I having first made known to such persons the contents thereof, such persons acknowledged that they are of sound mind, free of duress or undue influence, and that such persons signed, sealed, and delivered the same as their voluntary act and deed. All of which is hereby certified.

_____

(NOTARY)

SCHEDULE A

CHAPTER 13

How to Survive an Audit—Valuation

An audit is an independent verification of the amounts you put on your federal estate tax return. With an income tax audit, you are put to the test to substantiate the deductions you claimed. With an estate tax audit, the focus is different.

While the estate tax audit may concern substantiation of various deductions—for example, funeral expenses, executor's fees, and so on—it normally concentrates on one area: valuation. Remember, the estate tax is a levy on the transfer of wealth. The only real issue here is the valuation of that wealth. The higher the value, the greater the wealth, the bigger the tax.

One caveat before we get into valuation techniques themselves. If our objective is to minimize the estate tax, you would think that our aim should be to minimize the value of the estate assets. While at the second death that would be true, at the first death our answer is reversed.

We have structured our estate planning so that a married couple will pay zero estate taxes at the first death, regardless of the value of the estate. Therefore, because of the step up in basis allowed by Section 1014 of the Internal Revenue Code, we want to set the value of the assets in the estate of the first to die as *high* as possible. This gives the surviving spouse a higher basis in the transferred assets and minimizes any potential future income tax gain.

Let's look at how assets are valued for gift and estate tax purposes. Remember that all assets transferred are valued at their fair market value. The fair market value is the price at which the property would change hands between a willing buyer and a willing seller, neither being under any compulsion to buy or sell and both having reasonable knowledge of all relevant facts. The fair market value may not be determined by a forced sale price, nor is it to be determined by the sale price of the item in the market other than that in which the item is most commonly sold to the public, taking into account the location of the item wherever appropriate. Thus, in the case of an item that is generally retailed, the fair market value is the price at which the item or a comparable item would be sold at retail.

For example, a car is the type of property generally obtained by the public on a retail market. Therefore, the fair market value of a car is the price for which a car of the same make, model, and age could be purchased by the public. This is *not* the price that a used car dealer would pay for it.

If tangible personal property is sold as a result of an advertisement in the classified section of the newspaper and the property is of a type often sold by this means, or the property is sold at a public auction, the price for which it is sold will be presumed to be the retail sales price of the item at the time of the sale. This retail sales price will also be presumed to be the retail sales price of the item on the applicable valuation date if the sale is made within a reasonable period following the applicable valuation date and if there is no substantial change in market conditions or other circumstances affecting the value of similar items between the time of the sale and the applicable valuation date.

For gift tax purposes, if a gift is made on the expressed or implied condition that the donee pay the gift tax, the amount of this tax may be deducted from the value of the gift made as partial consideration for the gift. It should be noted that such an agreement does not release the donor from the principal liability of paying the gift tax if, in fact, the tax is not paid.

The question of value is one of fact and is therefore subject to solution only in light of all circumstances having a bearing on the issues as of the valuation date. It is, furthermore, a matter that is to be resolved in all cases, according to the Internal Revenue Service, "on the basis of sound judgment and common sense. There is no 'right' answer, only a range of possible right answers that are supported by convincing and logical reasoning. We cannot expect another appraiser to come up with the same conclusion that we do on the valuation issue, however we must be sure that there is ample justification for the value placed on the property in each case."

Valuation, therefore, is frequently viewed by the Internal Revenue Service as a problem of negotiation and compromise. The role of the independent appraiser in this matter is crucial. Furthermore, the evidence and proof provided in the form of expert opinion as to value of the assets, if made promptly after death, would likely have a greater probative value than evidence obtained at a later date.

The Internal Revenue Service has outlined what information should be contained in a competent appraisal report (Rev. Pro. 66-49, 1956-2 CB 1257). Among the items detailed are: (1) a summary of the appraiser's qualifications, (2) the basis upon which the appraisal was made, (3) the date as of which the property was valued, and (4) the statement of the value and the appraiser's definition of value. The burden of proof as to value always lies initially with the taxpayer. Unless you can support the values claimed, the value as determined by the Internal Revenue Service is presumed correct. If sufficient evidence to rebut this presumption is provided, the tide turns and the Internal Revenue Service must prove that its determination is correct.

The federal estate tax return Form 706 contains nine schedules of assets. The valuation of these assets will be considered in the order contained in the federal estate tax return.

Real Estate

The valuation of real estate is primarily a local proposition. The best evidence of a fair market value of a specific piece of real property will be found in the records of comparable sales or in the opinions of qualified experts familiar with the area and the type of property involved. The specialist in each type of property, whether that property is a warehouse in New York or a personal residence in San Francisco, will be able to furnish the most authoritative opinions as to market value.

I suggest that you consult a real estate appraiser, or, if you are dealing with residential property, your local real estate agent. Get three comparative market analyses done on your property by three different real estate brokers. You can then average the analyses, use the median price, or use the extremes, depending upon what your valuation objective is. Remember, at the first death, it may be advantageous to use the higher valuation rather than the lower one.

Stocks and Bonds

The value of stocks and bonds is their fair market value per unit on the applicable valuation date. Methods used to determine the valuation of stocks and bonds depend on:

- Whether the security has an established market and quotations are available to value that security as of the date in question;

- Whether the security has a market value but for some reason market prices are claimed not conclusive for valuation purposes; *and*

- Whether the security has no established market.

If there is a market for stocks and bonds on a stock exchange, in an over-the-counter market, or otherwise, the mean (midpoint) between the highest and lowest quoted selling price on the valuation date is the fair market value per unit. If there are no sales on the valuation date, but there are sales within a reasonable period before and after the valuation date, the fair market value is determined by taking a weighted average of the means between the highest and lowest sales price on the nearest date before and the nearest date after the valuation date. The average is to be weighted *inversely* by the respective numbers of trading days between the selling date and the valuation date.

For example, assume the nearest transactions took place two trading days before the valuation date at a mean selling price of $10 and three trading days after the valuation date at a mean selling price of $15. The price of $12 is the fair market value, obtained by the following computation:

$$(3 \times \$10) + (2 \times \$15)/5 = \$12$$

Note that the weighted average is computed on the basis of intervening trading dates and not actual dates. If no transactions occurred within a reasonable period before and after the valuation date, the fair market value may be determined by taking a weighted average of the means between the bona fide bidding and asking prices on the nearest trading dates before and after the valuation date, if both these dates fall within a reasonable period.

If the highest and lowest selling prices on the valuation date are not available for bonds for which there is a market on a recognized exchange, but the closing selling prices are available on the valuation date and the trading day before the valuation date, then the fair market value of the bond is the mean between the quoted selling price on the valuation date and the quoted closing selling price on the trading day before the valuation date.

If the stocks or bonds are listed on more than one exchange, the records of the exchange on which the stocks or bonds are principally dealt should be used to value the stocks and bonds if the records are available in a listing or publication of general circulation. If these records are not available for the stocks and bonds, or in a complete listing of combined exchanges in a generally available listing or publication, then the records of the combined exchanges should be used.

If no sales exist on the valuation date or within a reasonable period, value is determined by the bidding and asking prices on the valuation date.

The valuation of closely held stocks—stocks not traded on a recognized market—is more difficult. The problem in properly establishing the value of an interest in a closely held corporation lies in the complexity and subjective nature of any evaluation process. Value itself is subjective; it is based on individual human experience. Valuation is the composite of many judgments, not the reaching for an illusory fixed and invarying basis value on which the judgment of everyone must agree. Valuation of closely held stock is clearly an art, not a science.

According to the Internal Revenue Service, the fair market value of any interest in a closely held business, whether a corporation, a sole proprietorship, or a partnership, is the net amount that a willing purchaser will pay for the interest to a willing seller, neither being under any compulsion to buy or sell and both having reasonable knowledge of all relevant facts. The net value is determined on the basis of all relevant factors, including:

- A fair appraisal of all the assets of the business;

- The demonstrated earning capacity of the business; *and*

- Other factors used in considering the value of corporate stock to the extent applicable.

Every evaluation presents a unique problem, and no formula exists to be mechanically applied. Seven primary characteristics distinguish closely held stocks from publicly traded securities:

1. Lack of marketability;

2. Concentration of voting power;

3. Concentration of management in a family or close group;

4. Disproportionate effect of salaries on earnings because of small capitalization;

5. Leverage from small capitalization leading to potentially wide fluctuations in earnings;

6. Influence of shareholders' tax rates and personal circumstances on corporate planning and dividend policy; *and*

7. Limited access to public markets for capital funds.

In the valuation of closely held securities, it is essential to consider all factors. This requirement is stated in the applicable provisions of the Internal Revenue Code and the estate tax and gift tax regulations.

A complete listing of all factors is not feasible, because each issue will involve circumstances or items unlike any other. There are, however, broad areas that are present in closely held security valuations that must be examined in practically every case. Throughout the consideration of these factors of value, the essential ingredients of common sense and judgment cannot be overemphasized. These are fact questions that must be decided by reasoning power after all pertinent data have been established. These factors are purely informational in character and should not be construed as establishing a strict guideline to be followed in every case.

Internal Revenue Service Revenue Ruling 59-60 sets forth the basic approach, method, and factors to be examined in valuing stock of a closely held corporation for estate and gift tax purposes. This is the fundamental government decree that the Internal Revenue Service will follow in making its determination value.

The ruling begins by stating that a formula approach is not valid for valuing a private business. It suggests instead the use of common sense, informed judgment, and reasonableness in evaluating the relevant factors of the business. The following eight relevant factors are suggested for consideration in setting the value. While these factors are not all-inclusive, they are considered basic to any analysis:

1. *The history of the company and the nature of its business.* This factor is helpful in determining the degree of risk involved in the business. Historical trends will show past stability or instability, depth and abilities of management and the labor force, degree of diversity of operations, condition of facilities, and trends in business volume, profitability, and dividends. Recent events should be given more weight in predicting the future, and nonrecurring events of the past should be discounted.

2. *The economic environment in which the business will operate.* The industry outlook and the company's position with respect to its competitors are important determinants of value. The loss of a key person (e.g., a manager) by a "one-person" business will adversely affect the future of the company. This is especially true where there are no potential management successors. Consequently, the value of the stock should go sharply down unless the loss is modified by life insurance. Some common economic factors that may affect the company are:

   a) The degree of fragmentation;

   b) Ease of entry into the industry;

   c) The degree of capital or labor intensiveness of the business;

   d) The stage of the company in its life cycle;

   e) The nature and extent of the market for the company's product or services;

   f) The ability of the company to protect itself against price level changes;

   g) The existence of proprietary products or services;

h) The uniqueness of the company's industry position;

i) The cyclical nature of the industry and the company's position on the cycle;

j) The ability of the company to control cost; *and*

k) The vulnerability of the company to government regulation and control.

3. *The book value of the stock and the financial condition of the business.* The book value of the firm's stock is the historical value of the corporation's assets in excess of corporate liabilities. While this book value may bear little relationship to fair market values, it does provide a starting point for determining the net value of the corporation's tangible assets and identifying existing intangible assets. The historical book value should be adjusted to reflect economic value.

4. *The earnings capacity of the company.* According to Revenue Ruling 59-60, "In general, the appraisal will accord primary consideration to earnings on valuing stocks of companies which sell products or services to the public." The basic focus under this element of valuation is what a buyer would pay for the stock based upon income or return that he or she expects to receive in the future on the investment. Future income potential—for instance, earnings capacity—is a significant element in stock valuation. The primary tangible evidence of future events is past earnings history. Therefore, income statements of the business for the five years prior to the date of the appraisal should be used, with emphasis on the most recent statements. A distinction should then be made between recurrent and nonrecurrent items, operating an investment income, and any consistent loss areas of the business. It may be helpful to analyze deductions from gross income in terms of a percentage of sales so that the risk of the business can be better determined.

5. *The company's dividend-paying capacity.* The company's ability to pay dividends will obviously influence its ability to attract buyers for its stock. Dividend-paying capacity should be emphasized over the amount of actual dividends paid out in the past. The reason for this is the tendency of closely held corporations to pay little out in dividends, which would be taxed as ordinary income. Where controlling interest is being valued, the dividend factor is immaterial since the buyer would be in the position to influence the dividend-paying capacity of the firm by substituting salaries and bonuses for dividends, thus reducing the net income of the firm.

6. *The existence of goodwill or other intangible values.* Goodwill may be measured by the amount by which the appraised value of a business's tangible assets exceeds the net book value of such assets. It is the transferable expectancy of earnings in excess of normal return on tangibles. Such things as the prestige and renown of the business, ownership of a trade or brand name, and a successful operation for a prolonged period in a particular area are evidence of the presence of valuable intangibles. In the final analysis, goodwill is based on earning capacity. Note, though, that where goodwill is attributable solely to the services of a key person, it will not usually survive as an asset if that person leaves the firm. Even if a series of loss years preceded the valuation date, goodwill can still be present. Alternatively, even a favorable earnings record does not necessarily support assignment of intangible value to a business.

7. *Sales of the stock and the size of the block to be valued.* Sales of comparable stock may provide an excellent indication of value. For a valid comparison, these should be arm's-length transactions, not of a forced or distressed nature, and not isolated sales of small amounts. The best buyers are knowledgeable, unrelated third parties. According to Revenue Ruling 59-60, "Actual sales are generally a far more reliable index of market value than any alternative form of evidence, such as estimates based on a capitalization of perspective earnings. They have the advantage of combining greater reliability with greater ease of ascertainment."

8. *Comparison with another company's stock.* In making this comparison, it is important to deal only with the market price of stock of corporations engaged in the same line or similar lines of business having their stock actively traded in a free and open market, either on an exchange or over the counter. Establishing comparability with another company involves more than merely showing the existence of the same or a similar line of business. Other factors need to be examined to ensure that the comparison is valid. The essential factor is whether there is a free, active, public market for the comparable stock as of the valuation date. Comparability does not require virtual identity of operations and financial conditions—only approximately similar business risks. If several comparable companies are available, industry averages might be computed for use in valuing the subject company. In all cases, adjustments must be made for differences in comparability.

Other items may impact on the valuation of closely held stock. Such things as restrictive agreements or the cost of marketing the stock will have an impact and will cause a discount to the value of the securities. Revenue Ruling 59-60 states that primary consideration will be accorded to earnings when valuing stocks of companies that sell products or services to the public. On the other hand, for holding or investment-type companies, the greatest weight will be placed on the fair market value of the underlying assets of the stock to be valued.

When capitalizing earnings or dividends to determine stock value, the rate of return and dividend yield of listed corporate shares should be checked. Because of the variation among companies and the degree of annual fluctuation that will occur, this method may not be appropriate. The alternative is to set a subjective capitalization rate based on the nature of the business, the risk involved, and the stability or irregularity of earnings.

Mortgages, Notes, and Cash

The face amount of a note or mortgage is its value unless either the value of the underlying security is inadequate or the interest rate is below prevailing rates for comparable obligations.

The primary valuation factor is the ability of the debtor to pay his or her obligation at maturity. The test is collectibility as of the valuation date regardless of the actual collection at a subsequent date. If the debtor is insolvent, the value of the note will be limited to the value of any collateral.

A mortgage is a security interest in property given to secure a note. If the mortgagor (the maker of the mortgage) is not liable on the note or is insolvent, the mortgage itself becomes the measuring rod of value. The value is then determined by the size, shape, and location of the lot, as well as the physical qualities, actual and potential use, present interest yield, and liens on the property serving as a security interest. In addition, any taxes or interest in arrears, foreclosure proceedings, or assignment of rents and gross and net rentals themselves, as well as other pertinent factors, must be weighed by an appraiser.

For gift and estate tax purposes, cash is valued as of the date of transfer or death. It will be included regardless of where it is or who has possession if it belongs to the decedent at the date of death.

U.S. Government Series E bonds are valued at their redemption price (market value) as of the date of death since they are neither negotiable nor transferrable and their only definitely ascertainable value is the amount at which the Treasury will redeem them.

Insurance on the Decedent's Life

The full proceeds on any insurance on the life of a decedent that was receivable by or for the benefit of an estate will be taxed to the insured decedent's estate. Furthermore, if the decedent held any incidents of ownership, that ownership will cause the amount receivable by the beneficiary to be taxed in the decedent's estate. This amount includes both dividends and premium refunds, and no distinction is made between an ordinary life policy, a term policy, group insurance, and an accidental death benefit. This is why we have created the Irrevocable Life Insurance Trust—to keep all these insurance proceeds out of your estate!

Jointly Owned Property

Jointly owned property is property in which there is an automatic transfer of the decedent's interest in the joint property to the cotenant. The ownership of the property transfers by operation of law. If you and I own property jointly, even if your will directs your interest in that property to go to your spouse, it will come to me.

Generally, you must include the full value of the jointly owned property in your gross estate. However, the full value should not be included if you can show that a part of the property originally belonged to the other tenant or tenants and was never received or acquired by the other tenant or tenants from the decedent for less than adequate in full consideration in money or money's worth, or unless you can show that any part of the property was acquired with consideration originally belonging to the surviving joint tenant or tenants. In this case, you may exclude from the value of the property an amount proportionate to the consideration furnished by the other tenant or tenants. Relinquishing or promising to relinquish dower, courtesy, or statutory estate created instead of dower or courtesy or other marital rights in the decedent's property or estate is not consideration in money or money's worth.

If the property was acquired by the decedent and another person or persons by gift, bequest, devise, or inheritance as joint tenants, and their interests are not otherwise specified by law, include only that part of the value of the property that is figured by dividing the full value of the property by the number of joint tenants.

If you believe that less than the full value of the entire property is includable in the gross estate for tax purposes, you must establish the right to include the smaller value by attaching proof of the extent, origin, and nature of the decedent's interest and the interests of the decedent's cotenant or cotenants.

Other Miscellaneous Property

All items of the probate estate not reported under any of the preceding categories should be contained here. Such items may include debts to the decedent, claims or other rights, royalties, pensions, lease holds, judgments, household and personal effects, automobiles, and many other kinds of property. Paintings, literary material, collections, patents, household property, and personal effects should all be valued and included in your estate.

Here's a hint to save you some income tax money. If you are not going to be subject to the estate tax, then it is advantageous to value your household property and personal effects at a higher value. Upon your death (remember, no estate tax is going to be paid), your beneficiaries can use these higher values for charitable deduction purposes if they contribute your household property and personal effects to a charity. Increasing the valuation of these items means that your beneficiaries' income taxes are reduced without any corresponding increase in your estate tax.

Transfers During the Decedent's Lifetime

Interest in property that you transfer within the three-year period ending on the date of your death may be included in your gross estate. The rules for inclusion are as follows:

- Property interests transferred before 1977 are includable in the estate of a decedent if the transfer was made in contemplation of death.

- Property interests transferred by a decedent after 1976 may be includable without regard to the motivation for the transfer. Such transfers include only the following:

a) Any transfer by the decedent with respect to a life insurance policy within three years before death.

b) Any transfer within three years before death of a retained life estate, reversionary interest, or power to revoke, if the property subject to the life estate, interest, or power would have been included in the gross estate had the decedent continued to possess the life estate, interest, or power until death.

c) Estates of decedents dying during 1977, 1978, or 1979. These are subject to the contemplation of death rule for the pre-1977 portion of the three-year period ending on the date of death and to the automatic inclusion rule for the post-1976 portion of the period.

Powers of Appointment

The gross estate includes the value of property interests over which you possessed a general Power of Appointment at your death. The existence of the Power is not dependent on the capacity of the decedent (you) to exercise the Power. Included is the value of property interest over which you exercised or released such a Power during your lifetime if the exercise or release was:

- Within three years of death;

- With a retained life interest in the property appointed;

- With a retained reversionary interest in the property appointed; *or*

- With a retained power to alter, amend, revoke, or terminate the appointment.

A Power of Appointment is a power to determine who will own or enjoy, presently or in the future, the property subject to the Power. The term *Power of Appointment* includes all powers that are, in substance and effect, Powers of Appointment regardless of the terminology used in a particular instrument and regardless of local property law.

The valuation of Powers of Appointment is dependent upon the valuation of the assets over which the Powers of Appointment exist. It is the valuation of the property interest subject to the Power of Appointment that is included in the gross estate.

Annuities

The value of an annuity, such as a life insurance policy on the life of a person other than the decedent, issued by a company regularly engaged in the selling of such contracts, is the amount the issuing company would charge for a comparable contract on the date of the decedent's death. Such life insurance policies are defined by the Internal Revenue Code as annuities.

The value of contracts issued by organizations other than commercial insurance companies (e.g., private foundations, corporations, trusts, or funds) is the present value on the applicable valuation date of the annuity's future payments. To compute the present value of an annuity, the Internal Revenue Service provides a special table, contained in the federal estate tax regulations, Section 20.2031-10. For purposes of this table, the age of a person is the age attained at the birthday nearest to the valuation date.

In the event that a fact, computation, or ruling is necessary to complete a tax return, assistance may be obtained from the IRS by writing to:

Internal Revenue Service
Assistant Commissioner (Technical)
Estate and Gift Tax Branch
T:I:EG
111 Constitution Avenue
Washington, DC 20224

Remember, valuation is an art, not a science. A good valuation should yield a range of "answers," the accuracy of each only as good as the correctness of the financial, economic, and social factors—components used in deriving those "answers." Those interested in a more detailed analysis of the valuation process should take a look at another book I have written, *The Professional Handbook of Business Valuation* (Addison-Wesley, 1982). That book also includes the IRS Audit Technique Handbook for Estate Examiners and the IRS Appellate Conference Valuation Training Programs, both of which give you the inside scoop on what the IRS is looking for when it does an audit of an estate tax return.

CHAPTER 14

Special Situations

This book is not a compendium of everything I know about the estate tax. I have left out as much as I have put in, but that was my intent. Rather than show how much *I* know, I have focused on what *you* need to know, if you have an estate of $3 million to $4 million, to pay zero estate taxes.

The items that have been omitted has been left out because those items are for more sophisticated and larger estates. However, I do want to discuss certain items to fill in the penumbras of your estate planning knowledge. These are as follows.

Deductions from Your Estate

The estate tax is a tax on your net transfer of worth. That's the difference between your gross estate and the allowable deductions from that gross estate. You are allowed the following deductions from your gross estate.

Funeral Expenses and Expenses Incurred
in Administering Property Subject to Claims

Funeral expenses that you pay for a decedent are deductible on the estate tax return. Reduce these expenses by any amounts that were reimbursed, such as death benefits payable by the Social Security Administration and the Veterans Administration.

Executor's commissions that have actually been paid or that are expected to be paid may be deductible as well. You can't deduct commissions if none will be collected. If the amount of the commissions has not been fixed by decree of a proper court, the deduction will be allowed on the final examination of the return, provided that:

- The IRS is reasonably satisfied that the commissions claimed will be paid;

- The amount entered as a deduction is within the amount allowable by the laws of the jurisdiction where the estate is being administered; *and*

- It is in accordance with the usually accepted practice in that jurisdiction for estates of similar size and character.

Attorney's fees that have actually been paid or that are reasonably expected to be paid are also deductible. They are allowable under basically the same conditions as executor's commissions. Attorney's fees incidental to litigation incurred by the beneficiaries are not deductible. So, for example, if there is a will contest between the beneficiaries, legal expenses incidental to that contest are charged against the beneficiaries personally and are not administration expenses authorized by the Internal Revenue Code.

Interest expenses incurred after the decedent's death are also generally allowed as a deduction if they are reasonable, necessary to the administration of the estate, and allowable under local law. Interest incurred as the result of a federal estate tax deficiency is also a deductible administrative expense. Penalties, however, are not deductible, even if they are allowable under local law.

All miscellaneous administration expenses necessarily incurred in preserving and distributing the estate are deductible. These expenses include, but are not limited to, appraiser's and accountant's fees, certain court costs, and costs of storing or maintaining the assets of the estate. The expenses of selling assets are deductible only if the sale is necessary to pay the decedent's debts or the expenses of administration or taxes or to preserve the estate or carry out distribution.

Debts of the Decedent

Any valid debts owed by you at the time of your death reduce your estate. For example, your final hospital bills, any amount owed on your credit card, your final utility bills, and so on would all be debts that would reduce your taxable estate. Note the special technique we discussed under Family Limited Partnerships to actually convert a bequest into a deductible debt.

Mortgages and Liens

Any debts or obligations that are secured by mortgages or other liens should be deducted as well. For example, your portion of the balance on your home mortgage would be deductible here. So too would notes and other obligations secured by the deposit of collateral, such as stocks, bonds, and so on.

Net Losses During Administration

Under this category, you may deduct those losses from thefts, fires, storms, shipwrecks, or other casualties that occurred during the settlement of the estate. The amount that is deductible is only the excess not reimbursed by insurance or otherwise.

Expenses Incurred in Administering Property Not Subject to Claims

Under this category, you may deduct expenses incurred in administering property that is included in the gross estate but that is not subject to claims. The expenses deductible here are usually expenses incurred in the administration of a trust established by the decedent before death. They may also be incurred in the collection of other assets or the transfer or clearance of title to other property included in the decedent's gross estate for estate tax purposes, but not included in the decedent's probate estate. These expenses may include those that are the result of settling the decedent's interest in a property or vesting good title in the property to the beneficiaries. Expenses incurred on behalf of the transferees (except those described previously) are not deductible.

Bequests and the Like to the Surviving Spouse

This is our marital deduction. Remember, any amounts left to a spouse, either outright or through a qualified terminable interest trust, are not included in your estate.

Charitable, Public, and Similar Gifts and Bequests

You can claim a charitable deduction from your estate for the value of property that was transferred to a charitable organization. This charitable deduction is allowed not only for direct transfers, but also as a result of either a qualified disclaimer or the complete termination of a power to consume, invade, or appropriate property for the benefit of an individual. The bottom line is that if the property is going to end up in the hands of a charity, you are going to get a charitable deduction. Note the use of the Charitable Remainder Trust as a technique to take taxable assets out of your estate during your lifetime and replace them with tax-free insurance proceeds at your death.

Credits

A credit is a dollar-for-dollar offset to your tax. In the 50 percent estate tax bracket, a $100 deduction saves you $50. A $100 credit saves you $100.

There are certain credits that are allowed against your estate tax. First and most important is the *unified credit*. Each person has a unified credit that will reduce the amount of estate or gift taxes that must be paid. For 2000, this credit is $220,550, equivalent to having $675,000 of assets not subject to the federal estate tax. The amount not subject to the gift and estate tax is technically known as the *applicable exclusion amount*. Table 14.1 summarizes the unified credit changes as they are currently scheduled.

You are also entitled to a state death tax credit. The Internal Revenue Service allows you a deduction against your federal estate tax for part of the state inheritance or estate tax that you pay. That deduction is computed by taking your total federal taxable estate, subtracting $60,000 from that amount, and then applying that adjusted taxable estate to Table 14.2. For example, if you had a federal taxable estate of $500,000, you would subtract $60,000 from that amount, leaving $440,000. Using Table 14.2, the credit would be $3,600 plus 3.2 percent of $200,000, or $10,000. This credit is a dollar-for-dollar reduction in the amount of federal estate tax that you have to pay.

You are also allowed a credit for any foreign death taxes paid. The credit for foreign death taxes is allowable only if the decedent was a citizen or resident of the United States. These would be taxes paid to foreign governments for assets that you have located in those governments' jurisdictions subject to their own estate tax. You should convert death taxes paid to the foreign country into U.S. dollars by using the rate of exchange in effect at the time each payment of foreign tax is made.

Finally, you get a credit for certain gift taxes paid on prior transfers, but only to the extent of the smaller of:

1. The amount of the estate tax of the transferor's estate attributable to the transferred property, *or*

2. The amount by which an estate tax on the transferee's estate determined without the credit for tax on prior transfers exceeds an estate tax on the transferee's estate determined by excluding from the gross estate the net value of the transfer.

Table 14.1   Unified Credit Changes

Year	Unified Credit	Applicable Exclusion Amount
2000 and 2001	$220,550	$ 675,000
2002 and 2003	229,800	700,000
2004	287,300	850,000
2005	326,300	950,000
2006 and later	345,800	1,000,000

Table 14.2 Computation of Maximum Credit for State Death Taxes

(1) Adjusted Taxable Estate Equal to or More Than	(2) Adjusted Taxable Estate Less Than	(3) Credit on Amount in Column 1	(4) Rate of Credit on Excess over Amount in Column 1	(1) Adjusted Taxable Estate Equal to or More Than	(2) Adjusted Taxable Estate Less Than	(3) Credit on Amount in Column 1	(4) Rate of Credit on Excess over Amount in Column 1
0	$ 40,000	0	None	$ 2,040,000	$ 2,540,000	$ 106,800	8.0%
$ 40,000	90,000	0	0.8%	2,540,000	3,040,000	146,800	8.8%
90,000	140,000	$ 400	1.6%	3,040,000	3,540,000	190,800	9.6%
140,000	240,000	1,200	2.4%	3,540,000	4,040,000	238,800	10.4%
240,000	440,000	3,600	3.2%	4,040,000	5,040,000	290,800	11.2%
440,000	640,000	10,000	4.0%	5,040,000	6,040,000	402,800	12.0%
640,000	840,000	18,000	4.8%	6,040,000	7,040,000	522,800	12.8%
840,000	1,040,000	27,600	5.6%	7,040,000	8,040,000	650,800	13.6%
1,040,000	1,540,000	38,800	6.4%	8,040,000	9,040,000	786,800	14.4%
1,540,000	2,040,000	70,800	7.2%	9,040,000	10,040,000	930,800	15.2%
				10,040,000		1,082,800	16.0%

What does this mean in simple English? Basically, it means that if you have paid a gift tax on assets that for one reason or another are now included in your estate and are subject to estate taxes, then to prevent double taxation you may qualify for a credit for the gift tax paid.

The Generation-Skipping Tax

In 1976, Congress declared that the federal estate tax should be imposed at each generation. It was felt that generation-skipping transfers constituted a loophole in the federal estate tax system. Congress therefore enacted a generation-skipping transfer tax on property that passed in trust to a younger generation at the death of a beneficiary. In 1986, this generation-skipping transfer tax was found to be too complicated to administer and was repealed, and a new and perhaps even more complicated and draconian tax was enacted in its place.

The current generation-skipping tax is a flat 55 percent (the maximum federal estate tax rate) imposed on every taxable dollar of three types of transfers:

1. Gifts during lifetime or at death to grandchildren or other persons considered to be two or more generations younger than the grantor (*skip persons*). This type of generation-skipping transfer is called a *direct skip*.

2. Any distributions from a generation-skipping trust to a grandchild or other skip person. These are called *taxable distributions*. Under this rule, if a generation-skipping trust that can make distributions to both children and grandchildren makes a discretionary distribution to a grandchild, the distribution is taxable and the generation-skipping tax applies. Moreover, the generation-skipping tax applies regardless of whether the distribution is considered to be income or principal.

3. If the beneficial interests of a child in a generation-skipping trust come to an end (for example, upon the death of the child) and, as a result, all of the remaining beneficiaries of the trust are grandchildren (or other skip persons), there is a *taxable termination*. In that case, the generation-skipping tax is immediately imposed on the value of the trust, regardless of whether the trust ends or continues for the benefit of the grandchildren.

As noted, the tax rate on generation-skipping transfers is a flat rate equal to the maximum estate and gift tax rate in effect at the time of the transfer (55 percent under present law) multiplied by the *inclusion ratio*. The inclusion ratio with respect to any property transferred in a generation-skipping transfer indicates the amount of generation-skipping tax exemption allocated to a trust. The allocation of the generation-skipping tax exemption reduces the 55 percent tax rate on a generation-skipping transfer.

Each individual has a $1 million lifetime generation-skipping tax exemption. You can therefore make taxable gifts or leave $1 million to grandchildren without incurring any generation-skipping tax. The amount of generation-skipping tax exemption is indexed for inflation beginning in 1999, rounded down to the nearest $10,000. The exemption for 2000 is $1,000,030. Therefore, in 2000 a husband and wife each have their own $1,000,030 exemption, for a total exemption of $2,000,060.

It is important to note that the generation-skipping transfer tax on taxable terminations and distributions and on direct skips is calculated in two different ways:

1. The generation-skipping transfer tax on a taxable distribution or taxable termination is based upon the amount of distribution or termination before taxes. The calculation is therefore *tax inclusive,* because the tax is based on an amount that may include an amount that must be paid in taxes. For example, if a $1 million generation-skipping trust terminates and is subject to the 55 percent generation-skipping transfer tax, the tax will be $550,000 and the grandchildren will get only $450,000.

2. Alternatively, on a direct skip the generation-skipping transfer tax is based on the amount actually received by the grandchildren (or other skip persons) after the tax has been paid. The calculation here is therefore *tax exclusive.* For example, if an estate of $1 million (after federal estate tax) is left to (or in trust for) the grandchildren and is subject to the 55 percent generation-skipping transfer tax, the tax will only be $354,839, leaving $645,161 for the grandchildren. This is because 55 percent of $645,161 is $354,839. So, if you start with $1 million and give $645,161 to the grandchildren, you will have $354,839 left to pay the generation-skipping transfer tax on that $645,161. Therefore, the effective rate of tax for direct skips is really 35.484 percent, not 55 percent.

Because the effective tax rate for direct skips is only 35.484 percent, not 55 percent, it is often better to make direct skips to grandchildren (and great-grandchildren) than it is to create taxable generation-skipping trusts that must pay the generation-skipping transfer tax at 55 percent upon the death of children.

Besides the $1 million-plus exemption that you have, what other transfers are exempt from this generation-skipping transfer tax? The $10,000 annual gift tax exclusion applies to direct skips. So, gifts to a grandchild (or great-grandchild, etc.) of not more than $10,000 each year are not subject to the generation-skipping transfer tax. Gifts in trust for the benefit of grandchildren (or great-grandchildren, etc.) may also qualify for this exception, but only if the trust is for only one grandchild or great-grandchild and the assets of the trust will be included in the beneficiary's federal taxable estate at his or her death. Most trusts for minors that qualify for the federal gift tax annual exclusion should also qualify for this generation-skipping transfer tax.

A gift to a grandchild also escapes generation-skipping transfer taxation if that child's parent is already dead. This is sometimes known as the *predeceased child exception*. There is also an exemption for payments made directly to an educational institution for tuition or made directly to a doctor or hospital for medical expenses. This means that a payment from a generation-skipping trust for a grandchild's college tuition is not a taxable distribution for generation-skipping transfer tax purposes if the payment is made directly to the institution.

The generation-skipping transfer tax is bad news. It is a very expensive flat rate of 55 percent. Moreover, remember, this tax is in addition to estate taxes, which also can be as high as 55 percent.

What I want you to get out of this discussion is the potential draconian impact of the generation-skipping transfer tax and the importance of the appropriate allocation of the generation-skipping tax exemption. Failure to claim this exemption could be disastrous. For example, assume that in 1983 you create a trust with income distributed to your daughter for life and then distributed to your grandchildren when your daughter dies. You transfer $1 million into the trust in 1983. Your daughter dies in 1998, and at that time the value of the trust fund is $5 million. If you fail to allocate your generation-skipping tax exemption to the transfer, the tax imposed when your daughter dies in 1998 is 55 percent of the $5 million, or $2,750,000. Had you allocated your entire $1 million generation-skipping tax exemption to the transfer into the trust on a timely filed gift tax return, no generation-skipping tax would be due upon your daughter's death. The tax cost for not filing the tax return and claiming the allocation is $2,750,000!

The moral of the story here is that it is imperative for you to recognize the existence of the generation-skipping transfer tax, when it is imposed, and the prudent necessity of filing the gift tax return (Form 709) to use and allocate your generation-skipping transfer tax exemption when appropriate. If you make a direct skip during your lifetime, any unused generation-skipping transfer tax exemption is automatically allocated to a direct skip to the extent necessary to make the inclusion ratio for such a property equal to zero. (You may elect out of the automatic allocation for lifetime direct skips.) Congress has moved to provide automatic allocation of your generation-skipping transfer tax exemption to transfers made during your lifetime to *indirect skips* as well. An indirect skip is any transfer of property (that is not a direct skip) subject to the gift tax that is made to a generation-skipping transfer tax trust. In either case, it would be prudent to file the gift tax return to confirm these allocations and to start the running of the three-year statute of limitations with respect to the valuation of the property transferred.

Conclusion

This book has been written as a guide to show those of you with estates of not more than $3 million to $4 million how to pay zero federal estate tax. Because of my focus on that limited target market, I have left out discussion of certain items such as special use valuation, the qualified family-owned business exclusion, and special techniques for the deferral of the estate tax. Those are topics that are of major importance with larger estates but that have minimal relevance for my targeted readers. Those with net estates of $3 million to $4 million can reduce their federal estate tax to zero without the need to resort to these more complicated and sophisticated techniques by using those strategies already presented.

But what is the efficacy of the tax itself? According to Princeton economist Harvey Rosen, "The estate tax is a bad tax. It is capricious." James Glassman, a Fellow at the American Enterprise Institute, has said: "It has the deleterious effect of discouraging investment, since being able to pass wealth on to heirs is an important reason to work and save. It's inequitable, since the money was already taxed when it was earned and probably again when it was saved. And don't forget that studies also show that entrepreneurs, at least, put inheritance to good use."

Those likely to pay the highest estate tax rates are those with medium-size inheritances. These are passed down from owners of small businesses and family farms who amass wealth during their lifetimes through hard work and thrift. Because such wealth is often unexpected, these people may not be aware of or take full advantage of ways to reduce taxes. In contrast, the very rich who have inherited their wealth mitigate the death tax through careful estate planning.

According to Gary and Aldona Robbins of the Institute for Policy Innovation, if the federal estate tax had been eliminated in 1999, then by the year 2010:

1. Annual gross domestic product would be $117.3 billion, or 0.9 percent above what it would be with the tax.

2. The stock of U.S. capital would be higher by almost $1.5 trillion, or 4.1 percent above the baseline.

3. Between 1999 and 2008, the economy would have produced $700 billion more in gross domestic product than otherwise.

In December of 1998, Congressman Jim Saxton of New Jersey in conjunction with the Joint Economic Committee of the United States Congress studied the economics of the estate tax. The committee concluded that the tax costs more to administer than it actually raises in revenue!

My personal opinion is that the estate tax is a bad tax. The wealthy have the time, the talent, and the money to avoid and/or minimize this fiscal imposition. *How to Pay Zero Estate Taxes* has been written to give you the same knowledge and techniques that the wealthy use to eliminate estate taxes.

My objective has not been to make you an expert in the minutiae of the estate tax itself, but rather to give you the tools, documents, strategies, and techniques that will enable you to pay zero federal estate tax. Any errors, omissions, or mistakes are mine; any credit for a job well done goes to my typist and my editor.

This book is dedicated to the proposition: NO TAXATION WITHOUT RESPIRATION!

Index